Hudson Valley Mediterranean

Hudson Valley

Mediterranean

The Gigi Good Food Cookbook

Laura Pensiero

WILLIAM MORROW
An Imprint of HarperCollins*Publishers*

HarperCollins books may be purchased for educational, business, or sales promotional use. For information please write: Special Markets Department, HarperCollins Publishers, 10 East 53rd Street, New York, NY 10022.

FIRST EDITION

Designed by Jennifer Daddio/Bookmark Design & Media Inc.
Photography by Leonardo Frusteri

Library of Congress Cataloging-in-Publication Data

Pensiero, Laura J.
   Hudson Valley Mediterranean: the Gigi good food cookbook/Laura Pensiero.—1st ed.
      p.   cm.
   ISBN 978-0-06-171917-2
   1. Cookery (Natural foods) 2. Cookery, Mediterranean. 3. Cookery—Hudson River Valley (N.Y. and N.J.) I. Title.
   TX741.P464 2009
   641.5'636—dc22

                                                                      2009002198

09 10 11 12 13   ID3/QWF   10 9 8 7 6 5 4 3 2 1

To the loyal Gigi customers
who share Mediterranean flavors, buon vino, and spirited fun;

_____

the dedicated and talented Gigi Hudson Valley team,

_____

and the farmers and food and beverage producers
whose hard work and passion result in
"harvests" that make us all look and feel good

Contents

Introduction

New York's *Hudson Valley* is in the midst of a rural renaissance. The farms and pastures stretching north along the Hudson River from New York City up to Albany have undergone a radical shift over the past thirty years, creating a new kind of American agricultural landscape. Committed farmers, ranchers, and artisan food producers have joined with one another and a growing community of innovative chefs to create a fresh food movement that is focused on local ingredients and supportive of farming practices that are both environmentally and socially sustainable.

The proof is on the plate. The Hudson Valley now produces some of the best-tasting food in America. This book is a celebration of the pleasure, practice, and joy of eating right here: a place of green rolling hills, deep, rich topsoil, exceptional agricultural diversity, and four very distinct seasons.

Life in the Valley today mirrors our national preoccupation with sustainable living, but does so with an exaggerated intensity. This trend toward sustainability and green living is particularly strong because we cull from a population that's passionate about food, cooking, and the environment and because we attract people who thrive on the excitement of the changing seasons, complete with dramatic thunderstorms, nor'easters, brilliant fall colors, and endless sunny summer days with slow twilight evenings. Our proximity to New York City means that our farmers have long supplied urbanites in search of quality and flavor. As a result the Hudson Valley has grown into a sophisticated agricultural community with a certain urbane style. Sure, you can buy sweet summer corn here, but you can also try local handcrafted Calvados and pear liqueur or organic foie gras.

Leading this charge to ensure a sustainable landscape are many of my friends, neighbors, and growers throughout the Valley who work hard to protect the land, encourage local traditions, and advocate for the need to maintain open spaces. It is an exciting time.

Looking outside our valley, I recognize the growing community of concerned Americans all across the country who seek to restore, and in some cases create anew, sustainable agricultural landscapes that will invigorate rural communities and provide consumers with healthier, fresher, and humanely raised food. I am thrilled to be a part of this national, and even global, movement of change. My friend Diane Hatz, who champions sustainable agriculture through her organization Sustainable Table, led a biofueled bus journey across the United States in 2007, highlighting the best farming practices, and found enthusiastic audiences everywhere. Fittingly, the Eat Well Guided Tour of America ended right here, with a September harvest celebration on the field behind our Gigi Market barn. I was curious to find out what Diane had observed in the many communities where she organized events and farm tours during her two-month journey. "You know what surprised me?" she said. "This really isn't a niche trend any longer. Whether we were on a sustainable ranch in eastern Washington State, an organic pizza restaurant in Chicago, or a hog farm in rural Iowa, people everywhere are growing, raising, promoting, and eating fresh, local sustainable food from small family farms. It has become part of daily life for hundreds of thousands of Americans."

I was born and raised in the Hudson Valley and spent the early years in my career working as a registered dietitian and culinary consultant to chefs and in hospitals throughout New York City. My central goal was to convince people that good, healthy food and great-tasting food weren't mutually exclusive. In 1999 I left New York to spend a year running a restaurant in northern Italy. That was an eye-opening experience for me. The food in Italy was extremely fresh, very locally grown, and often simply prepared. It was this natural seasonal approach to eating that made food exciting. Since 2001, I have owned Gigi Trattoria in Rhinebeck, New York, and as a restaurateur, I have never forgotten the lessons of my Italian sojourn and remain an advocate of fresh, locally grown food. In fact, it's the cornerstone philosophy of Gigi Trattoria and lies at the very heart of the food we prepare and serve. In 2006 I opened Gigi Market, a year-round farmers' market to provide everyday access to "straight from the farm" products and to forge a stronger link between growers and consumers in my community. Both businesses have thrived. I find that my "great food, great flavor" mantra is now part of a revitalized national discussion about health, nutrition, and food. How exciting it has been for me to see all this happening, especially right here!

I laugh every time someone characterizes rural life in the Valley as "sleepy." No way. There is a tremendous amount of activity going on. My neighbor, farmer Chris Regan at Sky Farms, is trying new sorts of organic farming methods to coax baby lettuces and leafy greens onto my plate when there is still frost on the ground. Owen O'Connor and KayCee Wimbish of Awesome Farm are collecting eggs so fresh that the yolks look like sunshine. Gary Wiltbank of Wiltbank Farm is harvesting chanterelles, shiitakes, and oyster mushrooms for a clientele that snaps them up as soon as they hit the farm stand. The rich pastures and open grazing spaces of the Hudson Valley are ideal for raising animals. The lamb you eat here is gamy and rich, the beef has an intense mineral quality, and the pork breeds are traditional, which means plenty of succulent, natural fat. Humane animal husbandry is the theme among our ranchers. Animals are given sufficient space to move around and given high-quality feed, making them an exceptional choice for our tables.

The Hudson Valley today boasts excellent cheeses and dairy products. Two local producers, Old Chatham and Coach, are recognized nationally for the quality and flavor of their cheeses. One of my favorite cheesemakers is Colin McGrath of Sprout Creek Farm. This 200-acre working farm in Dutchess County makes cheeses from the rich and creamy milk of their herd of grass-fed Jersey, Guernsey, Milking Shorthorn, and Brown Swiss cows. These Hudson Valley artisanal cheeses are crafted in time-honored European traditions. Their buttery Toussaint and young Barat make their way into many Gigi menu items and are sold at Gigi Market.

Sam Simon, a local dairyman and former surgeon, helped form the Hudson Valley Fresh dairy consortium. Dairy farming is a notoriously tough business in upstate New York. The consortium has helped independent dairy farmers get their excellent milk, cheese, and yogurt onto the tables of residents from here to New York City. It's all natural, distributed locally and regionally, and provides the chance for people to taste fresh, preservative-free milk.

For me it all adds up to high-quality products made a stone's throw from my back door. What's not to love? Like many Americans, our community is also thinking differently about the very long journey our food takes from the field to the table. Some long-established farms are changing their approach to land management. Even more encouraging, I now see young men and women becoming farmers and working to translate a philosophy of sustainable agriculture and sound environmental stewardship into reality. I'm glad to see that Russell Bieszynski will return from SUNY Cobleskill's College of Agriculture and Technology ready to take over the property adjoining his parents' ranching (beef, pork, and poultry) business, Northwind Farms. After mentoring Russell for years, his father, Richie, looks forward to everything his son will be able to teach him. Perhaps all these enthusiastic new farmers have been inspired by farmers' markets packed with customers from here to the city, clamoring for food picked at the peak of flavor and ripeness. I know I have.

THE HEALTH CONNECTION

Eating locally and seasonally is a natural, easy way to move toward better health. The reason, I believe, is that locally raised food harvested at the peak of its flavor and natural sugars will just taste better, and if it tastes better, the pleasure of eating it goes way up. We all know that we should eat more fruits and vegetables, but I think biting into a crunchy peach or a mealy apple is a form of torture. But a peach at its ripest . . . that's bliss.

A health connection to eating locally and seasonally is underscored by the traditional Mediterranean diet. Lots of ripe fresh fruits and vegetables, olive oil, whole grains, and restrained amounts of red meat have led to healthy old age for many generations of people living around the Mediterranean. I believe it's an inherently healthy way to eat. It doesn't need to be reworked in any way.

It's unfortunate that for many people, eating healthy food implies sacrifice and lack of flavor. That's never good. Feeling satisfied and well nourished is critical to making lasting lifestyle changes. Let's face it: if you aren't enjoying yourself, you'll revert to old habits. Often, this means more food rather than good food. A philosophy of flavorful food and better health is so important to me that I tell my nutrition clients to remember just four rules: Eat Healthy, Enjoy Food, Live Well, and Never Sacrifice Flavor. There. Now you have your marching orders!

Really, there isn't any magic to healthy eating. The focus shouldn't be on nutrients but rather on enjoying what you eat with an eye to balance and moderation. You've heard it all before: eat plenty of fruit and vegetables, whole grains, and a limited amount of animal products, and most important, choose food that you find deeply flavorful and satisfying.

Are there studies that support the concept that locally grown foods are more nutritious than traditional supermarket fare? Not exactly, since studies like this are difficult to do, in part because absolute nutrient content has so many variables, such as soil fertility, ripening times, and so on. But research has shown that produce picked at its peak has its highest possible nutrient content and certainly its highest level of antioxidants. Once picked, the quality of fresh produce gradually starts to degrade. Common sense tells me that an apple picked ripe and consumed soon afterward will have lost fewer nutrients due to oxidation than one that sat on a slow boat from South America. Plus, that local apple tastes better!

Working in the field of food and nutrition for almost twenty years, I have seen a slew of trends and diets, but as a chef and dietitian my goal has always been to lead people to a healthier (and tastier) life. Over the years I have see many "miracle" diets touted—high-carb, low-carb, low-fat, high-protein. During the same period, overweight and obesity rates have skyrocketed.

Just telling people to eat more fruits and

vegetables doesn't work, either. Despite numerous education campaigns designed to increase fruit and vegetable consumption, our national intake hasn't ticked upward. In fact, the Centers for Disease Control has published data showing that the average fruit intake among people two years of age or older has actually declined slightly from the early '90s. How do we change this? Chefs, doctors, nutritionists, farmers, food providers, environmental and sustainable groups, health agencies, and local governments need to work closely together to help consumers connect the dots and make food choices that are "whole," doable, tasty, and convenient. People need strategies to help translate health information from the page to the market and stovetop.

When all our magic bullets fail, what do we do? Well, perhaps it's time to look at the problem from a different perspective, one that focuses on enjoyment, balance, and health. The truth is that eating well is a pleasure, not a pain. Taking the first steps might require some adjustments, but trust me, none that hurt. We do need to change some of our eating habits, and I compare changing those habits to learning a new language: once you have enough vocabulary, you are speaking. But there is no elusive perfection to chase after, no absolute dos and don'ts. There is just learning, having fun, and building on successes.

The first step? Indulge in great flavor. There's no point in cooking healthy if it isn't as tasty as anything else you would like to eat.

At the restaurant I never tell customers that our food is good for them even though about half the menu would qualify as heart-healthy. But I do tell them to try our Northwind Farms roasted baby chicken with corona beans and braising greens. It's delicious and balanced.

This flavor-first philosophy came about through my work as a nutritionist. In the mid-'90s I was lucky enough to help develop the nutrition counseling program at the Strang Cancer Prevention Center, affiliated with Cornell University's medical school. There I eventually spearheaded and co-authored *The Strang Cancer Prevention Center Cookbook*. Working on that book gave me the opportunity to meet some of the most creative chefs in the country, chefs who were cooking great-tasting healthy food. From that experience and others, I realized that you can't teach healthy eating habits if you don't give pleasure its due. Food can be healthy, but it must always be delicious.

When shopping, remember that farmers at your local farmers' markets know what you don't. Ask them about fruits or vegetables you've never tried. They can give you lots of helpful tips and even recipes. For instance, the technique for peeling and seeding butternut squash applies to almost all other kinds of hard-skinned squashes. So you can try new kinds of squash that only your local farmer will have. Use him or her as a culinary resource. Farmers can tell you where their food comes from, when it's available and at its peak, and how best to use it. Armed with all that good information, you can cook with greater confidence.

Adopt a reasonable approach. Don't be drastic. Don't feel you have to cut out food you love and then suffer and feel deprived. Instead, look at the problem a different way. Maybe you should just put more "good" food on your plate. Add a colorful vegetable, a great salad, or a whole grain. Get what you need not through duty but with pleasure.

Resist dubious or extreme nutritional claims. If you're eating lots of fruit and vegetables, don't feel bad because you're cooking them! I've heard from too many clients who actually feel guilty because they like their green beans well cooked, not crunchy. In fact, fruits and vegetables have all sorts of benefits in their raw, slightly cooked, and well-cooked states. For example, ripe fresh tomatoes are delicious and healthy, but cooked tomatoes are great as well, since the lycopene within the fruit's cell walls is more accessible when broken down in cooking. And even better, all of that tomato goodness is boosted when you add fat, such as olive oil; the body can absorb the lycopene more fully. So please, just enjoy plenty of fresh food and trust your taste buds to lead the way.

I laud people who focus on organic food, but I think you can be reasonable here and still sleep at night. If buying only organic means your food choices are drastically reduced, then rethink your approach. Better to eat more fruits and vegetables, even conventionally raised ones, than to be limited by the notion of organic. Most studies show that variety is the best thing when it comes to eating, and I personally don't like to be bound by too many rules. The good news is that the market for organic has grown in this country, and it's easier than ever to find organic produce at your traditional supermarket.

Around here many farmers simply don't have the time or money to go through the organic certification process. Instead they just focus on growing good food, and the result is that their food is often completely organic or what I term "near organic." For example, a farmer may be growing organically on land that had been sprayed with pesticides a few years back. While certification requirements stipulate a six-year pesticide moratorium before the land is declared "organic," I know that grower is still sending me carefully grown, tasty food.

THE LIBERATED COOK

When I opened my restaurant back in 2001, I was committed from the start to focus on great ingredients found at hand. And that "buy local" mantra helped me build a reputation for fresh, flavorful food. Without fail local farmers, cheesemakers, dairymen, and ranchers brought me their very best. What a debt of gratitude I owe them! Every time I taste a strawberry picked from a nearby farm, I relearn a simple truth: for flavor, nothing beats local. It's true. While plums grown in neighboring Tivoli may be exactly the same variety as those grown in the Central Valley of California, their flavor will be better because they remain on the tree longer, ripening fully until their stems release from the branch with the gentlest of pressure. They are fragile, yes. They are highly perishable, yes. And they must be eaten immediately, preferably over the sink with the juices running down to your elbows.

That "picked at its peak" flavor makes eating healthy easy. During my four years as the culinary coordinator at the Memorial Sloan Kettering Wellness and Prevention Center, I gave cooking demonstrations focusing on fresh fruit and vegetables and I saw firsthand how even dedicated meat-and-potato eaters respond to vegetables that have been cultivated and prepared with care. The usual wide-eyed response is "I didn't think I would ever like that." That's the power of fresh food. By the way, I hear that same expression just about every night from customers at Gigi Trattoria.

Just like working on a farm, eating seasonally is something most of us no longer do. In fact, we often associate eating seasonally with privation. After all, winter in upstate New York is cold, with limited daylight, and the fields are blanketed with snow. You definitely know you don't live in San Diego. How could seasonal eating be at all fun? Well, actually, it's a lot of fun. A healthy agricultural environment like the Hudson Valley is a diverse one. Different growers may develop an interest or expertise in a certain type of produce. My friends Miriam Latzer and Benjamin Shute of Hearty Roots Community Farm plant a myriad of root vegetables, varieties I didn't know existed. I have spent many free hours just cooking, tasting, and testing them all. For me, exploring all those culinary possibilities is one of the great pleasures of eating season by season. Plus, all those root vegetables in the winter mean I'll have plenty of delicious braises and stews to dine on, and I'll feel warm and well pampered in the midst of the wintry landscape outside. With their hoop houses now in place, Miriam and Ben plan to farm limited vegetables throughout the winter. Many are sold at the Red Hook winter farmers' market, which Miriam spearheaded in 2008–2009. Very encouraging for local eaters in a four-season climate!

I also think that eating locally makes you less reliant on recipes and more open to adaptation, creativity, and reinterpretation. For example, barley, one of my favorite whole grains, can be used effortlessly all year long. You can sit down to a barley, tomato, zucchini, and mint salad in the summer, a warm pilaf of barley, peppers, butternut squash, and dried fruit in the fall, a root vegetable and barley stew in the winter, and a quick sauté of peas, fava beans, asparagus, mushrooms, and barley in the spring. As a liberated cook, you start first by learning what is ripe in your growing area and then explore how to use it.

The Hudson Valley is famous for its orchards, especially apple orchards, and apple-tasting here is a pleasure. Talea and Doug Fincke have run Montgomery Place Orchards for the last twenty-five years. They encourage you to taste their many varieties—Mutsu, Macoun, Ida Red, Cortlandt, McIntosh, Rome, Northern Spy, Greening. Soon you realize that some are best eaten out of hand, while others are perfect for pies and cakes, and still others lend themselves to chutneys, preserves, and slow-cooked apple butters.

As a liberated cook you let ingredients lead the way. This makes for a more improvisational style of cooking, though you can still stay true to your own culinary roots. For example, I describe the cuisine we serve at Gigi Trattoria as Hudson Valley Mediterranean. It is a style of cooking firmly rooted in local farm products, yet it draws on the Mediterranean for inspiration. Is it exactly what you would get in Palermo? No, that was never the point. Rather, it is a culinary viewpoint that features fresh, simply prepared food presented in an honest, uncluttered way. No fussy sauces, no complex recipes, nothing to dull the shine of great ingredients.

I have always felt that strong similarities exist between the Hudson Valley and the Mediterranean, especially Italy. Historically many generations of Italian immigrants bought farms and settled down here. Even the names of our towns—Athens, Cairo, Milan, Modena, Tivoli—reflect that Mediterranean connection. And while the familial roots of the farmers, ranchers, and food artisans living here today may not all lead back to southern Europe, those earlier farmers established a culture and sensibility that still endures.

When I opened Gigi Trattoria, I bought from local farmers because I figured that if my ingredients were fresher, my food would taste better and hopefully customers would line up for a table. I certainly didn't see myself as any kind of radical activist with a foodie agenda. In fact, I still don't. But I do recognize that eating local food challenges the agricultural status quo—environmentally, socially, and politically. By purchasing food grown closer to home you accomplish three things: you reduce the amount of spent fuel, you get great products, and you lend financial support to your local farm economy. When you support farms, you help save farmland and open spaces. It's estimated that over a million acres of U.S. farmland are lost each year to residential and commercial development. That is a real concern to Hudson Valley residents, who know firsthand the pressures of development. After all, New York City is only eighty miles to the south.

Don't forget to be practical. When it comes to food, take a moment to weigh local options against global ones before purchasing. See what is available in your community, especially from local growers. If the quality meets your standards, then buy what is nearby. If not, then by all means purchase a better product elsewhere. In some cases there is no choice—I will always buy Parmigiano from Parma and balsamic vinegar from Modena. You should always try to get the best quality of food available and consider (and minimize) waste. The food I buy from local sustainable farmers may not be the least expensive choice up front, but I know that the costs, both explicit and implicit, are calculated in the price, including the cost of maintaining a healthy environment.

Preserving farms means preserving history, cultural and culinary diversity, and local livelihoods. Dotted throughout the Hudson River Valley, towns like Beacon, Rhinebeck, Millerton, Red Hook, Chatham, and Kinderhook are heirs to some of the oldest agricultural traditions in America. This valley has been farmed almost continuously for four hundred years and was settled by some of the earliest immigrants to colonial America. Development in the Valley should be carefully planned to protect this precious resource. The wide-scale return to sustainable, often organic, growing methods in the Valley means that generations of children will still be able to bite into a crisp wine-flavored heirloom Spitzenburg apple grown here for—I hope—another four hundred years. When I think about that, I cross my fingers and smile.

A NOTE ON HOW TO USE THIS BOOK

This book is a resource for people who enjoy living in a four-season climate and want to try local eating either occasionally or in a more committed fashion. It can also work for people blessed with a more mixed harvest climate. The sections are organized seasonally, so you can easily find out what's going to be available at your local farm or farmers' market. To be sure, there are some regional differences in farmers' markets, most related to timing and local preferences. In October our Rhinebeck market will stock lots of hard-skinned squashes, fresh garlic, and onions; yet the farmers' markets in North Carolina might still have a few late-season peppers on hand and a plentiful selection of collard greens. Not a problem. Generally farmers' markets across the United States will have a great deal of the same kinds of produce, even though the warmer or cooler weather means that produce shows up at different times.

So take some time and get to know your local farmers' market and farm community. Even take a farm tour if you get the chance. Most farms love to have visitors and are proud to show off what they are doing. More and more farms are leaning toward eco-tourism, offering pick-your-own services and tours coordinated directly or through your local tourism board. From a consumer perspective, a hands-on understanding of good farming practices helps you make more informed choices.

Even if you never set foot on a farm, eating locally means you'll be spending some time at your local farmers' market or at shops that carry local products. Make it a weekly ritual; slow down and take your time. Farmers' markets are great places to talk to farmers and sample food that's likely within forty-eight hours of picking. Plus, you'll find unique varieties of produce that can't be found in any conventional store. Try them. You may help preserve a distinctive food that could otherwise be lost to us. And it can also inspire your inner chef! Remember that the key to a "sustainable" healthy diet is strengthened when you use all those insights gleaned from farmers and chefs to create a great-tasting dinner.

While I'm really proud of what we are doing here in the Hudson Valley, I encourage you to take a look at what is growing in your own locale. Each part of the country has its own food traditions, and as the desire for local foods grows, farmers and consumers will develop new ones. I hope this book enhances your efforts to seek them out.

I firmly believe that getting in touch with seasonal and local eating can bring more joy to your table and strengthen your connections to your community. Have fun, and remember: the recipes included here are flexible and forgiving. Substitutions are allowed! In fact I've included some substitution ideas with each recipe to get you started, and some cost guidelines ($ = $2 or less per serving, up to $$$ = $8 or more) for what you can expect to pay for the main ingredients, especially if they're in season.

Building on my belief that local eating is healthy eating, I've added some basic nutritional information on market produce and highlighted some specific fruits and vegetables that have great health-giving properties. I've also focused on some of my favorite local growers and food artisans. Their environmentally sustainable practices can give you a better understanding about what progressive farmers all over the United States are doing. While there has been a gradual winnowing away of independent farm culture over the last half century, these environmentally focused farmers are a bright light of ingenuity, individuality, and commitment. They deserve our attention.

There's a section on entertaining (page 295) that should make your seasonal celebrations a breeze. I've included menus to start your creative juices flowing; make these recipes a jumping-off point for your own "liberated" style of cooking.

And check out the sources section (page 303), which gives a listing of online sites to find local Hudson Valley specialties, from preserves to condiments to smoked foods, and additional online sites to encourage and support your local eating efforts, including help in locating your nearest farmers' market.

Spring

Predicting the true arrival of spring is like reading tea leaves. I'm never right. But after years of living in the Valley, I do rely on a couple of signs. The first is the air: one morning it smells just a little different to me, a touch more fragrant and a slight bit warmer against my face. Then I start to see the first baskets of fresh green produce trickling in from the fields, filling up our farmers' market cooler at Gigi Market with something other than root vegetables. Hurrah! The best sign of all is in my garden, as bulbs start their first tentative thrusts above ground. What a treat when you forget just how many you planted last season!

Make no mistake, March here is still cold, sometimes even icy. The sides of the roads are covered with sand and dirt from a winter's worth of plowings, and there is often a surprise snow or ice storm, just when I've put the shovel away in the barn. As the temperature slowly rises above freezing, the Esopus Creek in nearby Saugerties swells with water from the melting snow on the eleven Catskill peaks that feed into its watershed. The copious rain and the thaw seem to prompt trees to bud and animals to start their "spring fever." As for me, well, it seems time to bid winter adieu. I gather friends for a final hearty meal of choucroute garnie washed down with plenty of Riesling and beer. It's the last time we'll need that warm, stick-to-your ribs food for months.

As spring unfolds, green rolls over the Valley like a wave, slowly moving up the watershed. Tree leaves unfurl and soon form a backdrop for flowers and grasses. The yellow forsythia bursts into bloom and the local orchards flower into fields of white and pink. For me, the beauty of an orchard in full bloom is one of the most felicitous examples of man's work with nature. The spring cascade of colors will continue in the weeks ahead as dogwood, lilac, and many others bloom. The flowering of shadbush and ornamental magnolia announce the return of shad to the river to spawn. Spring continues its push northward and upward from the coast to the peaks of the Adirondacks.

The vernal equinox, around March 20, marks the very start of spring. Soon the skies are filled with Canada geese migrating to colder climes. The first warm rains encourage spring peepers to burst into song and jump-start the mating urges of frogs and salamanders in countless wetlands, ponds, and pools. I find that birds are once again nesting in my gutters, and their chatter wakes me up bright and early. With sleep no longer possible, I slowly make my way into the kitchen for a cup of coffee and watch the sun rise over the back meadow.

By late March I begin to hear the familiar sounds of tractor engines at Hearty Roots Farm and Migliorelli's. It's time to start turning the land and begin planting. As I look at my property—a mess of broken sticks, twigs, and branches—I realize it's time for me to get working as well. The act of setting things in order, bagging brush and raking up debris, working outdoors rather than rushing to my car, clears my head and lifts my mood. It's so good to be outside.

Spring planting means spring eating. Starting in April, peas, fiddlehead ferns, and tender baby greens such as escarole, bok choy, and Sky Farm's handpicked baby arugula and idiosyncratic mesclun mix start to come through the kitchen door. Mâche, mint, chervil, watercress, tender dandelion greens, and puntarelle, a slightly peppery green, are also available to be tossed into salads or used in a springtime panzotti, a wild green–filled ravioli with sage and Parmesan. Asparagus patches are producing beautiful stalks to serve roasted alongside tender racks of baby lamb or in one of our super-thin Skizzas with roasted Vidalia onions and braised leeks, topped with melted Fontina. The asparagus I love best have stalks so pencil-thin you can actually eat them raw. Along with baby carrots, fingerling potatoes, and baby turnips, asparagus works its way into our roasted vegetable side dishes, and asparagus tips and stems stud pasta and risotto dishes. I love asparagus Italian-style next to a sunny-side-up egg with a broken-yolk dressing spilling onto the green or even white spears. Last spring Gigi's wonderful chef, Wilson Costa, created a new favorite of mine: a fresh asparagus slaw.

It's great to taste cold food again. Overall, the menu lightens up. There are spring pea and leek soups, marinated lamb with new potatoes (page 50), and all kinds of relishes and crunchy salads. I'm ready for pesto, and many spring ingredients—arugula, watercress, even blanched asparagus—can be pureed into a great-tasting mix. Why wait for summer's basil?

Roasting vegetables is a good idea, even in spring, and while many of the same fall vegetables are used, this time they are almost miniature—tiny baby carrots, peas, cipolline onions and shallots, baby beets and mushrooms. Served alone or spooned into a risotto with fresh herbs, they make a beautiful plate filled with spring flavors. In an ecumenical nod to the bounty of the season, I also include fava beans and artichokes—two non-local but symbolic vegetables that I've associated with spring since the time I lived in Italy. There is some room for nostalgia in life, after all.

Spring is all about preparation—in the fields, at home, and in the restaurant and market. Gigi managers and I are busy hiring and training staff and finalizing our basic menus. I'm also one of the many gardeners thronging local nurseries to gather up seedlings and seed packets for my garden beds, picking out annual and perennial plants to tuck in. My garden "plan" never works out the way I expect it to. I always plant too early and get trumped by one late frost. Later in the summer, I'll learn that I didn't plant vegetables as close or as far apart as required or even in the right bed. Ah, well, who really follows those seed packet instructions anyway? At Gigi Trattoria, I help load up large vases with branches of apple and cherry blossoms. What fleeting beauty spring holds in those bouquets.

The pace along the streets of Rhinebeck starts to pick up, with more people and less parking. The locals are out and the New Yorkers are back. The Rhinebeck farmers' market opens on Sunday mornings in late May, and crowds descend to buy not only vegetables and fruit, but also honey, fish, game, cheeses, pickles, fresh bread, handmade chocolates, and more. At Gigi Market,

everyone is busy. Lots of produce is coming in from the fields, filling our retail and production coolers.

Toward the end of spring everyone comes looking for strawberries. Ashley Kearns, our pastry chef, starts making strawberry galettes and rustic strawberry-rhubarb tarts, which seem to go right from the oven into someone's shopping cart along with several containers of fresh berries. I love strawberries too and eat them fresh whenever I can, usually holding a napkin under my chin to catch any escaping juices. John, the Gigi catering director, is busy locking in dates for clients' summer entertaining. As he talks on the phone nonstop, his furrowed brow gives me a clue that summer might be busy indeed.

THE SPRING HARVEST

Peas and Beans

With their pale tendrils climbing up rows of trellises, pea and bean plants are among the earliest signs of green in local vegetable gardens. Garden peas, sometimes called English peas, are grown specifically for their seeds and are harvested as soon as the pods are full with seeds still tender and sweet. Chefs look forward to spring's fresh crop, using its versatility, color, and taste in myriad ways. At Gigi Trattoria, we mash fresh peas to make a crostini topping (see

The Missing Harvest

When Henry Hudson explored the river four hundred years ago, his first mate, Robert Juet, recorded in his journal that "the river is full of fish." As a broad and deep river estuary, the Hudson River was home to up to two hundred varieties of fresh- and saltwater fish. This provided people living nearby with a local food source that was even richer than the surrounding farmland. Part of the cycle of activity in the river was the arrival each spring of American shad entering from the Bay of Fundy, which separates the Canadian provinces of Nova Scotia and New Brunswick. All shad, whether they spawn in the Hudson River, in the Delaware, or in the Connecticut, return to the Bay of Fundy once a year. The local Indians harvested and preserved this exceptionally bony herring by "planking" it—nailing it onto pieces of wood and propping the wood near a smoky fire for hours, a method adopted later by farm communities along the river. The flesh, rich in fat and creamy in texture, was deeply flavorful and a great source of protective omega-3 fatty acids. As a bonus, a netted female shad might yield sacs of up to three hundred thousand eggs, called shad roe, which were gently wrapped in bacon and fried.

I use the past tense because by all indications the shad numbers in the past decade were the worst in hundreds, if not thousands, of years. The shad population is a fraction of what it was as recently as ten years ago, both in the river and entering the river. The numbers of live young have dropped drastically, and the overall weight of fish leaving the Hudson to return to the Bay of Fundy is puny.

There are a host of possible culprits. Environmental disregard is one. Traditional spawning grounds have been dredged or dammed, making the journey more difficult for shad. River-adjacent coal plants and a nuclear plant have sucked up huge volumes of cooling water, and with it fish eggs, larvae, and habitat. Manufacturing has dumped waste and communities have dumped sewage into the river, creating oxygen-depleted "dead" zones. Overfishing through the 1940s caused a steep decline in shad and other native fish, along with the arrival of new invasive species, such as the zebra mussel, which arrived here in 1991 via dumped ocean freighter ballast. Shad caught as bycatch by Atlantic trawlers may also mean that less fish are making it into the river in the first place.

As a result, a species that thrived here for an estimated ten thousand years is near collapse. And the culture and life of Hudson River fishermen who caught and filled crates of fresh shad bound for New York City has collapsed as well. We are interdependent, after all.

But perhaps there is yet time. If we are very careful, the shad can return. Today there are more people and communities in New York championing the cleanup and care of the Hudson River than ever before. One of its strongest champions is the Riverkeeper organization, which since the 1960s has systematically and aggressively prosecuted polluters, making the river cleaner today than it has been for decades. Then there is the most beautiful element of nature: the ability of an ecosystem to right itself over time. Today we see evidence that some species are recovering—striped bass in particular and slowly, but encouragingly, sturgeon. Ocean intercept fishing was declared illegal in 2005, thereby reducing bycatch and ensuring a safer passage for shad from open waters into the Hudson.

We are far from what Robert Juet saw when he came up the river in 1609. But the Hudson, with our concerted efforts at restoration and preservation, may one day be described in a visitor's journal as a river full of fish.

Sweet Pea Guacamole, page 16), slather them with shavings of Parmesan and a drizzle of olive oil, use them whole in spring risotto preparations or pasta dishes, puree them into soups, or serve them alongside roasts, just blanched and drizzled with olive oil and lemon juice. Peas are technically a legume, with high protein levels. It may come as a surprise, but a ¾-cup serving of peas contains more protein than a tablespoon of peanut butter or a single egg. I don't know whether you are willing to replace your morning eggs with a bowl of peas, but you could! More traditionally, I fold them into scrambled farm-fresh eggs with some snippings of the wild thyme that grows in a patch in my meadow.

Besides delivering protein, peas are also rich in the B vitamins, including folate and B_6 (which is supportive of cardiovascular health), and are a good source of vitamin C and fiber. They also contain plenty of vitamin K_1, which activates osteocalcin. Osteocalcin anchors calcium inside the bone, and adequate osteocalcin levels are critical for achieving strong, healthy bones.

Garden peas are somewhat unique. All other types of peas are either eaten with the whole pod or shelled to reveal a much starchier legume. So for me garden peas are a little bit special and worth the effort to shell. That isn't to say that I don't like the other kinds too: snow peas with their almost transparent pod and immature peas; sugar snap peas, which are big, fat, and crunchy when eaten raw; and classic Blue Lake green beans and romano beans, which are great cooked either briefly or until they are really, really tender. There are wax beans, purple spotted beans, cream peas, black-eyed peas, butter beans . . . too many to list.

Ask people what their favorite bean is and you'll get almost as many different answers as people. One bean that has a special place in my heart is the fava. Fava beans belong to a group of beans called broad beans and are beloved in Italian and Greek communities, where they have always been consumed raw when picked young, or cooked when left to fully mature on the vine. Like lots of beans, favas are a near-perfect food: high in fiber, low in fat, lots of iron and folate, and so much protein that Italians have long referred to them as "the meat of the poor." The plant itself is native to North Africa and doesn't do particularly well in the Hudson Valley, preferring the hot, dry weather of California. A lot of fava beans are now grown in the western United States, where farmers refer to them as a "feeder" plant because the bush produces lots of nitrogen to replenish the soil. All well and good, but that misses the point entirely: the bean. It grows in the downy interior of a large leathery pod. When

picked young, the pod is a light green and the favas themselves are plump and green. See if you can find them in the freezer section of the supermarket; there are some excellent brands of frozen shelled young favas. Eat them simply with fresh pecorino cheese, a drizzle of good olive oil, and a glass of wine for an extremely ancient yet civilized snack. When they are a little more mature, the beans develop a white covering that has to be peeled before cooking. That's a time-consuming task, but worth it. After peeling off the outer layer with the tips of your fingernails, sauté the fava beans in olive oil until tender with some shallots, a bit of garlic, and some flat-leaf parsley. Serve with a crumbly feta, some fresh tzatziki yogurt dip, and a stack of whole-wheat pita, and you can close your eyes and imagine yourself dining along the Mediterranean.

Spring Radishes and Daikon

Radishes show up at Gigi Market from April through June, and then again in October. We typically have a good crop for both harvests, but I treasure the spring one because the peppery flavor, color, and crisp snap of a spring radish is a welcome tonic for my body and taste buds. Yes, you find the Cherry Belle cultivar—the classic radish with the red skin and white interior—but I also like the White Icicle variety and the slightly elongated French Breakfast radishes to munch on while drinking a glass of beer or to include as part of a cheese plate. Hearty Roots and Migliorelli farms grow some amazingly tender French Breakfast radishes. There are also very mild radish varieties like the Gala and Roodbol, which are great when eaten thinly sliced on buttered bread.

Like most Americans, I eat radishes raw. Their pungent flavor derives from the same enzymes (albeit in milder form) that make mustard, horseradish, and wasabi so eye-opening. All radishes lose some of that zip when cooked, and I've seen some interest among chefs in braising radishes slowly until tender and then drizzling them lightly with aged balsamic vinegar for a gentle sweet/spicy flavor. Radishes can be added to stir-fries, chopped fine and added to dips and dressings, or shredded into green salads. They also make great pickles.

Daikon, a large elongated radish originally from Asia and now grown here, is really very mild when cooked and almost begins to taste like a potato. Some friends of mine make what they call "Chinese latkes" with grated daikon, salt, flour, and a bit of tapioca flour. Fried into small cakes, the daikon is crunchy on the outside, creamy soft on the inside, and perfect with a bit of garlic chili paste on top. Definitely a comfort food. Mr. Mink, a treasured local farmer who specializes in heirloom fruits and vegetables, especially tomatoes, grows a "watermelon" variety of daikon that has a light green rind and a surprising speckled pink interior. Gigi chef

Wilson Costa creates a mini "sandwich" appetizer of paper-thin daikon slices filled with our homemade herbed ricotta. It's interesting, beautiful, delicious, and does exactly what an appetizer is supposed to: get you excited about what is coming next.

As members of the Brassica family of vegetables, radishes are rich in antioxidants and phytochemicals that help to ward off cancer. They contain high amounts of vitamin C, folic acid, and potassium and are a good source of vitamin B_6, riboflavin, magnesium, copper, and calcium. All these nutrients are optimized when radishes are eaten fresh, so look for firm leaves, bright color, and a firm root. Avoid tired, wilting leaves and any soft spots on the root. If you have a little extra space on the patio or in the garden, by all means plant a few radishes. They are easy to grow, which is one reason why children's gardens usually include radishes. And with their little bulbous roots sticking out of the soil, they're kind of cute.

Strawberries

Strawberries come in from the fields beginning in late May in the Hudson Valley and may show up even earlier in the southern or western regions of the United States. No matter where they are grown, the first strawberries at the farmers' market are snatched up immediately. Sales will remain strong until some of the summer stone fruits appear. Strawberries are America's favorite berry, and demand for them has led to the development of hardy varieties that can be picked early and shipped great distances. But there is an obvious reason why local Hudson Valley farmers sell their strawberries so quickly and at such a premium: flavor, simple as that. Berries, after all, are fragile and when fully ripe they really can't travel long distances. To eat juicy, sweet strawberries, you've got to find what's growing nearby. Make a day of it, get some exercise, and save some money by going to a pick-your-own strawberry farm. There are many in the Hudson Valley; the two closest to me are Mead Orchards and Fraleigh's Rose Hill Farm.

And when you do fill your basket with fresh berries, my advice is to just go ahead and enjoy. They are an extremely healthy fruit. In fact, ounce for ounce, they contain more vitamin C than citrus. Foods rich in vitamin C may lower the incidence of gastrointestinal cancers.

You can also enjoy strawberries in classic shortcakes (with or without rhubarb, which is harvested at about the same time), in tarts and galettes, spooned on top of pound cake, or even as a savory dish, such as our Strawberry Balsamic BBQ Sauce (page 54). Any slightly bruised berries can go into the blender for smoothies. The classic combination of a bowl of berries with a drizzle of fresh cream on top is pretty good, but I prefer the Italian way—really good aged balsamic vinegar from

Modena drizzled over berries. Just a drop adds tremendous depth of flavor. Of course, adding a scoop of vanilla gelato makes it even better. But remember, great strawberries don't require a lot of fussing. In the end, simple is best.

Leeks, Scallions, and Chives

These are the members of the allium family that show up early to the party. Their cousins—onions, garlic, and shallots—arrive in the fall, fashionably late, and are in many ways a completely different kind of guest. I like the way scallions can act either as an herb or as a vegetable, graceful and versatile in both roles. I also love the beauty of chives, especially the long onion chives and the pale green–tipped garlic chives found in Asian markets. I keep them on my kitchen counter in water-filled cups, where I can enjoy their appearance. A just-pulled bucket of fat leeks with dirt still clinging to their roots reminds me that you can look tough but still have a tender heart.

All spring alliums are mellow, mellow, mellow. Leeks cooked slowly in butter or olive oil become a refined, subtle sweet mass. Use the dark green parts to flavor soups and stock, tying them into a bundle to easily remove and toss after cooking. Add the tender white and light green parts to soups and stews toward the end of cooking. Scallions, also called spring onions, green onions, baby onions, or salad onions, can provide a bright note when eaten raw but become mild when roasted or grilled. I've had smoky grilled scallions paired with everything from delicately flavored fish to robustly seasoned carne asada tacos to great effect. Chives' mild flavor adds a note of freshness to dishes and is great with potatoes, eggs, and rice dishes. Their flavor becomes even more muted when cooked, so use lots if you are going to add them to breads or focaccia, soups, or steamed or roasted dishes. I usually add them right before serving to hold on to that piquant touch of onion in the finished dish.

What spring alliums share with their fall peers is that they are a fat-free, high-fiber food containing two powerful antioxidants, sulphur and quercetin, that help neutralize cell-damaging free radicals in the body. These health benefits have been documented many times over in scientific studies. Leeks also have lots of vitamin C, B_6, folate, and iron, which make them helpful in stabilizing blood sugar, and many alliums offer up a laundry list of other benefits. They are antibacterial, antifungal, antiviral, support a healthy immune system, are naturally detoxifying, contain anticoagulant properties (which helps moderate the risk of heart attack and stroke), and help boost "good" fats in the blood and reduce "bad" ones. Wow! Bring on the onion soup (page 218)! Best of all, spring onions contain very low levels of sulphur compounds, so there are no telltale "onion tears" when you cook with these spring lovelies.

Asparagus

In her book *Animal, Vegetable, Miracle,* Barbara Kingsolver plants an asparagus bed at her small farm in West Virginia, something many early American households did as a way to ensure fresh spears every year. Planting an asparagus bed is quite a sustainable endeavor, since a well-maintained bed, once established, can be productive for up to fifteen years. It just keeps producing and producing. Good thing, too, because we tend to eat as much asparagus as we can get our hands on. Perhaps because it's so easy to prepare and has such an elegant appearance.

This part of New York, through to western Massachusetts, has good sandy growing conditions for asparagus. In fact, in the early 1900s the region was one of the premier asparagus growing areas, with lots of farmers near the Connecticut River harvesting the famous Mary Washington variety. In the 1970s the plants were hit with a soil fungus called fusarium that destroyed field after field. While most farmers stopped cultivation, those that remain are now reporting that asparagus production seems to be slowly coming back.

Now to the eternal asparagus question: thick or thin? I'm going to play it down the middle; I truly like both, for different purposes. For a quick turn on the grill or single presentation as the star ingredient, I'll use the thin ones. For dishes where asparagus is incorporated into the finished product (soups, slaws, relishes, risotto, and so on), thicker stems are just fine. I use a vegetable peeler to get to the tender stem and cut the stem and tips separately on the diagonal. Those thicker stems can be sautéed or cooked first, with the delicate tips added a few minutes later. The truth is that both thick and thin spears can be very tender, and I think the preference is just personal, not based on any solid facts.

Asparagus plays well with all its neighbors—English peas, fresh lettuces, and chives and spring onions. It's great with stronger flavors, too, such as those found in Chinese stir-fries, and it goes well with refrigerator odds and ends like cheese, eggs, and cream. An old Connecticut farm recipe is simply tender boiled asparagus served on toast with hot cream and a few grinds of fresh black pepper. Steaming seems to be how most people cook asparagus, but I love the way the late Edna Lewis roasted her asparagus spears with a little butter. When I lived in the Bassano del Grappa area of Italy, I fell in love with the local white asparagus, available ever so briefly in late May to early June. The spears were served steamed until just tender. There I learned to make my dressing on the side of the plate: Using a fork, you would whisk an egg yolk with a bit of vinegar, salt, and pepper. Then you dipped the asparagus in and ate. Lovely.

Prepping asparagus is easy. Just snap off the woody bottoms. The spears won't all be the same length, but that isn't a huge issue. Steam, sauté, or roast until they're as soft as you like them. Again, it's all about personal preference, just as some people like green beans crisp and some like them very tender.

Asparagus is a great source of vitamins A, C, and E, folate, and the minerals potassium and zinc. Interestingly, it is a rich source of an antioxidant called rutin, which actually strengthens the cell walls of capillaries, and of a cancer-fighting flavenoid called quercetin, which has significant anti-inflammatory properties. Glutathione, a peptide (a small string of amino acids), is also found in asparagus. It is of special interest to athletes and trainers because increased levels of glutathione may significantly reduce cellular oxidative stress and increase peak power and muscular performance. Asparagus is also moderately high in fiber, especially a type called inulin, which supports "good" bacteria in the gut and promotes gastrointestinal health.

Rhubarb

Who was the genius who first figured that rhubarb was edible? Probably the same woman who realized you can eat an artichoke! Think about it: rhubarb has extremely tart, astringent stalks crowned with toxic leaves and roots with laxative properties. What a promising plant! Used medicinally for centuries, rhubarb didn't gain favor as a food until the seventeenth century in England, when it was paired with sugar. At that point its reputation as a pie filling and food for jam was assured in Britain—and subsequently in the United States, where farmers and backyard gardeners in the northeastern states started planting it in the early 1800s. As a plant, rhubarb has even greater longevity than asparagus. Once established in a good spot, rhubarb will keep producing for years and years. Some farmers claim they're still cutting rhubarb from plants their grandparents put in.

For such a bitter plant, rhubarb is about 95 percent water. It's a good source of potassium, vitamin C, and dietary fiber. While it also contains a good bit of calcium, the oxalic acid in rhubarb binds with minerals like calcium, making it difficult for it to be absorbed by the body. It is that same oxalic acid that gives rhubarb its mouth-puckering tartness.

Rhubarb starts showing up at the Rhinebeck farmers' market in April and May. It's usually sold as a bunch weighing about two pounds, but I've also seen it sold loose, allowing you to pick out the freshest stalks. Some people string rhubarb, running a knife down the outside length of the stalk to remove the stringy fibers, which are similar to those found in celery. That might be a good idea with very mature stalks, but generally I don't bother when using the young, slim, tender spring ones. Rhubarb is usually stewed with ample sugar, and a two-pound bunch

will cook down to about ¾ cup, so if you're making a rhubarb-only cobbler, it might be wise to buy a couple of bunches. Rhubarb has classically been paired with strawberries for pie, a great combination of two seasonal ingredients. But these days cutting-edge chefs have also begun using rhubarb in a tart sauce paired with game, salmon, or even foie gras, and in spicy hot chutneys for Indian and Asian dishes. It's nice to see a plant that has always been used for dessert used in savory dishes, even though I still like it as jam slathered on breakfast scones and muffins.

Chef Alain Sailhac, a mentor, friend, and the senior dean of studies at the French Culinary Institute, once showed me how he likes his rhubarb. He strings the stalk with a paring knife, slices it on the diagonal, and sprinkles the slices with sugar. Then he places it under the broiler until the sugar caramelizes. From there, it is eaten directly out of the pan or on top of ice cream, gelato, or frozen yogurt. Simple and delicious.

GREAT SEASONAL INGREDIENT

Lettuce

Microgreens, baby greens, mesclun, salad herbs, rocket or arugula, baby spinach, butter lettuces, mâche, cress—the number of varieties, flavors, colors, and recipes for filling America's salad bowl has never been greater. From wedges of iceberg lettuce in the 1970s to the Asian spring mix available prewashed in breathable plastic bags today, the technological innovation brought to bear on large-scale cultivation and distribution of lettuce is one of the great stories of American agriculture. The loamy topsoil of the sunny Salinas Valley in California means that even when it is snowing outside we can have fresh tender greens on the table, a harbinger of spring.

And that's a good thing. But while you can enjoy organic mesclun at eight dollars a pound no matter the season, what you get is still just a faint notion of what a great salad can be. Because to taste a great salad you must start with great lettuce, and great lettuce is one of nature's most delicate, most ephemeral gifts. Its flavor and texture change quickly after harvest. Cut, it immediately begins to use the extra oxygen in its leaves to boost its metabolism and speed up its immune system. A plant still in the ground can grow new leaves and save itself, but cut lettuces don't have that connection anymore. Quickly the cellulose within its walls breaks down, releasing its energy and producing water. The more water the plant exudes, the more it wilts, and the more its flavor fades. Knowing this, I place mesclun at the top of my list of products to "eat local."

Complicating matters further is the fact that lettuce is mostly a creature of cool spring weather. There are certain varieties that continue growing in the warm summer months in places (like the Hudson Valley)

that get cooling breezes during the night, and some varieties even soldier on into the fall, when the temperatures drop to near freezing and the leaves develop an almost sweet toughness, with dark color and great flavor. But come winter, you'll have no more salad until the following spring. I switch over to some of the lettuces that are grown so well on the West Coast—romaine and red-leaf lettuce to name a couple—but I still dream of early spring lettuces grown by my friends, tasting like the earth around me and the sky above.

Mesclun, from an old French word meaning "mix," was one of the early advance shots fired by Alice Waters in the 1970s food revolution. Her restaurant, Chez Panisse, featured a mix of organic leaves from a dozen different plants that Waters had grown from French seeds. Served with baked rounds of goat cheese, mesclun was new and exotic.

In Provence, where mesclun has been cut for generations, gardeners literally scatter varieties of seeds together onto the planting bed and just harvest what comes up. Since certain lettuces are ready before others, the mix of greens always included some tender, some tough, some sweet, and some bitter leaves. My experience as a restaurateur is that Americans generally don't embrace the bitter or the tough, so mesclun mixes here tend to span the sweet to peppery range of flavors. Just a sample of what is grown in the Hudson Valley includes mesclun combinations like mizuna, purslane, mâche and chervil, red and green chicories, and endive. All of which are a good beginning to a great salad. Then local farmers add special plants like red amaranth, frisée, purple radish, buckwheat greens, tatsoi, purple mizuna, micro red mustard, micro peppercress, micro red Russian kale, baby dandelion, fennel, mini golden purslane, edible chrysanthemum, sorrel, pea shoots and greens, spinach, escarole, nasturtiums, impatiens, arugula blossoms, and ever-so-tiny mustard flowers, which spice up and beautify salads and sandwiches.

There is some nutritional sense to a wildly exuberant mix of salad greens. First, loose-leaf lettuces are loaded with vitamin A and fiber. They are high in potassium and low in calories. Dark lettuce leaves are rich in folate and contain useful amounts of beta-carotene as well as vitamin C and phytochemicals such as coumarins, flavenoids, and lactucin. If iceberg is the only type of lettuce in your shopping cart, you are choosing the least nutritious member of the lettuce family.

Don't blame the iceberg, though! It has been allowed to grow too long in order to gain weight and command a higher price. Actually, perfectly mature iceberg lettuce has a fuller, slightly open head with beautiful leaves, and most surprising of all is the color. It's not green at all. It's golden. If you garden, certainly harvest it at this younger stage.

I've spent many years creating, eating, and enjoying salad. I was even lucky enough to create salads for a New York City chain called Just Salad (www.justsalad.com) that are healthy "meals in a bowl." For me a great main-course salad includes a mix of lettuces and loose-leaf greens for flavor, texture, and nutrition along with whole grains and lean protein. Great lettuce doesn't need a lot of help, so I recommend a light hand with the dressing. You need just enough to barely coat the leaves, no more. Add some of your favorite veggies, fruits, nuts, or a crumble of cheese, and all that's left to do is dig in.

SKY FARM

Working with many Hudson Valley farmers over the years, I've noticed certain personality types that show up time and time again. There's the maverick who doesn't like to be told what to do. And the loner who is simply more at home in the natural quiet of a garden than in a noisy city. There's the exuberant plantsman who loves all kinds of buds and flowers and fruits and creates lush landscapes of amazing diversity. And there are even artists, sustained and inspired by the beauty of the natural world. Chris Regan of Sky Farm in Millerton is one of those—a painter whose chosen palette is endless shades of green and whose eleven-acre-wide "painting" changes subtly from spring to summer to fall.

Chris is a self-described salad farmer, which is sort of like Monet calling himself a picture painter—not entirely untrue, but vastly wide of the mark. For in fact, the lettuces from Sky Farm, grown at the foot of the Berkshire hills, have helped Gigi Trattoria and other Hudson Valley restaurants develop very devoted customers. I've tasted more lettuces than I can remember, and these are without peer. I've often wondered why Chris's salad tastes so good. True, it's a careful mix of different leaves and herbs that go well together. But that isn't all. Compared with a standard bagged organic mesclun mix from the supermarket, Sky Farm's mix is a collection of sturdy, turgid leaves, still alive and ready to release their full energy and flavor. The bagged mix is like a faded snapshot of lettuce. It's a hazy remembrance of what it once was.

At Gigi, the mesclun mix and arugula from Sky Farm deserve much of the credit for our two most popular salads, the Barbina (page 146) and the Rughetta, a simple mix of Chris's tender baby arugula, Parmesan shavings, and an olive oil and lemon vinaigrette. The delicate flavors and tender baby leaves are terribly missed when the growing season is over.

Chris, who before starting Sky Farm was a fine artist and metalworker, is a strong proponent of organic, sustainable methods and believes that farming can be a viable occupation, even today. So for eight months each year, he harvests about eight hundred pounds of salad greens a week, all hand-

Gigi Skizza: gamberetti (small shrimp) with pea shoots, red onion, and red pepper flakes (see page 28 for this Skizza and lots of other ideas)

Spring Pea Soup (page 30)

Spring Vegetable Stew (page 26)

*Sautéed Red Snapper with Herb Roasted Fingerling Potatoes
and Sweet Pea Guacamole* (page 46)

Spring (and Every Other Season) Lasagna (page 39)

Spring and Fall Baby Beet Salad (page 21)

Hearty Roots Farm Spring Harvest Risotto (page 44):
(clockwise from top right) spring, winter, summer, and fall

cut, and sells them exclusively to forty local restaurants. He doesn't own the land he farms but leases it from friends, a practice I notice is becoming more and more common in the Hudson Valley as land prices climb. Leasing is a great option for farmers. The landowner gets a tax exemption, the land remains in cultivation, and the investment barrier that confronts would-be farmers is dropped. Further helping Sky Farm's bottom line is that Chris grows a highly specialized product, one that is visually appealing and inspiring to chefs. In fact, he feels that the number of great restaurants along the Hudson and the appreciation of local cuisine have allowed farmers like him to grow food on a small scale and still prosper.

Chris would say that making a great salad is all in the mix, and that crafting a great mesclun mix is a challenge he enjoys. A typical box of Sky Farm mesclun can include up to sixteen varieties of lettuce; eight different types of Asian greens, such as bok choy and tatsoi; two kinds of chicories; edible flowers; and up to ten different herbs, including sorrel, parsley, chervil, fennel, salad burnet, and others. When you open a box, you behold a pristine assortment of tender lettuces that calls for only the very lightest, simplest dressing. These salads, reflective of Chris's polished tastes and his careful and attentive growing style, always carry themselves and require no propping up by heavy, intensely seasoned vinaigrettes.

When I last visited the farm, tucked in a beautiful nook of land between rolling hills just outside the village, I saw a hazy purple field of amaranth, a plant typically grown for its grain but interesting to Chris because of its color and taste. I asked Chris if I can expect to see it in one of his boxes later this summer. The answer: of course I can.

Sky Farm, 122 Boston Corners Road,
Millerton, NY 12546
845-698-0353

Sweet Pea Guacamole

*Enjoy this light and easy-to-prepare guacamole all spring. Gigi executive chef Wilson Costa
and chef de cuisine Kevin Hermann include it on many of our spring menu specials
as it adds flavor, vibrant color, and good cheer after the long winter.*

2 tablespoons	sugar
1 tablespoon	salt
2 cups	shelled fresh peas (or frozen peas, thawed)
1 tablespoon	chopped fresh mint
¼ cup	extra-virgin olive oil
	Freshly ground black pepper

Bring 1 quart of water to a boil in a medium saucepan. Season the water with the sugar and salt, and add the peas. Boil for 4 to 5 minutes, until the peas are just tender and bright green (if using frozen peas, cook for only 1 minute).

Meanwhile, prepare an ice bath by filling a medium bowl three-fourths full with ice cubes and water.

Drain the peas, reserving 1 cup of the cooking liquid. Transfer the peas to the ice bath and let them cool completely. Then drain the peas and add them to a food processor along with ⅓ cup of the reserved cooking liquid and the mint. Pulse to combine. Scrape down the sides of the bowl to make sure all the peas hit the blade. Turn the motor on and add more of the cooking liquid, a little at time, through the feed tube to work the peas into a thick puree with the consistency of guacamole. With the motor still running, drizzle the olive oil through the feed tube. Adjust the seasoning with more salt, if necessary, and pepper, and transfer the guacamole to a serving bowl.

SERVING SUGGESTION

Serve the spread with crackers, crostini, or toasted bread triangles.

VARIATIONS

• Use tarragon instead of mint.
• Give it a touch of cayenne to kick up the flavor.

• A handful of cooked whole peas for a chunky texture and finely diced red bell pepper for color contrast are both nice additions, increasing the dish's textural interest.

LEFTOVERS

Replace high-fat sandwich spreads with this yummy and nutritious guacamole.

NUTRITION

Peas are rich in the B vitamins folate and B_6 (both supportive of cardiovascular health) and are a good source of vitamin C and fiber. They also contain good amounts of vitamin K.

ECONOMY $

Fresh Fava Bean Spread

MAKES 6 TO 8 SERVINGS

*Use this as a dip or spread with some crusty bread, pour a glass of
white wine such as Fiano or Falanghina, and pretend you're in Rome.*

2 cups	shelled fresh fava beans, cooked and peeled (see Note, page 27), or frozen fava beans or garden peas, thawed
¼ cup	finely grated Grana Padano or Parmesan cheese
1 tablespoon	grated lemon zest
2½ tablespoons	fresh lemon juice
½ cup plus 1 tablespoon	extra-virgin olive oil
	Salt and freshly ground black pepper

Combine the fava beans, Grana Padano, and lemon zest and juice in a food processor and pulse until the beans are chopped. With the motor running, add the ½ cup oil through the feed tube in a slow stream, processing until the mixture is fairly smooth. Season with salt and pepper to taste, and transfer to a serving bowl. Drizzle the remaining 1 tablespoon oil over the top.

SERVING SUGGESTION

Serve this spread with crackers or toasted bread.

LEFTOVERS

Replace high-fat sandwich spreads with this flavorful spread.

NUTRITION

To create a lighter version of this recipe, you could substitute water, chicken stock, or vegetable stock for ¼ cup of the oil. Fava beans are rich in protein, B vitamins (especially folate), and fiber.

ECONOMY $$

Asparagus Soufflé

MAKES 6 APPETIZER SERVINGS (PREPARED IN 4-OUNCE RAMEKINS)
OR 4 ENTRÉE SERVINGS (PREPARED IN 8-OUNCE RAMEKINS)

This versatile soufflé adapts to the seasons (see the variations on page 20).
It makes an elegant starter or a soul-warming entrée on a spring evening.

10 ounces	fresh asparagus (about 1 bunch)
1 cup	milk
3 tablespoons	unsalted butter, plus extra for the ramekins
3 tablespoons	all-purpose flour
3	large eggs, separated
2 teaspoons	chopped fresh tarragon
1 teaspoon	salt
	Freshly ground black pepper
Pinch	cayenne pepper

Bring a large pot of salted water to a boil over high heat. Snap the tough ends off the asparagus. Place the asparagus in the boiling water and cook until just tender, 3 to 4 minutes for medium spears.

Meanwhile, fill a medium bowl with water and ice cubes.

Drain the asparagus and plunge it immediately into the ice water. When the asparagus is cool, remove it from the water with tongs and pat it dry with a clean dish towel. Remove the tips and halve them lengthwise; set aside. Slice the spears crosswise into 3 pieces, and place them in a blender. Add the milk and blend until smooth. Strain the puree through a medium sieve into a bowl, using a rubber spatula to push through as much pulp as possible.

Preheat the oven to 400°F. Butter six 4-ounce or four 8-ounce ramekins.

In a medium saucepan, melt the butter over low heat. Whisk in the flour and cook for a minute, whisking constantly. Slowly whisk in the asparagus puree and cook, stirring often, until the mixture is quite thick, and pulling away from the sides of the saucepan, about 5 minutes. Transfer the mixture to a bowl and let it cool slightly.

Stir the egg yolks into the soufflé base, and then stir in the reserved asparagus tips and the tarragon. Season with the salt and pepper and cayenne to taste. In a clean dry bowl or in the bowl of a mixer, beat the egg whites until they form soft peaks. Using a rubber spatula, gently fold the egg whites into the soufflé base. Fill the ramekins about three-quarters full, and set them in a baking dish that is large enough to hold all of them. Pour enough hot water into the baking dish to reach halfway up the sides of the ramekins.

Bake until the soufflés are puffed, set, and lightly golden, 15 to 25 minutes depending on the ramekin size; rotate the pan once during baking. Serve immediately.

SERVING SUGGESTION

Perfect with a salad of spring baby greens and some crusty bread.

VARIATIONS

Try the following as substitutions for the asparagus:

- *Spring:* 1½ cups pureed cooked beets (with a bit of crumbled goat cheese stirred in), sweet baby carrots, or peas
- *Summer:* 1½ cups pureed cooked corn or zucchini
- *Fall:* beets (again) or 1½ cups pureed sautéed mushrooms or ¾ cup pureed pumpkin or butternut squash
- *Winter:* 1½ cups pureed cooked greens such as collards, kale, or chard. Squeeze the cooked greens until most of the water is removed before pureeing

NUTRITION

Asparagus is a great source of vitamins A, C and E, and B, and the minerals folate, potassium, and zinc. It also contain flavenoids (antioxidants) and compounds with anti-inflammatory properties.

ECONOMY $

Spring and Fall Baby Beet Salad

MAKES 4 APPETIZER OR SALAD SERVINGS

So simple, and far better than candy when using the sweet, tender baby beets of spring. Beets are a busy cook's dream because like carrots, they are very forgiving—a few added minutes roasting, steaming, or boiling won't cause mushiness or ruin flavor. We buy our golden and red baby beets from nearby Migliorelli and Hearty Roots farms.

16   baby beets (about 9 ounces total), stems trimmed to 1 inch

1 cup   mesclun mix or baby greens with assorted herbs

Extra-virgin olive oil

Salt and freshly ground black pepper

Preheat the oven to 375°F. Separately wrap the beets tightly in aluminum foil and roast them in the middle of the oven until fork-tender, 30 to 40 minutes. Let the beets rest in the foil for 15 minutes. Then carefully open the foil, letting any residual steam escape. With a small sharp knife, cut off the remaining stems and peel the beets. Halve or quarter the beets and arrange them on a platter. Sprinkle the beets with greens or herbs and drizzle them with olive oil. Season with salt and pepper, and serve warm or at room temperature.

VARIATIONS

- Delicious with fresh ricotta (see page 288), shaved Parmesan, or crumbled goat cheese.
- For a tossed "green" salad, dress mesclun or arugula (1½ to 2 cups per serving) and cooked, halved beets with a citrusy vinaigrette, such as Gigi Lemon Vinaigrette (page 277).

NUTRITION

Loaded with folate, potassium, calcium, vitamin C, and other antioxidants like betacyanin (which is what gives beets their rich red color), beets are among the most nutritious roots.

ECONOMY $

Hudson Valley Club Sandwich

MAKES 4 SERVINGS

Friends always jokingly encourage me to open a soup-and-sandwich shop—usually after I've coerced them into hours of hard labor in my garden. We're famished, and I always come through with a "surprise" sandwich and cold beer. Save the avocados, which do not grow in the Hudson Valley, I try to use fresh local ingredients for the rest of the filling.

White bean spread

2 tablespoons	extra-virgin olive oil
1 tablespoon	fresh lemon juice
2	garlic cloves
1 teaspoon	minced fresh rosemary
¼ teaspoon	cayenne pepper
One	16-ounce can white beans (great northern or cannellini), drained and rinsed
2 tablespoons	dry white wine
½ cup	chicken or vegetable stock or reduced-sodium broth

Sandwich

12 slices	whole-wheat bread, lightly toasted
12	small inner leaves romaine lettuce
Eight	¼-inch-thick slices tomato
12	very thin slices red onion (a sharp chef's knife or mandoline will get the job done)
2	avocados, peeled, pitted, and sliced into thin wedges (6 to 8 each, depending on size)
8 ounces	thinly sliced cooked chicken breast
8	pork or turkey bacon strips, cooked until crisp (optional)
2 cups	broccoli or alfalfa sprouts (4 ounces)

To make the white bean spread, heat the olive oil, lemon juice, garlic, rosemary, and cayenne pepper in a nonstick skillet over medium-high heat. When the garlic just starts to brown, add the white beans. Cook, tossing or stirring, for 1 minute. Add the white wine and cook for another minute to reduce. Then add the broth and cook for 2 to 3 minutes. Transfer the mixture to a food processor and process until smooth. Set the white bean spread aside (it will thicken as it cools).

Spread 2 tablespoons of the cooled white bean spread over 1 slice of toast; top with 3 lettuce leaves, 2 tomato slices, 3 onion slices, another slice of toast, another tablespoon of white bean spread, 3 or 4 slices of avocado, one-fourth of the chicken, 2 bacon strips (if using), and ½ cup of the sprouts. Top with a final slice of toast spread with 1 last tablespoon of white bean spread. Cut the sandwich diagonally into quarters; secure the quarters with wooden picks. Repeat with the remaining ingredients to make 4 sandwiches.

SERVING SUGGESTION

Great with a seasonal pureed vegetable soup—think butternut squash, corn, leek, spinach—and/or chips.

VARIATIONS

- Omit the rosemary from the white bean spread and add 4 or 5 chopped fresh basil leaves.
- For a kick, stir some ancho or poblano chili paste, harissa, or salsa into the spread.
- Substitute preserved tomatoes or pickled vegetables (zucchini, cucumber pickles, eggplant, mushrooms, or onions, for example) when the local fresh ones are out of season.
- Use mesclun or arugula in place of the romaine, and omit the chicken and bacon to make a veggie decker sandwich.

NUTRITION

White bean spread is a diverse and flavorful alternative to mayonnaise and other sandwich moisteners. Along with the whole-wheat bread, you'll get more than half of your daily fiber, plus oodles of vitamins, nutrients, and phytochemicals.

Dingle Pies (Irish-Style Lamb Pies)

MAKES ABOUT TWELVE 3-INCH PIES

Agnes Devereux is one of a few restaurateur "soul sisters" in the Hudson Valley. We buy from many of the same farmers and food producers and share a goal of cultivating community spirit by providing delicious, nourishing food in a welcoming ambience. Like me, Agnes is an accidental restaurateur. After a career in interior design in New York, she opened the Village Tea Room in New Paltz, New York, in 2005. In addition to a vast tea list, Agnes serves the traditional Irish fare she grew up with.

I had the pleasure of tasting one of her Dingle pies at a Hudson Valley promotional event, and I was won over at first bite. Dingle is mountainous sheep country in the west of Ireland where the peninsula plunges into the Atlantic Ocean. Traditionally these pies were made with scraps of mutton. Shepherds slipped the cooled pies into their pockets for a tasty, portable meal. Agnes's version is made with ground lamb flavored with cumin. They make an excellent lunch or snack on a hike or picnic.

Flaky cream-cheese pie dough

2 cups	all-purpose flour
¼ teaspoon	salt
¼ teaspoon	baking powder
4½ ounces	cold cream cheese, cut into 1-inch cubes
12 tablespoons	cold unsalted butter (1½ sticks), cut into cubes
3 tablespoons	ice water
1 tablespoon	cider vinegar

Pie filling

2 tablespoons	unsalted butter
1	medium onion, finely diced
2	carrots, finely diced
1	celery stalk, finely diced
	Salt and freshly ground black pepper
1½ pounds	ground lamb
1½ teaspoons	cumin seeds
Pinch	cayenne pepper
1 cup	chicken stock or low-sodium broth
1	large egg, lightly beaten

To make the dough, place the flour, salt, and baking powder in the bowl of an electric mixer fitted with the paddle attachment. Add the cream cheese and process until the mixture resembles coarse meal. Add the butter and process until the pieces of butter are no larger than pea-size. Add the ice water and the vinegar, and mix briefly. The mixture will be crumbly, but a piece should hold its shape when squeezed together. Transfer the dough to a clean, lightly floured surface and bring it together with your hands. Divide it into 2 disks, wrap each one in plastic wrap, and refrigerate for at least 1 hour.

Preheat the oven to 250°F. Melt the butter in a large ovenproof skillet over medium heat. Add the onion, carrots, and celery and cook until softened, 10 to 12 minutes, seasoning with salt and pepper and stirring often. Increase the heat to medium-high and add the ground lamb, breaking up the meat. Cook until the lamb is lightly browned, 5 minutes. Add the cumin seeds and cayenne and season again with salt and pepper. Stir in the chicken stock and place the skillet, uncovered, in the oven. Bake, stirring occasionally, until the lamb is deeply browned and the liquid has evaporated, 35 to 40 minutes. Transfer the mixture to a bowl, cover, and let cool to room temperature; then refrigerate for up to 2 days.

On a lightly floured surface, roll out one of the disks of dough to ⅛ to ¼-inch thickness. Cut out six 5-inch rounds. Repeat with the remaining dough. Chill the rounds, with a piece of parchment or wax paper between the layers, for at least 1 hour.

Holding a round of dough in the palm of one hand, spoon a heaping ¼ cup of the filling into the center. Fold the edges over to form a half-moon shape and pinch the edges together securely (brush the bottom edge with a bit of water to help adhere if necessary). Place the pies on a baking sheet lined with parchment paper, and crimp the edges. Freeze for at least 2 hours, or the pies will burst open in the oven.

Preheat the oven to 375°F. Brush the tops of the pies with the beaten egg, and bake for 30 to 35 minutes, or until the pastry is golden and the filling is bubbling. Enjoy hot or at room temperature.

FILLING VARIATIONS

- *Indian:* Add curry and turmeric.
- *Tex-Mex:* Add chili powder, black beans, corn kernels, and cilantro.
- *Italian:* Omit the cumin. Add some tomato paste, oregano, parsley, and basil.

NUTRITION

Slightly on the rich side, but they are great carry-alongs for hiking! To make them lighter, try ground turkey or chicken.

ECONOMY $$$

Spring Vegetable Stew

MAKES 6 SERVINGS

The classic summer vegetable stew is often referred to as "ratatouille." What could be better than cooked-down garden tomatoes, summer squash, eggplant, onions, garlic, and herbs? With its more delicate flavors, this spring stew eases us away from the root vegetables of fall and winter and toward a summer filled with bold flavors.

2	large lemons, halved
4	medium artichokes
2 tablespoons	olive oil
2	shallots, thinly sliced
9	small red potatoes (1 to 2 inches in diameter), quartered
½ cup	dry white wine
3 cups	vegetable or chicken stock or reduced-sodium broth
12	fresh asparagus spears, trimmed and sliced on the diagonal into ¾-inch pieces
1 cup	fresh or frozen peeled fava beans, thawed (see Note)
1 cup	shelled peas (fresh or frozen)
¼ cup	snipped fresh chives
¼ cup	chopped fresh flat-leaf parsley
3 tablespoons	finely grated Grana Padano or Parmesan cheese
	Salt and freshly ground black pepper
	Shaved Grana Padano or Parmesan cheese, for garnish

Fill a large bowl with 1 quart of water, and squeeze 2 lemon halves into it. Add the squeezed lemon halves to the water.

Working with 1 artichoke at a time, bend back the outer leaves close to the base until they snap off where they break naturally. Discard the layers until the exposed leaves are pale green at the top and pale yellow at the base. Using a small sharp knife, trim the stem and the base until it is smooth and no dark green areas remain. Trim the leaves. Rub the base with the remaining lemon halves. Cut the artichoke lengthwise into 4 wedges. Using a small knife, cut out the choke and the small purple-tipped leaves; then halve again for a total of 8 wedges. Place the artichoke wedges in the lemon water.

Heat the olive oil in a large skillet over medium heat. Add the shallots and cook, stirring often, until softened, about 3 minutes. While the shallots are cooking, drain and rinse the artichokes. Add the artichokes and the potatoes to the skillet and cook, stirring, for 1 minute. Pour in the wine and simmer until the liquid is reduced to a few spoonfuls, about 6 minutes. Add the stock and bring to a boil. Add half of the asparagus, fava beans, and peas, cover the skillet, and simmer the stew for 10 minutes. Stir in the remaining asparagus, fava beans, and peas, 2 tablespoons of the chives, and 2 tablespoons of the parsley. Let the mixture simmer, partially covered, for about 4 minutes, or until the potatoes and artichokes are tender. Stir in the remaining herbs and the grated Grana Padano, and season with salt and pepper to taste. Serve topped with shaved Grana Padano.

Note: High-quality frozen fava beans do not require any work. Add them to the soup after they have thawed out. If you buy fresh fava beans, cook the shelled beans in boiling salted water for 3 minutes, or until just tender. Drain, and cool in a bowl of ice water. Then drain, and peel off their tough outer skin (it should slip off easily).

SERVING SUGGESTION

Serve this delicious stew with crusty bread and some wedges of local cheese.

VARIATIONS

- Add your favorite spring vegetable to this stew, such as sliced carrots or sugar snap peas.
- Add protein: this dish can quickly turn into a fricassee when some bite-size pieces of cooked chicken are added to the vegetables.
- Substitute thawed frozen artichokes for the fresh ones; it will cut down on the prep time considerably.
- Substitute basil and tarragon for the chives and parsley.

LEFTOVERS

This stew would be delicious over pasta or served as the brothy base for roasted or grilled chicken and fish.

NUTRITION

Loaded with folate, fiber, and flavor!

ECONOMY $

Chock-full of the season's best vegetables, which cost less when purchased at their prime. Some frozen peas and artichokes can be mixed in with the fresh.

Gigi Skizza Through the Seasons

I recently calculated how many Skizzas we've sold at Gigi Trattoria over the past eight years: more than 150,000! Not bad for an eighty-seat restaurant. Kids love them, adults crave them, and even after all these years, I still need at least one Skizza fix a week. Skizza is our unleavened-flatbread "pizza," which cooks like the delectable super-thin Neapolitan-style pizza. The crispy shell provides the canvas for just about any seasonal ingredients. In 2007 I trademark-protected the terms "Gigi Skizza" and "Skizza" in the hope of bringing home kits, the kind we sell at Gigi Market, to your local supermarkets. It's a work in progress. The dough is our secret, but here are some of my favorite toppings, which you can use on your favorite pizza dough or even on a large flour tortilla.

SPRING

- Tomato sauce, mozzarella, gamberetti (small shrimp), pea shoots, red onion, and red pepper flakes
- Asparagus, Vidalia onions, Fontina, and truffle oil
- Chopped garlicky clams and Migliorelli Farm baby spinach
- Melted Hearty Roots Farm leeks, Mountain Smokehouse Products bacon, and Fontina
- Pickled RSK Farm ramps, Corola potatoes, and Taleggio cheese
- Spring onions, salmon, lemon vinaigrette–dressed baby spinach (see page 277), drizzle of crème fraîche

SUMMER

- Arugula pesto, thinly sliced Northwind Farms chicken breast, and Gigi Homemade Fresh Ricotta (page 288)
- Heirloom tomatoes, buffalo mozzarella, fresh oregano, and fresh basil
- Eggplant caponata, oil-cured tuna, and red pepper flakes
- Arugula pesto, zucchini and fresh herb ricotta, and grated Grana Padano or Parmesan
- Northwind Farms sausage, Hearty Roots Farm bell peppers, mozzarella, and shaved Grana Padano or Parmesan
- Garden string beans, eggplant, summer squash, zucchini, and cherry tomatoes
- Peach BBQ sauce (see page 289), rotisserie porchetta, and smoked mozzarella

FALL

- Spaghetti squash, Brie, and coppa
- Sweet potato slices, prosciutto, and crispy fried sage leaves
- Braised Migliorelli Farm Tuscan kale, Northwind Farms chorizo, and Old Chatham Ewe's Blue
- Roasted Red Pepper Pesto (page 279), smoked salmon, and capers
- Northwind Farms duck confit, Wiltbank Farm shiitakes, and mozzarella

WINTER

- Gigi Fig Jam (page 287), prosciutto, gorgonzola dolce, rosemary, and a drizzle of honey
- Gigi Market sauerkraut, Northwind Farms kielbasa, and Burrata cheese
- Roasted endive, chicken-sage ragù, and shaved Piave cheese
- Gigi mini-meatballs, tomato sauce, and provolone
- Sliced roast beef, grated fresh horseradish, prepared horseradish cream, and pickled cipolline onions
- Nutella, sliced bananas, and toasted crushed hazelnuts

EVERY SEASON

The following Skizzas are on our menu year-round by popular demand

- *Margherita:* Tomato, basil, oregano, and mozzarella
- *L'Ortaggio:* Oven-roasted seasonal vegetables and Pecorino Romano
- *Mamma:* Tuscan-style porchetta, fennel salami, red onion, tomato, and mozzarella
- *Rustica:* Northwind Farms fennel sausage, broccoli rabe, shaved Grana Padano or Parmesan, and red pepper flakes
- *Vongole:* Shucked clams, grated Grana Padano or Parmesan, garlic, extra-virgin olive oil, and herbs
- *Bianca:* Coach Farm goat cheese, mozzarella, rosemary, preserved figs, pears, arugula, and white truffle oil

Spring Pea Soup

MAKES 4 SERVINGS

I'm not quite ready to give up hot soup in the spring, but I definitely want an "enlightened" change from the hearty ones of winter. We buy local peas from Migliorelli Farm and sell them at Gigi Market, and this soup frequently appears on our restaurant "specials" list throughout the spring. Chef Wilson Costa also adds farm-fresh peas to our Spring Trifolati (page 48) and prepares a Sweet Pea Guacamole (page 16) that accompanies some fish dishes, such as seared sea scallops and red snapper. To test the quality of snap peas, snap one open and see whether it is crisp. The pods should be bright green, firm, and plump.

2 tablespoons	olive oil
2	medium shallots, sliced
One	8-ounce russet potato, peeled and cut into ¾-inch cubes
3 cups	shelled fresh peas (or frozen peas, thawed)
¼ cup	dry white wine
2 tablespoons	finely chopped fresh tarragon, plus extra for garnish
	Salt and freshly ground black pepper

Heat the oil in a medium saucepan over medium heat. Add the shallots and cook, stirring, until softened, about 3 minutes. Add the potato cubes, peas, and wine and simmer, stirring, until the wine is reduced by half, 1 to 2 minutes. Add 4 cups of water and the tarragon, and bring to a boil. Lower the heat to a simmer and cook until the potatoes are falling apart, 15 to 20 minutes.

Transfer the soup to a food processor or blender, and blend until smooth. Season with salt and pepper to taste. Spoon into serving bowls and garnish with more tarragon.

SERVING SUGGESTION

Drizzle with some extra-virgin olive oil or top with a dollop of sour cream or crème fraîche.

VARIATIONS

• Mint would be a great substitute for the tarragon.
• Substitute frozen peeled fava beans and a dash of fresh lemon juice.

LEFTOVERS

Simmer the soup to the desired thickness and use it as a sauce for pan-seared red snapper or grilled chicken.

NUTRITION

When cooked and pureed, potato "creams" the soup without adding any dairy. If you prefer a traditional cream soup, add $\frac{1}{3}$ cup cream or $\frac{1}{2}$ cup whole milk during the last 2 minutes of cooking. Peas are rich in the B vitamins folate and B_6 (both supportive of cardiovascular health) and are a good source of vitamin C and fiber. They also contain good amounts of vitamin K_1, which activates osteocalcin, a protein that is critical for bone health.

ECONOMY $

When in season, fresh peas are relatively inexpensive and are a great excuse to get the young 'uns in the kitchen shelling. Good-quality frozen peas have plenty of nutrient value (they are simply picked and flash-frozen).

Whole-Wheat Fettuccine
with Spring Vegetables

MAKES 4 SERVINGS

At Gigi Trattoria, this pasta delights our vegetarian and carnivore clients alike. We make our own whole-wheat fettuccine, but store-bought dry long whole-wheat pasta, such as spaghetti or fettuccine, is fine. Wiltbank Farm mushrooms (both shiitake and oyster) give an earthy heartiness to our dish. Check out your farmers' markets for local mushrooms in the spring and fall.

1 pound	dry (or 1½ pounds fresh) whole-wheat fettuccine (or other whole-wheat pasta)
¼ cup	olive oil
1 pound	assorted mushrooms, such as shiitake and oyster, shiitake stems removed, coarsely chopped
2	garlic cloves, finely chopped
8 ounces	sugar snap peas, trimmed
	Salt and freshly ground black pepper
2 tablespoons	chopped fresh flat-leaf parsley
⅓ cup	slivered almonds, toasted
½ cup	freshly grated Grana Padano or Parmesan cheese (optional)

Bring a large pot of salted water to a boil. Add the pasta and cook, stirring occasionally, until al dente, following the package instructions.

While the pasta is cooking, heat the oil in a large heavy skillet over moderate heat until it is hot but not smoking. Add the mushrooms and cook, stirring occasionally, until tender, about 7 minutes. Stir in the garlic and snap peas and cook, stirring, for 1 minute.

Drain the pasta and transfer it to a serving bowl. Toss the mushroom mixture with the pasta until well combined, and season with salt and pepper to taste. Sprinkle with the parsley and almonds and cheese, if using. Serve immediately.

- Bring this pasta dish back in the fall, substituting ribbons of radicchio and small dice of butternut squash for the snap peas.
- For a creamier version, toss with ¼ cup grated Parmesan and 2 to 3 tablespoons of the pasta cooking water before serving.
- Use 1½ pounds fresh pasta: Fresh pasta cooks quickly, so start cooking the mushrooms before you add the pasta to the boiling water.

NUTRITION

Why do 40 percent of Americans never eat whole grains, and most eat less than one of the recommended three to five servings per day? Having just tested (and eaten) this dish, it beats me! Seriously, whole grains and the products made with them offer toasty, elegant flavor. This dish, with the sweetness of the snap peas and the earthy mushrooms, is a clear example. While I would never give up regular semolina pasta, some dishes are better with the whole-grain product.

ECONOMY $$

This is a delicious, quick, healthy, and cost friendly meal. Using white domestic mushrooms can further save money.

Asparagus Pesto Linguine

At Gigi Trattoria and Gigi Market we use the fresh herbs, leaves, and vegetables of spring, summer, and fall to make delicious pestos that can be tossed with our hand-made pastas. I love the versatility of pesto. It works well on just about any pasta shape, can be spread on sandwiches, stirred into dips, or used as a marinade. Our talented kitchen team substitutes pesto for sauce on our evening Skizza specials. The oil in the pesto "fries" the dough, producing a yummy, crunchy thin-crust "pizza."

3 tablespoons	pine nuts, toasted
1 pound	fresh asparagus
3	garlic cloves, chopped
1 teaspoon	Dijon mustard
½ cup	olive oil
⅓ cup	freshly grated Grana Padano or Parmesan cheese, plus more for topping
3 tablespoons	chopped fresh flat-leaf parsley
	Salt and freshly ground black pepper
1 tablespoon	fresh lemon juice
1 pound	dry linguine or spaghetti

Toast the pine nuts in a small skillet over medium heat, shaking them as they brown, 2 to 3 minutes; set aside.

Snap the tough ends off the asparagus. Remove the tips; reserve the tips and stems separately.

Bring 4 quarts of salted water to a boil in a large pot. Add the asparagus stems and cook until they're just tender, 3 to 5 minutes, depending on thickness. Using tongs, transfer the asparagus stems to a large bowl. Cover them with cold water, and when they have cooled, drain them. Slice the stems into ½-inch-long segments and place them in a food processor.

Add the asparagus tips to the boiling salted water and cook until tender, about 2 minutes. Fish them out with a strainer or slotted spoon and place them in a small bowl. Cover with cold water, and when they have cooled, drain them. Set aside. Keep the cooking water at a low boil.

Add the garlic, mustard, and ¼ cup of the olive oil to the food processor, and pulse to combine. Add the Grana Padano, parsley, and pine nuts. With the motor running, drizzle the remaining ¼ cup olive oil through the feed tube. Season with salt and pepper, and the lemon juice to perk up the flavor. Pulse again to combine. (If you want a thinner consistency, a few tablespoons of the pasta cooking water can be added later.)

Return the cooking water to a full boil and add the linguine. Cook, stirring occasionally, until al dente, following the package instructions. Reserving ½ cup of the pasta cooking water, drain the pasta. Return the drained pasta to the pot, and add the pesto and the reserved asparagus tips. Cook, stirring, over medium-high heat until hot and well combined, about 1 minute. Add a spoonful of the pasta water, if necessary, to loosen the sauce. Season to taste with salt and pepper, top with grated Grana Padano, and serve immediately.

VARIATIONS

- Brush whole fish, fish steaks, or fish fillets with the pesto as the fish grills or roasts.
- Marinate asparagus spears in the asparagus pesto and then roast or grill them. See also Pesto for All Seasons (page 278).

LEFTOVERS

The pesto will keep, covered and refrigerated, for up to 4 days.

NUTRITION

A typical serving of asparagus provides more than 50 percent of the daily requirement for folate, a B vitamin that helps in the duplication of healthy cells and protects against heart disease. It's also a rich source of antioxidants, including vitamins C and A, and phytochemicals.

ECONOMY $$

Purchased in season, asparagus is tasty and inexpensive.

Gigi Potato Gnocchi with Chicken and Pea Ragù

MAKES 4 TO 6 SERVINGS

This sauce works really well with gnocchi, clinging to every crevice.
Also enjoy it with your favorite pasta shape, or cook off (or drain)
the liquid and use the ragù as the base for a shepherd's pie.

Gnocchi

4	medium russet potatoes, peeled and halved
	Salt
1½ cups	all-purpose flour, plus more as needed
2 pinches	ground nutmeg
2	large eggs
1	large egg yolk

Ragù

2 tablespoons	olive oil
1	medium onion, diced
½ cup	diced carrots
½ cup	diced celery
2	garlic cloves, minced
2 ounces	pancetta or slab bacon, diced (optional)
¼ teaspoon	garam masala (see Note, page 38)

1½ pounds	ground chicken (if possible, use local natural, antibiotic- and hormone-free), or 1½ pounds chopped boneless, skinless chicken thighs
2 tablespoons	tomato paste
⅓ cup	dry white wine
1½ cups	chicken stock or reduced-sodium broth
1 cup	shelled fresh peas (or frozen peas)
2 tablespoons	chopped fresh flat-leaf parsley
	Salt and freshly ground black pepper

To finish

1 tablespoon	olive oil
1 tablespoon	finely chopped fresh chives, parsley, or thyme
⅓ cup	freshly grated Grana Padano or Parmesan cheese

To prepare the gnocchi, place the potatoes in a medium saucepan and add water to cover by 2 to 3 inches. Season the water with salt and bring to a boil over high heat. Cook until the potatoes are just tender, 15 to 20 minutes. Drain the potatoes and let them dry slightly. While they are still hot, pass the potato halves through a ricer into a large bowl. Stir in the flour, 1½ teaspoons salt, and the nutmeg until just combined.

In a small bowl, lightly beat the whole eggs with the egg yolk. Pour the eggs into the center of the potato mixture. Knead the mixture with your hands until it holds together. Then turn the dough out onto a lightly floured surface and, with lightly floured hands, gently knead until it is smooth and well blended, working in more flour if it is too sticky.

Divide the dough into 8 pieces. Roll 1 piece into a rope that is about ½ inch wide. Using a knife, cut the rope into ¾-inch segments. Holding a fork on your work surface with the tines curved toward you, gently roll 1 segment of dough against the tines to mark it lightly with ridges. Transfer the gnocchi to a lightly floured baking sheet, and repeat until all the dough is used. Refrigerate the gnocchi, uncovered, until ready to cook. (The gnocchi will keep, refrigerated, for 1 day, or in the freezer for up to 3 months. They cook well from the freezer.)

To prepare the ragù, heat the olive oil in a large skillet or saucepan over medium heat. Add the onion, carrots, and celery, and cook until softened, about 7 minutes. Add the garlic and cook for another minute. Then turn up the heat to medium-high and add the pancetta, if using, and garam masala. Cook, stirring, until the pancetta renders its fat and begins to crisp and brown, about 5 minutes. Stir in the chicken and tomato paste and continue to cook, stirring often, until the chicken begins to brown and the tomato paste caramelizes lightly, about 10 minutes. Pour in the wine, scraping the bottom of the pan to dissolve any browned bits. Stir in the stock, cover the skillet, and simmer for 30 minutes. Then uncover and cook until the sauce thickens, about 15 minutes. During the last 5 minutes of cooking, stir in the peas and parsley. Adjust the seasoning with salt and pepper. Cover the sauce to keep it hot while you cook the gnocchi. (Alternatively, let the sauce cool and then refrigerate it for up to 3 days. Reheat before cooking the gnocchi.)

To cook the gnocchi, bring a large pot of salted water to a boil. Add the gnocchi and cook until they float to the surface; then cook for 1 minute more (about 4 minutes total). Immediately drain, toss with the olive oil, and mix with the chicken ragù. Stir in the chives and the grated cheese, and serve immediately.

Note: Masala is the Indian term for spice blend. It can include any simple or complex combination of spices. The most common blend is garam masala, which varies by region but typically includes ground peppercorns, cloves, bay leaves, cumin seeds, nutmeg, mace, coriander, cardamom, and star anise. Garam masala is available in some supermarkets and most gourmet stores. Chutney Unlimited, a gourmet company just east of the Hudson Valley, makes a delicious garam masala blend that can warm up any dish (see Sources).

SERVING SUGGESTIONS

Enjoy with a simple salad, some crusty bread, and a medium-bodied Italian red wine.

VARIATIONS

- Substitute local ground beef, pork, turkey, or lamb for the chicken.
- Use half-moon slices of zucchini instead of the peas.
- Substitute ground cumin or allspice for the garam masala.

NUTRITION

This dish provides a balanced mix of protein, carbs, and veggies.

ECONOMY $$

Spring (and Every Other Season) Lasagna

MAKES 6 TO 8 SERVINGS

We all love delicious bubbly lasagna, and on a chilly day there is nothing better than the traditional Bolognese style with a glass of fantastic Italian red. But meat-and-cheese versions tend to feel heavy after the winter months. Lasagna, like other pasta shapes, and like other starches such as rice and polenta, can take on the fillings and/or toppings of every season. Asparagus, fava beans, mushrooms, and baby peas make this version sing of spring. I use Wiltbank Farm oyster and shiitake mushrooms, but you can certainly substitute spring mushrooms. Miriam Altshuler, my literary agent, who lives down the street (how local can you get!), stopped over shortly after I pulled this out of the oven for its photo shoot and begged for the recipe prepublication.

	Salt
1 bunch	fresh asparagus (about 8 ounces)
2 tablespoons	olive oil
1	medium onion, thinly sliced
2	garlic cloves, minced
1/8 teaspoon	red pepper flakes
1 pound	mushrooms, sliced
2 teaspoons	fresh thyme leaves
	Freshly ground black pepper
1 cup	shelled fresh baby peas (or frozen baby peas, thawed)
1 cup	shelled fresh fava beans (or frozen peeled fava beans, thawed) (see Note, page 27)
1/4 cup	chopped fresh flat-leaf parsley
1/2 cup	all-purpose flour
5 cups	2-percent milk

Pinch	ground nutmeg
3/4 cup	freshly grated Grana Padano or Parmesan cheese
1 cup	well-drained chopped cooked spinach; or one
One	10-ounce package frozen chopped spinach, thawed, drained, and squeezed dry
1 cup	2-percent cottage cheese
1 cup	shredded part-skim mozzarella cheese
One	8-ounce package oven-ready no-boil lasagna noodles

Bring a saucepan of water to a boil and salt it. Slice off the asparagus tips and break off the tough ends; discard the ends. Slice the stems on the diagonal into 1-inch pieces. Cook the asparagus stem pieces in the boiling water for

2 minutes. Add the tips and cook for another minute. Drain well and set aside.

In a large nonstick skillet, heat the olive oil over medium-high heat. Add the onion, garlic, and red pepper flakes and cook, stirring occasionally, until the onion is slightly softened, 2 to 3 minutes. Add the mushrooms and thyme, season with salt and pepper, and cook, tossing or stirring occasionally, until the mushrooms soften and the liquid evaporates, 5 minutes. Add the asparagus, peas, fava beans, and parsley and cook for 1 minute. Set aside.

To prepare the sauce, place the flour in a medium saucepan and stir in just enough milk to make a smooth paste. Gradually add the remaining milk, whisking until blended and smooth. Season with salt, pepper, and nutmeg. Place the pan over medium heat and cook, stirring often, until the mixture is thick and creamy, about 8 minutes. Remove from the heat and add ½ cup of the Grana Padano. Adjust the seasoning with salt and pepper if necessary, and stir with a whisk to blend. Stir in the spinach and set aside.

In a small bowl, mix together the cottage and mozzarella cheeses. Set aside.

Preheat the oven to 375°F. Coat a 13 x 9-inch baking dish with cooking spray.

Measure out and set aside 1 cup of the spinach sauce. Spread ½ cup of the remaining spinach sauce over the bottom of the prepared baking dish. Arrange 4 lasagna noodles over the spinach sauce, trimming them if necessary so that they fit in one slightly overlapping layer. Dot with half of the cottage cheese mixture, half of the remaining spinach sauce, and half of the mushroom and asparagus mixture. Repeat the layers, ending with noodles. Spread the reserved 1 cup spinach sauce over the noodles. Cover the dish with aluminum foil, and bake for 35 minutes. Remove the foil, sprinkle the top with the remaining ¼ cup Grana Padano, and bake until lightly browned and bubbly, about 10 minutes. Let stand for 10 minutes before serving.

VARIATIONS

- *Spring options:* Thinly sliced artichoke bottoms, fava beans, and mushrooms
- *Summer:* Roasted or grilled eggplant and summer squash (zucchini and yellow squash) with tomato-basil sauce instead of the white sauce
- *Fall:* Butternut squash, mushrooms, sage, or blanched broccoli (or broccoli rabe), walnuts, and gorgonzola
- *Winter:* Braised cooking greens (chard, collards, mustard, spinach) and cauliflower; roasted root vegetables (parsnips, sweet potatoes) and mushrooms; or chicken, radicchio, and mushrooms
- *Any season:* Seafood and leeks
- Double or triple the recipe and make a few pans, as it freezes well. Reheat for about 45 minutes in a preheated 350°F oven.

LEFTOVERS

Even better the next day. Freezes well.

NUTRITION

You won't miss the fat with this veggie-loaded lasagna, which is prepared with a creamy béchamel made with reduced-fat milk and without butter. You can reduce the fat further if you use 1-percent milk. Use this béchamel as a base for macaroni and cheese and other recipes calling for a creamy white sauce. And why not "enlighten" the classic dietary taboo, fettuccine Alfredo?

Fusilli with Leek and Pea Sauce

Fresh vegetable purees make delicious and healthy sauces. In this sauce, the natural starch in peas and the silkiness of cooked leeks are blended into creamy goodness to coat your favorite pasta shape. I like fusilli because the sauce gets caught in the grooves, giving every bite the spring flavor of peas and leeks.

	Salt
2 tablespoons	olive oil
3	leeks, cleaned, white and light green parts thinly sliced
2 cups	chicken or vegetable stock or reduced-sodium broth
2 cups	shelled fresh peas (or frozen peas, thawed)
1 pound	dry fusilli
¼ cup	snipped fresh chives
	Freshly ground black pepper
¼ cup	heavy cream (optional)

Bring 4 quarts of water to a boil in a large pot. Season with salt.

Heat the olive oil in a medium skillet over medium heat. Add the leeks and cook, stirring, until softened, 4 to 5 minutes. Add the stock and bring to a boil. Add 1½ cups of the peas, reduce the heat, and simmer for 5 minutes for fresh peas or 2 minutes for frozen. Remove the skillet from the heat and set aside to cool slightly.

Cook the fusilli in the boiling water until al dente, following the package instructions (usually 8 to 12 minutes). While the pasta cooks, combine the pea mixture and the chives in a food processor or blender, and puree. Adjust the seasoning with salt and pepper. Return the sauce to the skillet and warm it gently. Add the remaining ½ cup peas to the sauce and cook for 5 minutes for fresh peas or 2 minutes for frozen peas. Stir in the cream, if using, and cook for another minute.

Drain the pasta and add it to the sauce, stirring until just combined and hot, 1 to 2 minutes. Serve immediately.

Top each serving with some snipped fresh chives and a spoonful of grated Parmesan.

VARIATIONS

- Substitute tarragon or mint for the chives.
- Add some sautéed mushrooms to the pea sauce.
- Stir some of the pea sauce into mashed potatoes—great for St. Patrick's Day!

LEFTOVERS

Thin the mixture with broth to make soup.

NUTRITION

Peas, part of the family of legumes, are good sources of fiber and folate, a B vitamin with many protective properties, including lowering lipids in the blood. Leeks also provide ample fiber and folate, as well as healthy amounts of calcium, potassium, and vitamin C. Like onions and chives, leeks have antiseptic, diuretic, and anti-arthritic properties.

ECONOMY $

Hearty Roots Farm Spring Harvest Risotto

MAKES 6 APPETIZER SERVINGS

Hearty Roots Community Farm is our neighbor at Gigi Market in Red Hook. In addition to providing fresh and delicious fruits and vegetables to restaurants and markets throughout the Valley, Hearty Roots operates a farm share program based on the Community-Supported Agriculture (CSA) model. A CSA creates a mutually beneficial relationship between farmers and community members that keeps working agricultural land in production.

We use Hearty Roots' tenderly raised vegetables each season in many of our dishes, including our well-known risottos. Enjoy shopping for these ingredients at your local farmers' market.

8 cups	vegetable or chicken stock or reduced-sodium broth
2 tablespoons	olive oil
2 tablespoons	unsalted butter
1	small onion, minced
1½ cups	thinly sliced radishes (purple, red, and white)
1 cup	shelled fresh baby peas (or frozen baby peas)
1	small bunch flowering chives, stems chopped and flower tops reserved for garnish
2 cups	Carnaroli rice
⅓ cup	dry white wine
	Salt
½ cup	freshly grated Grana Padano or Parmesan cheese

In a medium saucepan, bring the stock to a simmer over medium heat.

Heat the olive oil and 1 tablespoon of the butter in a heavy 6-quart saucepan over medium heat. Add the onion and cook, stirring, until very soft but not browned, 4 to 5 minutes. Add the radishes, ½ cup of the peas, and half of the chopped chives. Cook, stirring, for 1 to 2 minutes.

Stir the rice into the vegetables. "Toast" the rice, stirring constantly, until it looks chalky, about 1 minute. Add the wine and cook until reduced to a tablespoon or two, about 1 minute.

Add 2 cups of the simmering stock. Cook, stirring often, until the liquid is almost completely absorbed. Continue adding the stock, ½ cup at a time, stirring after each addition and allowing the rice to absorb the liquid before adding more.

After about 15 minutes, when the rice is almost done, add the remaining peas and chives and cook for another 2 minutes. Then taste the rice; it should taste cooked (not starchy) and have a slight resistance to the bite. If the rice seems too hard, add a little more stock and continue cooking for another minute or two. When the rice is creamy and al dente, remove from the heat.

Season the risotto with salt. Stir in the Grana Padano and the remaining 1 tablespoon butter. "Whip" the risotto with a wooden spoon to bring out the creaminess of the rice and to incorporate all the ingredients. Divide the risotto among serving plates, garnish with the chive flowers, and enjoy immediately.

VARIATIONS

- *Spring*: Use asparagus and peas, or peas and mushrooms, along with fresh herbs. Add shrimp or scallops (raw) to any of these spring risottos during the last 3 to 4 minutes of cooking.
- *Summer*: Corn, zucchini, shrimp, and basil; or fresh tomato and chorizo
- *Fall*: Butternut, sausage (or chicken), and sage; pumpkin and cooking greens; or beets and goat cheese
- *Winter*: Radicchio and mushrooms; or Parmesan or saffron risotto topped with leftover braised meat (such as lamb shank or beef stew). Or try cooked winter greens and sausage or duck.

LEFTOVERS

Pack leftover risotto 2 inches thick onto a parchment paper–lined pan. Place a sheet of parchment paper on top and chill for at least 4 hours or overnight. Cut out 2- to 4-inch rounds of chilled risotto (smaller rounds for an appetizer, larger when using as a side dish) and cook in a bit of melted butter in a nonstick pan over medium heat until golden, crispy, and heated through.

NUTRITION

Like polenta, whole-grain pilafs, pasta, and potatoes, risotto can be a yummy base for healthy seasonal ingredients.

ECONOMY $$

Sautéed Red Snapper with Herb Roasted Fingerling Potatoes and Sweet Pea Guacamole

MAKES 4 SERVINGS

I love a short ingredient list, especially when the end product is delicious, quick, and healthy. If the Sweet Pea Guacamole pushes you over your time limit, just sauté some fresh peas with a bit of olive oil, fresh herbs, and salt. We use spring fingerlings from RSK Farm in Prattsville and peas from Migliorelli Farm in Red Hook. The freshness helps make the dish, so select the freshest ingredients you can find.

1 pound	fingerling potatoes, halved lengthwise
3 tablespoons	olive oil
8	small thyme sprigs
	Salt and freshly ground black pepper
4	red snapper fillets with skin (about 6 ounces each)
½ cup	Sweet Pea Guacamole (page 16)
	Toasted bread triangles

Preheat the oven to 400°F.

In a bowl, toss the potatoes with 1½ tablespoons of the olive oil, the thyme sprigs, and salt and pepper. Transfer the potatoes to a small baking dish and roast in the middle of the oven until fork-tender and golden brown, about 25 minutes.

Meanwhile, season the fish with salt and pepper. Heat the remaining 1½ tablespoons oil in a large nonstick skillet over moderately high heat until it is hot but not smoking. Sauté the fish, turning the fillets once, until golden brown and just cooked through, 4 to 5 minutes total.

Serve the snapper with the roasted fingerlings, and spread the pea guacamole on toasted bread triangles.

- Substitute salmon, bass, halibut, or cod for the snapper.
- Brush the fish with olive oil and grill instead of sautéing.
- For a Mediterranean dish, add some capers, pitted olives, halved cherry or grape tomatoes, and lemon juice to the skillet after cooking the fish for a quick pan sauce.

LEFTOVERS

Snapper is best enjoyed immediately. Slice any leftover potatoes and throw them into a frittata or omelet. Spread the Sweet Pea Guacamole on sandwich bread.

NUTRITION

A light and balanced meal.

ECONOMY $$$

Seared Salmon over Spring Trifolati

MAKES 4 SERVINGS

Perfectly seared salmon is always popular on our menu, but it is this simple spring preparation that excites our customers most. Trifolati is typically a quick pan "stew" of mushrooms or zucchini. We enjoy making it with spring's first harvest.

Trifolati

8 ounces	fresh asparagus
3 tablespoons	olive oil
2	garlic cloves, minced
2	shallots, thinly sliced
1 head	radicchio, halved, cored, and cut into thin ribbons
2 cups	halved cherry tomatoes
¼ cup	chopped fresh flat-leaf parsley
	Salt and freshly ground black pepper

Salmon

2 tablespoons	olive oil
Four	6-ounce center-cut salmon fillets

To prepare the trifolati, blanch the asparagus in boiling, salted water until tender but still firm, 2 to 5 minutes depending on thickness. Drain and transfer to a bowl of ice water.

When cool, drain again and slice on the diagonal into 2- or 3-inch segments. Heat the olive oil in a medium skillet over medium-high heat. Add the garlic and shallots, and cook for 1 minute. Then add the asparagus segments and cook, tossing or stirring, for 3 to 4 minutes. Increase the heat to high and add the radicchio, cherry tomatoes, and parsley. Cook just long enough to wilt the radicchio and soften the tomatoes, 1 to 2 minutes. Season with salt and pepper. Cover loosely to keep warm, and immediately prepare the salmon.

Heat the oil in a large nonstick skillet over medium-high heat. When the oil is hot but not smoking, season the salmon with salt and pepper and sear it, skin side down, for 2 to 3 minutes; shake the pan and gently lift the salmon with tongs or a spatula to loosen it from the skillet. Reduce the heat to medium. Partially cover the skillet and cook until the salmon is cooked through, 3 to 4 minutes. The skin should be crisp and the flesh medium-rare.

Serve the seared salmon over the trifolati.

SERVING SUGGESTION

Top the fish with a good squeeze of fresh lemon juice.

VARIATIONS

- Add mushrooms and herbs such as thyme or tarragon.
- Substitute snapper, halibut, cod, or sea bass for the salmon.

NUTRITION

A seasonally and nutritionally balanced meal, including healthy omega-3s from the salmon.

ECONOMY $$

Marinated Roasted Lamb with Yukon Gold Potatoes

MAKES 6 TO 8 SERVINGS

This is a truly simple dish. The marinade can be whipped up in minutes; then, after the lamb absorbs the Mediterranean/Middle Eastern flavors, the whole mixture is transferred to the oven. By leaving the marinade on the lamb, flavorful browning is achieved in the oven (with no mess) and the sauce prepares itself in the pan. After just about an hour, you will find that the house is perfumed with wonderful smells and an elegant meal is ready.

1	boneless leg of lamb (about 3 pounds), butterflied
	Grated zest and juice of ½ orange
	Grated zest of ½ lemon
2	rosemary sprigs, leaves removed and stems discarded
3	thyme sprigs, leaves removed and stems discarded
3	garlic cloves, crushed
1 tablespoon	Dijon mustard
1 teaspoon	dried oregano
1 teaspoon	ground coriander
1 teaspoon	ground cumin
¼ cup	olive oil
	Salt and freshly ground black pepper
12	small Yukon Gold potatoes (about 2¼ pounds), quartered
4	small onions (about 12 ounces), quartered

If necessary, trim excess fat from the lamb, but leave a ⅛-inch-thick coating of fat to melt and baste the lamb during cooking.

To prepare the marinade, combine the orange zest and juice, lemon zest, rosemary and thyme leaves, and garlic in a food processor. Pulse to combine. Then add the mustard, oregano, coriander, and cumin. Turn the motor on, and after about 30 seconds, drizzle the olive oil through the feed tube. Transfer the marinade to a large self-seal plastic bag. Place the lamb in the bag, seal it securely, and turn the bag numerous times to coat the meat evenly. Refrigerate for at least 12 hours and up to 24 hours.

Preheat the oven to 375°F.

Using cooking twine, tie the lamb so that it is a uniform shape for even cooking. Do this by folding in the thinner, tapered tail piece toward the top; fold the right and left sides toward the middle and tie. Place the lamb and the marinade in a medium roasting pan. Season the lamb generously with salt and pepper, and place the pan in the oven. After 10 minutes, add 1 cup water to the pan. Roast for another 20 minutes. Then add the potatoes and onions to the pan, season them with salt, and stir to combine. Continue roasting until the internal temperature of the lamb reaches 125°F (it will continue cooking after it's removed from the oven), about

45 minutes. During cooking, stir the potatoes and onions occasionally to ensure even cooking and browning.

Transfer the vegetables to a bowl and cover to keep them warm. Allow the lamb to rest on a carving board for 10 minutes.

Pour any released juices back into the roasting pan, and reheat if necessary. Slice the lamb into ¼-inch-thick slices, and arrange them on a platter. Spoon some of the pan juices on top. Surround the lamb with the potatoes and onions, and serve. (Note: If you like lamb cooked to medium, add the vegetables about 15 minutes later in the roasting process and increase the total cooking time by 15 minutes.)

VARIATIONS

- Extend this preparation into warm-weather cooking by wiping the marinade from the lamb and leaving it open (butterflied). Cook it on a grill, over medium heat, for about 25 minutes per side, or until desired doneness, and serve with grilled tomatoes.
- Seasonal additions might include 1 fennel bulb, cut into 8 to 10 wedges; 4 medium turnips, peeled and quartered; or 2 large red bell peppers, cored, seeded, and cut into large pieces—all added at the same time as the potatoes—or about 10 ounces mushrooms (left whole if small, halved if large), added 15 minutes before you take the lamb out of the oven.

LEFTOVERS

Perfect sliced for sandwiches.

NUTRITION

Lamb is an excellent source of protein, vitamin B_{12}, niacin, zinc, and selenium and a good source of iron and riboflavin.

ECONOMY $$$

Goodbye-Winter Choucroute

MAKES 12 TO 14 SERVINGS

What a dramatic and aromatic presentation this dish makes in the dead of winter! On particularly cold nights, we prepare our Mediterranean version (seasoned with pancetta and prosciutto) as a special for our customers. At the last of winter, we kick the season away with a full-on party at my farmhouse, serving the choucroute with crusty breads, pickled vegetables, and Alsatian cheeses and wines and beers. We use all sorts of fresh, cured, and confit meats from local producers. The ingredients list is long (and flexible), but the preparation is really not fussy: you chop the vegetables and meats into large rustic-looking chunks and cook the choucroute slowly for several hours, melting the vegetables, tenderizing the meat, and perfuming the house. Enjoy the whole process.

3 pounds	sauerkraut, preferably organic
1	medium onion, studded with 12 to 14 cloves
¼ cup	olive oil
6 ounces	nitrate-free bacon, cut into 2- to 3-inch chunks (I use Mountain Products Smokehouse slab bacon, or pancetta)
1 pound	pork shoulder, trimmed and cut into 3-inch chunks (I use boneless shoulder chops from Northwind Farms)
7 ounces	bratwurst, sliced into 3-inch-long segments (I use Mountain Products Smokehouse)
7 ounces	bockwurst, sliced into 3-inch-long segments
6 ounces	kielbasa (I use Northwind Farms), sliced into 3-inch-long segments
One	8-ounce end piece of prosciutto
3	celery stalks, chopped
1	large carrot, chopped
1	large onion, chopped
1 tablespoon	dried juniper berries
1 cup	Alsatian white wine, such as Riesling or Gewürztraminer
1	bouquet garni (our mix: 6 parsley sprigs, 6 thyme sprigs, 6 fresh sage leaves, 2 bay leaves, and a cinnamon stick, tied together with a string)
4 cups	chicken or beef stock or reduced-sodium broth, heated

Rinse the sauerkraut thoroughly, and drain it. Spread the sauerkraut over the bottom of an attractive 6-quart casserole, preferably one with a lid (otherwise have aluminum foil ready to cover). Place the clove-studded onion in the center. Set aside.

Preheat the oven to 275°F.

Heat the olive oil in a large skillet over medium-high heat. Add the bacon and cook, stirring occasionally, until slightly browned, about 5 minutes. Add the pork shoulder and cook until the pork and bacon are nicely browned, another 5 minutes. Add the bratwurst, bockwurst, and kielbasa, and continue to cook until all the meats are well colored, 5 to 7 minutes. Finally, add the prosciutto chunk and the celery, carrot, onion, and juniper berries.

Cook, stirring often, for 5 minutes. Add the wine and cook, stirring to deglaze the skillet, until the liquid is reduced by half, 2 minutes.

Transfer the meat, vegetables, and pan juices to the casserole. Add the bouquet garni. Pour the stock over the meat and vegetables. The liquid should come to about 1 inch below the top of the meat and vegetables; add water or more stock if it doesn't. Cover the casserole with a lid or foil, transfer it to the oven, and bake for 3 to 4 hours (this is a dish that will only improve with more cooking). Add a bit more liquid, ½ cup at a time, if needed, during the cooking time to prevent drying.

Remove the lid and the bouquet garni. The dish will not likely need salt. Serve immediately, straight from the casserole.

SERVING SUGGESTIONS

Serve with any combination of the following: parslied boiled young potatoes, caramelized apple slices, pickled vegetables, grated horseradish, and/or a variety of mustards. (To caramelize apples, peel, core, and cut them into 1-inch-thick rounds. Cook in butter over medium heat until browned on both sides and soft but still structured.) And of course, serve Alsatian wine or beer.

VARIATIONS

Add or substitute salted pork belly, smoked pork loin, smoked ham hocks, boudin noir (blood sausage), smoked garlic sausage, German frankfurters, confit of duck legs, duck or turkey sausages.

NUTRITION

Well…

ECONOMY $$

The cuts, and thereby cost, of the meats used in this recipe are frugal, especially when you consider that this soul-stirring dish will feed 12 to 14 and still probably provide leftovers.

Grilled Pork Tenderloin with Strawberry Balsamic BBQ Sauce

MAKES 4 TO 6 SERVINGS

I have adapted the classic pork-and-applesauce combination by pairing pork with strawberries for this late-spring version. The strawberry balsamic glaze is the perfect sweet-and-sour accompaniment to pork. In the summer, substitute peaches or fresh plums for the strawberries.

2 tablespoons	olive oil, plus extra for brushing the grill
3 tablespoons	finely chopped shallots
1	garlic clove, minced
1 tablespoon	minced fresh chives,
Pinch	cayenne
2 pints	strawberries, cleaned, hulled, and halved
2 tablespoons	sugar
¼ cup	good-quality balsamic vinegar
2 teaspoons	freshly grated lemon zest
	Salt and freshly ground black pepper
Two	10-ounce pork tenderloins

Heat 1 tablespoon of the oil in a medium to large nonstick skillet over moderate heat. Add the shallots, garlic, chives, and cayenne and cook, stirring often, until the shallots have softened, about 2 minutes. Add the strawberries and sugar and cook, tossing or stirring occasionally, until the liquid evaporates to a few tablespoons, about 3 minutes. Deglaze the pan with the vinegar, and simmer until thickened and syrupy, about 4 minutes. Stir in the lemon zest and adjust the seasoning with salt and pepper. Put half of the barbecue sauce in a small bowl for brushing on the pork, and set it aside to cool. Set the remaining sauce aside to serve with the pork.

Preheat a grill to medium and brush the rack lightly with oil. Rub the pork tenderloins with the remaining 1 tablespoon oil, and season them with salt and pepper. Grill the pork, turning it occasionally, until golden brown all over, about 6 minutes. Reduce the heat to medium-low and brush the pork with some of the sauce. Continue to grill, turning and brushing with the sauce occasionally, until an instant-read thermometer inserted 2 inches into the center of the pork registers 145°F, about 5 minutes. Transfer the pork to a platter, cover it loosely with foil, and let it rest for 5 minutes. (Discard any remaining basting sauce.)

Cut the pork diagonally into ¼-inch-thick slices. Arrange the pork slices on plates, and serve with the reserved strawberry sauce.

SERVING SUGGESTIONS

The sweetness of the strawberry sauce makes this a perfect match for the slight bitterness of quickly sautéed spinach or Swiss chard. Arugula with some Parmesan shavings and a lemony vinaigrette would be a well-paired cold side dish.

VARIATIONS

- Substitute grilled bone-in pork chops, chicken, or duck for the pork loin.
- Substitute tarragon for the chives.

LEFTOVERS

Sandwich leftover sliced pork napped with some of the BBQ sauce and sliced red onion with a toasted onion or seeded roll. Stir-fry chopped leftover pork with cooked brown rice and scallions. Or shred leftover pork and cook it in leftover BBQ sauce until tender, about 20 minutes, and fill tortillas or tacos.

NUTRITION

Strawberries are high in vitamin C (by weight more than some citruses) and low in calories (less than 50 per cup). They are also high in fiber, folate, potassium, and antioxidants. Phytonutrients called phenols are abundant in strawberries. Two specific types, anthocyanins and ellagic acid, lead the charge and are associated with strawberries' antioxidant and anti-inflammatory properties. Like many colorful berries, they are a heart-protective, anticancer fruit.

ECONOMY $$

Strawberries bought locally in season hardly seem like the same fruit as the flavorless variety available year-round. Take advantage when both the fruit and the price are at their sweetest.

Strawberry Mascarpone Bars

MAKES 12 BARS

Gigi Market is an enchanting setting, but definitely on the informal and rustic side. Froufrou desserts just don't work there. Gigi pastry chef Ashley Kearns brilliantly switches gears from down-home farm desserts like these yummy bars to stepped-up desserts for the trattoria and catering menus on a daily basis.

Crust

12 tablespoons	unsalted butter (1½ sticks), at room temperature
⅓ cup	sugar
1	large egg yolk
½ teaspoon	pure vanilla extract
2 cups	all-purpose flour

Filling

1⅓ cups	mascarpone cheese, at room temperature
½ cup	confectioners' sugar
1 tablespoon	fresh lemon juice
1 teaspoon	pure vanilla extract
2 cups	strawberries, cleaned, hulled, and sliced

Preheat the oven to 350°F.

To make the crust, butter and flour a 9 x 12-inch baking dish. In a standing mixer fitted with the paddle attachment, cream the butter and sugar together on low speed. Add the egg yolk and vanilla, and mix well. Sift in the flour and mix to combine. The dough will be stiff. Pat the dough evenly over the bottom of the prepared baking dish, and prick it all over with the tines of a fork. Bake in the center of the oven for 15 to 20 minutes. (This is a short dough, so you don't want any color—just perhaps the slightest bit of brown at the edges.) Allow the crust to cool completely.

In a mixing bowl, cream together the mascarpone, confectioners' sugar, lemon juice, and vanilla to form a soft, spreadable filling. Spread it over the cooled crust. Cut twelve 3 x 4-inch bars, and set them on a platter. Arrange the sliced strawberries on top of the bars. Serve warm or at room temperature.

- *Summer:* Use blueberries, plums, or sliced peaches instead of the strawberries.
- *Fall:* Use juicy ripe sliced pears or raspberries instead of the strawberries.

NUTRITION

Strawberries are a great source of vitamin C and anthocyanins, which are potent antioxidants.

ECONOMY $

Pound Cake with Strawberry Rhubarb Compote

The term "pound" cake is derived from the fact that the traditional American version included one pound each of flour, eggs, butter, and sugar. While I wouldn't call this recipe "light," it is "enlightened." I love a simple cake with a juicy sweet-tart compote. Rhubarb and strawberries appear in abundance during spring in the Hudson Valley. Gigi pastry chef Ashley Kearns always raids our retail cases at Gigi Market to prepare her rustic and sophisticated desserts.

Pound cake

1 cup	unsalted butter (2 sticks), at room temperature
1 cup plus 1 teaspoon	sugar
3	large eggs
3	large egg yolks
2 teaspoons	pure vanilla extract
½ teaspoon	salt
1⅓ cups	cake flour, sifted

Strawberry rhubarb compote

¼ cup	cornstarch
¾ cup	sugar
⅓ cup	honey
2½ pounds	rhubarb, washed, dried, and cut into ½-inch pieces
1 cup	strawberries, cleaned, hulled, and quartered

Preheat the oven to 350°F. Butter and flour a standard-size loaf pan.

In a standing mixer fitted with the paddle attachment, cream the butter and sugar together at medium speed. Add the eggs and egg yolks, one at a time, beating after each addition and scraping the bowl down occasionally. Add the vanilla, salt, and 1 teaspoon water. Remove the mixing bowl from the stand and gradually fold in the cake flour by hand, a third at a time, until it is incorporated. Pour the batter into the prepared loaf pan and place it on the center rack of the oven. Bake until a toothpick inserted in the middle of the cake comes out clean, 45 to 60 minutes.

Remove the cake from the oven and allow it to cool for 5 minutes. Then tip the cake out of the pan and place it on a wire rack to finish cooling.

While the oven is still hot, warm a medium metal bowl in the oven until it is hot.

Carefully remove the bowl from the oven and add the cornstarch, sugar, and honey. Mix together, and then add the rhubarb. Coat the rhubarb with the cornstarch-sugar mixture, and let it sit at room temperature for 30 minutes. (The rhubarb will release its juices and the cornstarch will help thicken them prior to cooking.)

Pour the rhubarb mixture into a saucepan, along with all the accumulated liquid. Cook over low heat, stirring constantly, until the rhubarb is fork-tender but not overcooked, 10 to 15 minutes. Pour the compote into a heatproof bowl and set it aside to cool at room temperature.

Stir the strawberries into the cooled compote. Slice the cake, and top the slices with the compote.

SERVING SUGGESTION

A little whipped cream is a nice addition.

VARIATIONS

- Use the compote as a pie or tart filling (see the rustic fruit tart on page 112). Simply pour the compote into an unbaked pie crust and bake at 425°F for 30 minutes.
- Enjoy the compote on its own with vanilla gelato or frozen yogurt.

LEFTOVERS

Stored in a cake container, the pound cake will hold for 2 days. The strawberry rhubarb compote is good, covered and refrigerated, for up to 4 days.

NUTRITION

Rhubarb is a great source of lutein, potassium, calcium, and magnesium. Strawberries are rich in vitamin C and anthocyanins, which are potent antioxidants.

ECONOMY $

Grilled Strawberries with Vanilla Gelato and Aged Balsamic

This simple dessert has great depth of flavor and a homey elegance that is perfect for any springtime evening. If you cannot find aged (at least 5 years) balsamic vinegar from Modena, Italy, which is available in most gourmet stores, enjoy the berries and gelato on their own.

	Wooden skewers for grilling
2 teaspoons	fresh lemon juice
2 teaspoons	canola or vegetable oil
2 teaspoons	sugar
1 pint	large ripe (but firm) strawberries
2 cups	vanilla ice cream, gelato, or frozen yogurt
4 teaspoons	excellent-quality aged balsamic vinegar from Modena

Heat the grill or a grill pan to medium-high heat. Soak the skewers in water for at least 15 minutes to prevent burning.

Combine the lemon juice, oil, and sugar in a medium bowl, and whisk with a fork to combine. Add the strawberries and turn to coat them evenly. Thread the strawberries onto the skewers and place them on the grill. Cook, turning frequently, until the berries are just warmed and grill-marked, about 2 minutes. Remove the berries from the skewers and cut them in half. Serve the grilled berries over gelato, drizzled with the balsamic vinegar.

VARIATIONS

Substitute other firm seasonal fruits, such as peaches or nectarines, for the strawberries.

LEFTOVERS

Mix the strawberries into quick breads. Mash the berries and spread on toast instead of jam.

NUTRITION

Strawberries are low in calories and an excellent source of vitamin C. They are also high in fiber, folate, potassium, and antioxidants.

ECONOMY $

Take advantage of seasonal fruit.

Summer

Whoever coined the phrase "lazy days of summer" never ran a restaurant. Or a farm or a market, for that matter. The population of the Hudson Valley swells by 50 percent, and life gets incredibly busy. My summer passes in a mad sprint from Memorial Day weekend to Labor Day. The trattoria and the market are open seven days a week, all day long, to accommodate diners who eat at all different times. Breakfast turns into brunch then segues into lunch and slips into cocktails and dinner. And while the days disappear in a haze of activity, our focus remains on eating locally, seasonally, and with great flavor.

Hudson Valley farmers, ranchers, and food artisans help us make that happen. The Gigi van is out daily gathering produce from more than thirty local producers. Mr. Mink stops in with baskets of his fragrant ripe tomatoes ready to be paired with just-made mozzarella for everyone's favorite summer salad, caprese. Migliorelli Farm is loaded with produce, especially some of the more exotic Italian vegetables that Ken Migliorelli loves to grow.

There are typical yellow crookneck squash and zucchini, but he will undoubtedly also have cucuzze squash, which is an enormous pale green squash in either your standard baseball shape or coiled like a sea serpent. Cucuzze will also yield a second harvest of trailing squash runners called tenerumi. The tendrils will be cut down and the small pea shoots, tiny buds, and lemony-tasting leaves will be culled to produce an old-fashioned dish, Sicilian summer minestrone. Ken also brings us beautiful bunches of broccoli rabe, romanesco cauliflower, brilliantly colored chards, all sorts of basils and other herbs, garlic, Italian frying peppers, and small cherry peppers to stuff and preserve.

Hearty Roots delivers boxes through the market's back door. In them are lettuces, sweet red peppers, zucchini, cherry tomatoes, heirloom tomatoes, salad tomatoes—more and more tomatoes. Taliaferro Farms in New Paltz grows green beans, Chioggia beets, dill, garlic, and cantaloupes, and Phillies Bridge Farm in Gardiner is filling boxes with Asian greens, cucumbers, cilantro, fava beans, snap beans, tomatillos, and chiles. Sprout Creek Farm is still sending their fresh cow's milk cheeses, and I sometimes like to pair their cheese, or even the sheep's milk Camembert from Old Chatham, with spicy hot jellies, relishes, and chutneys from Beth's Farm Kitchen. She makes great use of the enormous number of chiles and hot peppers grown by local farmers. Tons of plums, peaches, cherries, and blueberries are from Mead Orchards unloaded from the van. I have a weakness for plums and have been known to keep eating and eating them. Their soft, juicy flesh is honey sweet, and I justify my gluttony by telling myself that the season is indecently short.

Crates of fresh brown eggs from Feather Ridge keep us going. I can't believe how many cartons we sell to customers at Gigi Market. We also use them in pastry chef Ashley Kearns's delectable baked goods and desserts. Milk from Hudson Valley Fresh sells quickly, and Old Chatham's sheep's milk yogurts go pretty fast too. I like the plain yogurt, but our customers also love the maple- and ginger-flavored versions.

The natural beauty of the Hudson beckons to visitors. That means there are people, people, and more people amid all the lush wooded hiking trails, under the canopies of trees, and paddling or fishing along our expanses of river and ponds. And we see a lot of each other—often at the expense of wildlife, who tolerate us but decide to retreat to quieter places. They'll venture back in the fall, when there's more space to move around. As for me, my precious spare moments are spent in more modest ways. I see a few friends, catch the occasional performance at the SummerScape Festival put on by Bard College, and spend as much time as I can in my garden.

Gardens and gardening are one of my passions. I'll head out for a minute to tie up some unruly vines, and before I know it two hours have passed. My summer vegetable garden is planted by mid-May with heirloom tomatoes, all sorts of peppers and chiles—including banana peppers, green peppers with a really thin skin for meltingly tender stuffed peppers—and eggplants, either a round striped variety or the classic Italian *melanzane*. Pumpkins are ripening, along with butternut squash, zucchini, and several varieties of cucumbers. My favorite home-grown herb is flat-leaf parsley. It has an amazing full, sweet flavor, and I've never met its peer in the supermarket. I snip my sage bushes all summer long for our Tuscan Fries (page 285). If the sage bolts, I chop it down and use it as a basting brush for barbecues (chef Wilson Costa showed me that this is how it's done in his native Brazil).

Besides working in my own garden, I love visiting other people's gardens too. Many houses in the Valley were built in the 1700s and 1800s, and their gardens have been shaped and reshaped over the centuries, creating man-made landscapes that blend harmoniously with nature. The beautifully manicured lawns and ponds, the riotous trumpet vines climbing over stone walls or garden entrances, lilacs in bloom, and gnarled apple trees with small blush-stained fruit are all tended with care. There are massive old oaks that anchor a whole garden, creating naturally cool spaces for relaxation. Gardens here reflect a deep appreciation of native flora, with a touch of the northeasterner's exuberance at finally, finally being able to stay outdoors all day long! It is the best time of year to entertain—it's summer, the outdoors beckons, and the mood is relaxed and easygoing.

Eating local now is a no-brainer. Lots of dishes can be put together with little effort. But even accomplished cooks drop by Gigi Market in the summer for us to help them along. The market is a great option for many people who just need a dessert, maybe a few side dishes and salads, or even the whole meal, with the Northwind Farm pork chops and chicken already marinated and ready for the grill. I love to craft meals that are easy to eat, yet give people a real feeling for the Hudson Valley. It's what one of my creative friends recently called "food with a face to the place."

My advice to summer cooks is keep it cool and simple. Oppressive summer heat can blunt anyone's appetite, and on those days it needs to be cold food or no food at all. There are lots of great options to choose from: ceviche, cold salads, cold soups, shellfish platters, and antipasto platters. My favorite summer meal is made with grilled pork loin or poached turkey breast, cooked in advance and then thinly sliced and served at room temperature with *tonnato* sauce, an Italian tuna, lemon, and caper sauce (see page 99). Add some tomato bread salad with fresh parsley and perfectly ripe tomatoes, or a simply dressed arugula or loose-leaf salad, and you have a meal that is simple, healthy, and completely satisfying.

Grilled food also fits the description of perfect summer food. It can be served hot, cold, or at room temperature and is simple to prepare. We serve great local beef burgers for barbecues on the Gigi Market patio when groups of visitors come up for the weekend. The beef comes from Northwind Farm, as does some incredible kielbasa. Gigi Skizzas with arugula and basil pesto and thinly sliced chicken are another simple yet full-flavored meal. I love Gigi Gigandes beans in any season; in the summer we prepare them BBQ-style (see page 105). They go with everything, especially butterflied baby chicken quickly grilled over high heat. And I often opt for that true summertime dish: grilled vegetables. Liberally doused with fruity olive oil and served at room temperature as a main or side dish, or loaded into panini with melting cheese, grilled vegetables are my go-to meal when pressed for time. Sometimes I skip the cheese, but not often.

What do you drink with all that summer produce? Well, here my advice still holds: Keep it cool and keep it simple. After years of matching food with wine, I can tell you one very simple rule that works for me: the region of the food pairs well with the local wine. This is especially true of Mediterranean cuisine. Choose crisp-tasting whites or fruit-driven structured rosés that have nice body to them. They work well with simple Mediterranean flavors. Of course, feel free to step outside the box. For example, a Super Tuscan, a Barbaresco, or a Nero d'Avola can cross over to many dishes, especially red meats from the grill. Amarone feels more like a winter wine, but its hint of sweetness can work well with sweet and spicy flavors such as BBQ ribs. But again, it's summer. Don't work too hard.

These long sunlit days are a fleeting treasure. While I'm busy running around during the day, most evenings I can be found at the trattoria, getting in the way of my capable staff and manager John Storm. Before they came along, I used to be needed! By Friday evening, an early crowd fills the Gigi patio. Servers move along the narrow space between tables, carefully clearing and delivering plates, discussing our specials, and taking requests. With the humidity hanging heavy in the air, our bartenders are busy sending out tray after tray of chilled drinks, such as Hendrick's gin and cucumber-water martinis or currant Cosmopolitans, to cool everyone down and rev up their appetites. Friday starts the weekend, and we are busy. Some friends have just driven up from the city and have stopped off for dinner before heading to their summer house. I see some of our regulars relaxing on the patio with cold glasses of fresh peach sangria, watching the evening *passegiatta* of people and cars along Rhinebeck's main street and enjoying a friendly conversation with some of their favorite longtime Gigi waiters.

Inside the dining room, all the available tables are seated—there are just a few spots at the bar. Most nights it feels like controlled chaos, and the trattoria is humming. Wilson Costa is running the kitchen in his calm, cheerful way. That attitude is a treasure to me and to everyone who works for him. Almost three hundred meals will be cooked on an average night, a daunting task that can make just about anyone cranky. John is busy trying to seat a group of diners who have just run into one another at the bar and now all want to eat together. It will be a convivial, if tight, fit. As for me, I'm at the door explaining to a hungry customer that we take reservations only for large groups. After all, we are a trattoria; we serve anyone who shows up at the door. Don't worry, it's a beautiful night and the patio is open. The wait won't be long, I promise.

THE SUMMER HARVEST

Corn

Summertime means fresh corn in the Hudson Valley. With so many fields of tall green stalks, it may seem as if corn is the only thing we grow. That and cows, of course! At the restaurant, corn will go on the menu as soon as it shows up at the market, and it will stay on the menu until the fields are picked clean. We'll make batches of Mead Orchards creamed corn with Taleggio (page 107) and corn ceviche (raw kernels marinated in olive oil, orange juice, a bit of orange zest, and some minced garden jalapeños), which is perfect with seared scallops or just about any grilled, seared, or roasted fish.

There are two predominant types grown here: sweet corn, for your classic summertime corn on the cob, and flint corn or dent corn, grown primarily for livestock feed but also used for polenta, hominy, masa, and some varieties of popcorn. And there are now "supersweet" hybrids, sweet corn that holds on to its sugars a little longer, so you can pick it today and eat it in a few days with virtually no loss of sweet flavor. I like both, depending on the dish. When it's a spicy mixture like the corn ceviche, I like a really sweet corn to play up the contrast between it and the heat of the chile. But for simple cob-in-hand eating, I do prefer the classic.

No matter what kind of sweet corn you pick, fresher is better. When just picked, sweet corn needs only a quick dip in hot water, typically the time it takes the water to return to a boil, in order to be ready to eat. Once the season gets under way here, there's little difficulty in finding truly fresh-picked corn. It seems to be piled high on every roadside stand and in every farmers' market. And not just here in the Valley. It's a big country, and we grow a lot of corn, so just about everyone can get their hands on fresh corn during the summertime.

It's important to remember that our bodies often absorb the nutritive values of vegetables better when we cook them. Corn is a case in point. Eating cooked sweet corn significantly boosts the grain's health-giving antioxidant activity. Researchers at Cornell University found that cooking sweet corn actually increased antioxidant levels and levels of ferulic acid, which provides cancer protection benefits. You do lose vitamin C in cooking corn, but at the same time your body gains access to other important acids, minerals, enzymes, and antioxidants, such as lutein, a member of the vast carotenoid family. Lutein is found in high amounts in dark green leafy vegetables, and in egg yolks as well. Eating corn is also a tasty way to get more whole grains in your diet. Both the whole kernel and anything unprocessed that is made from it, such as cornmeal, counts.

We grow flint corn here too. One of my favorite mills is Wild Hive Farm in Clinton Corners, which purchases locally grown, open-pollinated organic flint corn from farmers and then grinds it traditionally, between two rotating granite slabs. We carry the packages of their freshly ground cornmeal in Gigi Market. I'm always supportive of local products, especially one as versatile as cornmeal. But I became a huge fan after

I tasted it. Local or not, this cornmeal simply makes the best nutty, rustic-textured cornbread I've ever eaten.

Tomatoes

During summer, farmers' markets and farm stands throughout the region have impressive displays of all kinds of tomatoes: small bunches of sweet grape tomatoes, deeply creased heirlooms in a variety of colors, heavy round blood-red beefsteaks, and pear-shaped Italian varieties, perfect for canning and sauce. Tomato plants give generously of themselves until it seems almost an embarrassment of riches. I'm lucky to have my businesses on the receiving end, because at my house it's *basta*—enough with all the tomatoes already! As much as I love them, it's hard to keep up with the harvest, especially as we get closer to busy Labor Day weekend and the mountain of tomatoes for canning seems to reach gargantuan proportions.

Tomatoes are botanically a fruit, and I think of them that way because like fruit, they are completed by nature. We just fool around a bit. Alan Chadwick, the biointensive gardener who has influenced so many organic gardeners, has been quoted as saying, "Food is really cooked in the garden. It is just finished in the kitchen." To me, that is especially true of tomatoes—and if you don't believe me, go ahead and eat a warm, freshly picked tomato and see.

Life without tomatoes? Unimaginable. When eaten truly ripe at their peak of flavor, tomatoes define summer. I have friends who exist on ripe tomato sandwiches in a "feast now, famine later" mentality. I totally understand that. Talk of tomatoes takes over the dining room at Gigi Trattoria, as customers ask me how my plants are doing and whether they're getting red. Things can get competitive among us tomato addicts. We're all waiting for that perfectly ripe tomato, and suddenly, wham—we are overwhelmed with bushels of them.

Truly ripe tomatoes do not travel. Those that are forced to are wan, unhappy things you don't want to befriend. I'm especially pleased to see more and more heirlooms at the farmers' market. Heirlooms are usually slightly older varieties that have been passed down over a period of years and are open-pollinated, which just means that the plants' seeds will produce identical seedlings. Not all tomato plants do this. Hybrid tomatoes are the result of cross-breeding, and their seeds, if open-pollinated, may not produce seedlings identical to the parent plant. It's good to have both hybrid and heirloom seedlings available, though I am concerned about plant and seed companies patenting their crosses so that only they have the right to reproduce their hybrids. Talk about holding tomato-loving folks over a barrel!

What can't you do with tomatoes? They're a source of endless culinary invention. I love them in salads, in cold soups such as gazpacho or a simple tomato-basil, in sandwiches, on bruschetta, chopped and folded into scrambled eggs for breakfast, or just in fat, juicy slices still warm from the garden with salt, pepper, and a drizzle of olive oil. One of my favorite summertime dishes is panzanella (tomato-bread salad). After cutting the tomatoes in wedges, I season them with salt to get the juices running and toss in some fresh-cut parsley and basil. When they are soft and slightly soupy, I add some day-old Gigi crostini or croutons and give it all a good stir. If I don't have any bread on hand, I use the marinated tomatoes for a great hot-weather pasta dish: warm spaghetti topped with a raw tomato-basil sauce. Given all the different ways you can enjoy tomatoes, my advice is to enjoy them as often as you can, ripe and ready.

The biggest nutritional benefit of tomatoes is that they contain lots of vitamin C and lycopene. Lycopene, which provides tomatoes with their red color, acts as a very powerful antioxidant. In fact, lycopene may carry twice the punch of another well-known antioxidant, beta-carotene. Studies conducted by researchers at Harvard and in Italy link consumption of tomatoes with reduced risk of developing a wide variety of cancers. And Harvard's Women's Health Study, which evaluates the dietary habits and health of more than 40,000 women, found that women who consumed 7 servings or more of tomato based foods, like tomato sauce and pizza, each week exhibited nearly a 30 percent risk

reduction in total cardiovascular disease compared to the group with intakes of less than 1½ servings per week. A final piece of great news is that lycopene is more easily absorbed by the body if you include a little fat, so don't forget to put a healthy drizzle of olive oil on your caprese salad or tomato sandwich. Your body and your taste buds will thank you.

Cucumbers

Cucumbers are botanically similar to watermelons; both are in the gourd family. They have a high water content, which makes them especially refreshing to eat during the dog days of summer. Here in the Hudson Valley we always get a stretch of the three H's: hazy, hot, and humid. The Valley traps the heat, the air is thick and sticky, and it's the perfect time to enjoy fresh-picked cucumbers.

Cucumbers are usually eaten fresh during the season and then pickled to enjoy for the rest of the year. There are varieties of cucumbers that are grown for pickling alone, including squat Kirbys, gherkins, and cornichons. All kinds of cucumbers are grown in the Valley, including your typical classic garden cucumber, long English cucumbers with few seeds, and some smaller Mediterranean and Persian varieties. I grow cucumbers myself, my favorite being the round lemon cucumber, which is sweet and flavorful and doesn't contain much of the chemical that can makes other cucumbers bitter and hard to digest.

Cucumbers are high in potassium, silica (a vital mineral), and vitamin A, which is found mostly in the vegetable's skin. The silica in cucumbers is an essential component of healthy connective tissue. Often supermarket cucumbers have been waxed, which means they must be peeled before eating. That is our nutritional loss. Buying cucumbers in season from your local farmers' market means you get more flavor and nutrition, as they do not require peeling. The watery flesh of a cucumber contains vitamin C and caffeic acid, both of which help soothe skin irritations and reduce swelling. That may explain why cucumber slices are considered a good beauty treatment for swollen eyes. The cucumber's high water content makes it naturally hydrating. Anyone who has crunched on a cold sliced cucumber during a hot summer afternoon can attest to that.

Summer Squash

Summer squash, such as yellow crookneck, zucchini, chayote, and pattypan, are also botanically related to cucumbers and watermelons. The entire vegetable is edible— even the flowers, which the Italians consider a summer treat, either fried or added to risotto and frittatas. The flowers also top our Skizzas, along with a delicate cheese such as Crescenza or Gigi fresh ricotta. Chayote, probably the least familiar summer squash here, is a light green squash with a lengthwise crease. It is sometimes referred to as mirliton and is a beloved favorite among the Acadians in Louisiana.

All summer squash are fragile and easily bruised when ripe. But if you grow zucchini, you know that a bruised squash is no problem. If you stand still for ten minutes and watch closely, your zucchini plant will grow another! An exaggeration, but only slightly. Summer squash plants are prodigious producers. A joke circulating a few years ago was that nobody here locked their car doors— except in summer, when someone might leave zucchini in the backseat.

If you have a lot of summer squash, what do you do with it? Well, I love it grilled as part of a veggie plate, chopped and added to summer grain salads, or tucked into a sandwich. I love zucchini slices slowly roasted with olive oil until meltingly soft. Please don't serve me crunchy zucchini; it has no flavor! After it has been grilled, roasted, or sautéed, summer squash can be tossed with pasta and some chopped mint and cheese, or with a light tomato sauce. Consider shredding summer squash and adding it to a batter to make fritters, or hollow it out and stuff it with barley, couscous, or rice, chopped tomatoes, herbs, a bit of crumbled Italian sausage, and a dusting of Parmesan. Light summer minestrone benefits from the addition of crookneck squash, and I also love zucchini *agrodolce,* a marinated sweet-and-sour preparation thought to have been brought to Sicily by the Arabs. This reduction of vinegar, sugar, citrus, a bit of onion, garlic, and dried fruit can be made with zucchini, eggplant, or peppers as the featured ingredient—a refreshing side dish to grilled fish or chicken.

Summer squash, like their relatives, are mostly water. But that doesn't mean they're nutritional weaklings. In fact, all summer squash are a great source of manganese, vitamins A and C, magnesium, fiber, potassium, folate, copper, and phosphorus. The magnesium in squash has been shown to help reduce the risk of heart attack and stroke. Together with potassium, magnesium is also helpful for reducing high blood pressure. The vitamin C and beta-carotene help to prevent the oxidation of cholesterol and may help to reduce the progression of atherosclerosis and diabetic heart disease. All in all, not too shabby for a vegetable with such an everyday reputation.

Peppers

Fat green, yellow, red, and even brown bell peppers, jalapeños, Italian frying peppers, Anaheim chiles, habañeros, Scotch bonnets, poblanos, Thai green chiles, cayenne peppers, banana peppers, Hungarian wax peppers, and that special chile the family has been growing for generations—all wind up at the farmers' markets in beautiful displays of color, size, and exuberant diversity.

How dull food would be without peppers, both sweet and hot. I love a smidge of the scorching hot ones to perk up fresh foods. Poblanos are a big favorite of mine, with their sweet-hot notes when eaten fresh. I love them, too, when they're dried into anchos. I toss seeded ancho chiles into soups, stews, and sauces, making sure to blend the flavorful flesh into the sauce.

The Scoville scale, named for its creator, Wilbur Scoville, measures capsaicin, the "heat" of chiles. Sweet bell peppers contain almost no capsaicin, while the Naga pepper from India is so hot that it's used for repellent pepper spray. Just out of curiosity I grew the supposedly super-hot habañero peppers one summer. They definitely lent a kick to things, but it wasn't unbearable, and I wonder if the heat of the chile pepper is somehow dependent on the soil. Perhaps mine is just too mellow.

Of all peppers, my favorite is the garden-grown green bell. What a difference in flavor from the big, heavy ones in the supermarket. The thin walls of the home-grown varieties make them perfect for stuffing and roasting. The filling cooks and remains moist, the top is crispy, and the pepper is cooked and tender, all at the same time (see Harvest Stuffed Peppers, page 156).

Spicy chile peppers contain beta-carotene, lutein, zeaxanthin, vitamin C, and of course lots of capsaicin, an antibacterial that may help prevent ulcers. Capsaicin is also an anti-inflammatory and is now widely used as a topical pain reliever. Eating chiles may also help lower triglycerides and act as an anticoagulant to prevent blood clots.

Bell peppers and other sweet peppers are low in calories and rich in vitamins A and C. They also have good amounts of vitamin K, which plays a role in bone health. Peppers are members of the nightshade family of plants, and as such, they have trace amounts of alkaloids. Some researchers have speculated that nightshade alkaloids can contribute to excessive loss of calcium from bone and excessive depositing of calcium in soft tissue. Cooking lowers alkaloid amounts significantly. Some people with arthritis have been advised by their nutritionists to follow a "no nightshade" diet because a substance called solanine, found in all nightshade plants, is believed to exacerbate their arthritic condition. To date, there is no substantial evidence supporting this belief, but I never argue with what people say works for them.

Currants

Currants are delicious but unfamiliar to most Americans. Grown in the Hudson Valley and touted as a new "superfood" by nutritionists, these little berries contain two times the antioxidant power of blueberries, four times the vitamin C of oranges, and twice the potassium of bananas.

Europeans have always grown currants, but their cultivation here was outlawed in 1911 after the timber industry argued (erroneously) that currants carried a botanical disease that could wipe out pine trees. The bill was repealed in New York in the 1990s, and we are now seeing currant bushes being planted and the fruit harvested. Since the currant bush likes hot, humid summers and cold winters, it's perfectly at home in the Hudson Valley. Black and red currants have a tart flavor that is great in jellies, sauces, and pies. They're also the main flavor in cassis, the French liqueur.

A fairly consistent rule of thumb with all fruits and vegetables is that the deeper the color, the greater the amounts of nutrients and phytochemicals. Black currants certainly support this. Their anthocyanins, which also cause the blue-purple pigmentation, have been shown to diminish oxidative stress, a syndrome that can cause neurodegenerative diseases, such as Alzheimer's, and some cardiovascular diseases. Anthocyanins are a subclass of the broad polyphenol group of phytochemicals, which are also found in foods like apples, blueberries, broccoli, cabbage, celery, cherries, coffee, cranberries, dark chocolate, grapes and red wine, legumes, olive oil, onions, parsley, strawberries, tea, and whole grains, among others. The level of anthocyanins found in black currants, however, surpasses most foods.

Potassium is another reason to eat black currants. The Harvard School of Public

Health studied the diets of more than 43,000 men and women and found that those eating diets rich in potassium and magnesium (also found in currants) had a reduced risk of stroke.

Peaches, Plums, Nectarines, and Apricots

Some foods bring out our most poetic nature. Just read the work of David Mas Masumoto, the peach and grape farmer in central California who writes movingly about growing and harvesting his organic Sun Crest peaches. Or classical Persian love poems, in which talk of "the honeyed juices of ripe apricots" is about nothing more than (very) thinly veiled seduction. Indeed, summer fruit brings out our emotions and memories. Its fragrant perfume sends poets and non-poets alike into serious swoons of delight. That means we barely make it out of the farmers' market before we bite into a ripe plum or peach and do a funny little dance to avoid getting the juice all over our clothes.

Fully ripe summer stone fruits are a stubbornly local product, rebuffing the best attempts of industrialized agriculture to conform to shipping dates and distances. Fruit ripens only on the tree; it doesn't get any better after you pick it. To enjoy absolutely ripe stone fruit, you have to head out into a pick-your-own farm field. Chuck Mead of Mead Orchards, who grows great-

tasting fruit, acknowledges that even he must pick his peaches one or two days before they are perfectly ripe. If he waited any longer, his fruit couldn't handle the ride from the farm to the farmers' market. They are that delicate.

There is no better way to enjoy fully ripe stone fruits than by simply eating them out of hand. But that doesn't mean we don't try. Their flavors, especially peaches, are great in salads, cobblers, compotes, tarts, and pies, and in summer drinks like sangrias or glasses of Prosecco. We make a peach BBQ sauce (page 289) to spread on the base of one of our summer Skizzas or to baste shrimp with while they cook on the grill. I also love our peach salsa (page 97), which has been kicked up with the addition of some hot garden chiles and lime juice.

All summer stone fruits are high in vitamins A and C. Peaches and nectarines contain phytonutrients that have been shown to diminish the growth of tumors and minerals, such as iron and potassium, that ensure good cell function and electrolyte balance. They also contain carotenoids such as lutein and zeaxanthin that help prevent macular degeneration, a generally age-related condition that can lead to impaired vision or blindness. Plums (and in their dried form as prunes) have many of the same healthy benefits along with high levels of unique antioxidants in the phenol family called neochlorogenic and chlorogenic acids.

Still, all their good nutritional qualities are just gilding the lily. I've never known anyone who needed to be convinced to eat a ripe plum or peach. And once you get started eating, it is awfully hard to stop.

Eggplant

By July the eggplants in my garden are starting to lean over, pulled down by the weight of their shiny purple fruit. The ground is very warm now, and the eggplants are growing bigger in the hot, humid air and long days of sunshine. This "food of the sun" flourishes among the farms and gardens all over the Valley now, a living link to the great number of Italian immigrants who farmed this land throughout the last century, taking eggplant from "ethnic" to mainstream.

I love eggplant. My eggplant epiphany, if you will, happened during a trip to Sicily years ago, where I tasted the vegetable perfectly prepared. It had been picked young and cooked until fork-tender. With no heavy or greasy preparations, the eggplant's own delicate flavor shone through. I thought of all the bad eggplant Parmesan dishes I'd had in my life—heavily breaded and fried slices, smothered in overcooked tomato sauce and loaded with stringy melted mozzarella. Here the slices were liberally brushed with olive oil and roasted until tender, then napped with a light, fresh-tasting tomato sauce and layered with shavings of my favorite cheese,

Parmigiano-Reggiano. Restrained, simple, utterly direct. Sicilians also don't wait for the eggplant to grow too big, but pick the fruit when it's small, taut, and heavy.

It isn't difficult to cook eggplant well, but you must cook it fully. On too many occasions I've been served grilled eggplant that looks very pretty but is still raw on the inside. No, no, please no. Instead, grill it slowly, brushing it with olive oil from time to time, or roast slices with a good film of olive oil in the bottom of the pan and an additional brushing of oil over the top. Eggplant does absorb oil initially and look dry, but as it cooks, the oil penetrates into the flesh, helping it soften and become creamy. If you like eggplant Parmesan (and I really do!), drop the overcooked sauce and bad cheese. Instead try the Enlightened Eggplant Parmesan on page 90 and experience your own "come to mamma" moment!

Which type of eggplant to choose? Well, the dark purple elongated globe eggplant is still the predominant variety you see at the farmers' markets, and to be honest, I like them a lot, especially when they've been picked young. But there are lots to choose from. You can now find slim, tapered Japanese eggplants; shorter, light purple Chinese eggplants; small round green-striped Thai eggplants; or even more exotic (and bitter) pea eggplants, which are typically sold as a cluster on a branch. There are white eggplants of all sizes and, of course, the classic Italian *melanzane*, which is small and round with white flesh and striking violet streaks and markings. I've had good luck planting that variety myself. Whatever variety you choose, select young, fresh fruit, which will not require the time-consuming salting and rinsing to remove the bitterness.

From Japan through Asia and Africa and into Europe, eggplant shows up in the traditional dishes of many cultures, where it is transformed into curries, pickles, rice dishes, chutneys, soups, and tempuras, and also hollowed out, stuffed, and baked. At Gigi Trattoria we even make Eggplant Fries (page 109) with cut globe eggplant batons dusted with cornmeal, flour, and herbs. They are an elegant surprise to our customers, combining a crunchy exterior with a melting soft interior and gentle flavor.

Eggplant belongs to the nightshade family, which includes tomatoes, potatoes, and peppers. The plant's leaves and stems contain alkaloids: colorless, bitter organic substances that include caffeine, morphine, and nicotine. But there is a negligible amount in the fully mature fruit, and the plant's medicinal benefits are many. Eggplant has ample bioflavenoids, which may be beneficial in preventing strokes and hemorrhages, and the phytochemical monoterpene, an antioxidant helpful in preventing heart disease and cancer. Eggplants, and many other nightshades, are rich in phytonutrients, including phenolic compounds, which may have antioxidant, antiviral, and antimutagenic (anticancer)

properties. They also contain the anthocyanin nasunin. Research in animals indicates that nasunin, a potent scavenger of free radicals, protects healthy cells from oxidative damage. Anthocyanins are also responsible for the vibrant red, purple, and blue coloring of many vegetables and fruit. When possible, enjoy the skins!

While eggplant is grown and eaten all over the world, it always reminds me of Sicily. Several years ago I stayed in Taormina, on the northeastern side of the island, for a few weeks. It was the middle of summer, high tourist season, and the town was packed with families and couples enjoying their holiday. The generosity and warmth of the local community was astonishing, but I was on this trip by myself, suffering occasional bouts of loneliness. As I sat in a restaurant eating dinner one evening, an old man sat down next to me and we began talking. He gracefully endured my halting Italian and we had a warm discussion about Taormina, local food, and politics, all the while eating delicious plates of eggplant Parmesan and drinking a lovely local Insolia, a delicate fruit-driven white wine whose color seems to have captured the Sicilian sun. He insisted, quite adamantly, that his mother's recipe was much better, scribbling it down for me on a piece of paper. After dinner he stood up, tucked my arm into his, and proceeded to give me a ride back to my hotel on his Vespa. I'll never forget it.

MEAD ORCHARDS

Beginning in June, cars start pulling up in front of the white-canopied farm stand at Mead Orchards. Families and couples head out into the orchard to spend the day picking whatever is ripe—strawberries first, then peaches and other stone fruits, soon blueberries, and by late fall, apples and pumpkins. While people certainly come for the fruit, they also come to be in the country, breathe the fresh air, and enjoy the orchard's great view of the Catskills rising to the west and the Berkshires sloping off into the east.

This family farm in Tivoli, just north of where I live in Red Hook, is the story of three generations of Mead men. G. Gordon Mead purchased the hundred-acre farm in 1916. It came with a small dairy, chickens, hogs, and a variety of grain and fruit crops. He loaded his apples into barrels each summer and fall and shipped them by boat down the Hudson River to New York City. With time and work the farm prospered, and in 1959 Gordon's son Sid took over. He expanded the number of apple trees, preserving many old varieties that others had abandoned. Twenty years later, Sid's son Chuck joined him on the farm, and

for the next thirty years the men worked side by side, growing the farm to include a broader range of fruit, planting peaches, pears, plums, apricots, and nectarines. The relationship between father and son was extremely close, sharing deeply held beliefs of the value of farming. In the 1990s Chuck began shifting the farm away from wholesale to retail sales. He also added more vegetables—pumpkins, corn, squash, tomatoes, peppers, greens—and some herbs, berries, and cherries. Sid also considered ways to grow and protect the farm. In 2001 Mead Orchards sold their development rights to Dutchess County Conservation, under a conservation easement. This means the land will never be developed. With the proceeds of that sale, they purchased an additional eighty-five acres, and the size of the farm operation nearly doubled. Sid passed away in early 2008, leaving the farm under Chuck's stewardship. In eight years the farm will be one hundred years old, and Chuck hopes to keep it going for much longer.

The history of this family farm brings up an element rarely mentioned in the national discussion about "sustainable" farming. This farm has longevity. It has provided a good livelihood to each successive generation of the Mead family, it has enriched the local community, and it has delivered wonderful food to generations of New Yorkers. Mead Orchards' harvests continue to be robust, and the land is carefully managed. By putting the land into a conservation easement, Sid and Chuck Mead have ensured that the land will be available as farmland in the future. But Chuck doesn't grow his fruit organically. By that measure alone, many would say his operation isn't being run "sustainably." All of which makes Chuck scratch his head. If he had been doing harm, would his farm still be viable after nearly one hundred years? Would he still be in business?

I think he has a point. We can't limit our focus on sustainability on only the environmental piece. We need to expand our view to recognize the value of economic sustainability. We need to encourage farming families, who are, by design, highly self-motivated to be good stewards of the land. Farming should provide a good life to those willing to work hard. This ensures that the next generation will take over the farm from their parents.

In fact, Chuck has tried to grow his fruit organically, but the results weren't good enough to convince him to convert his operations to organic. He is mindful of the risks of pesticides and exhaustively searches for and picks pesticides that present the least risk to his farm workers, his consumers, and his own family. He does grow many of his vegetables organically and is pleased with the results. It's just that the humid, wet environment of the Valley makes growing organic fruit a very difficult proposition.

Susan Oliveria, my co-author on *The Strang Cancer Prevention Center Cookbook* and a world renowned epidemiologist at Memorial Sloan Kettering, has written that less than 2 percent of cancers are environmentally based (this includes all environmental factors, including pesticides) while, by contrast, more than 30 percent of cancers may be prevented by eating fruits and vegetables. Believe me, I'm not advocating pesticides—just lots of juicy, perfectly mature fruits and vegetables.

And I get great fruit from Mead Orchards. Right now we have Mead onions and peaches at Gigi Market. Chef Wilson Costa has spoken with Chuck and offered to buy the rest of his organic corn, just so we can keep our Taleggio Creamed Corn (page 107) on the menu. The orchards and farm are magnificent, clearly managed by someone who knows what he's doing. Virtually all of Chuck's produce is consumed within one hundred miles of the farm, and his goods are snapped up at farmers' markets from the Bronx to Ossining. He jokes that you should have to bend over to eat a peach, otherwise the juices would drip all over you. You do bend over for a Mead Orchards peach. They're messy and wonderful.

Mead Orchards sits on good land. Fertile soil, natural rain, clouds, and sunshine make this corner of Tivoli a perfect place to farm. Chuck is placing the remaining eighty-five acres of his land into a conservation easement, and with that money, will spruce up his barn and facilities to ensure that the farm stays in good condition, now and into the future.

Mead Orchards, 15 Scism Road,
Tivoli, New York 12583
845-756-5641
www.meadorchards.com

Gigi Marinated Olives

MAKES 1 QUART

*These citrusy and slightly spicy olives dot the mixed antipasto platter
at Gigi Trattoria and are almost always requested by our catering clients.*

2½ pounds	mixed olives (any combination of picholine, Kalamata, Cerignola, Gaeta, and Niçoise)

Marinade

1	cinnamon stick
2 teaspoons	black peppercorns
2	small bay leaves
2 tablespoons	fennel seeds
2 tablespoons	dried rosemary
2 teaspoons	red pepper flakes
2 teaspoons	dried oregano
1½ teaspoons	dried thyme
	Peel from ½ lemon, cut into thin strips
	Peel from ½ lime, cut into thin strips
	Peel from ½ orange, cut into thin strips
2 cups	medium- to full-bodied red wine, preferably with some spice (such as a Zinfandel or Primitivo)
1 tablespoon	good-quality balsamic vinegar
2 cups	olive oil

Rinse the olives for several minutes under cold running water to remove the salt or brine. Set them aside in a storage container with a lid.

In a large nonreactive pot, combine all the ingredients except the olives and the olive oil. Bring to a boil; then reduce the heat and simmer until the wine is reduced by half, about 10 minutes. Set aside to cool to room temperature.

Add the cooled marinade and the olive oil to the container of olives. Stir gently to blend. Let the olives marinate, covered and refrigerated, for 2 days before serving. Store in the refrigerator for up to 3 weeks.

SERVING SUGGESTIONS

- Great on cheese or antipasto plates.
- Set numerous little bowls out for cocktail parties.
- Remove the pits and toss the olives into salads and pasta dishes.

Mr. Mink's Panzanella

MAKES 6 TO 8 SERVINGS

This tomato-bread salad is easy to make with Gigi Tomato Salsa. Enjoy it as a side dish, or spoon it over mesclun or baby greens. It is great on a summer buffet to accompany barbecued or grilled meat, poultry, fish, or vegetables.

1½ cups	croutons, torn day-old peasant bread, or grissini broken into segments
1 recipe	Gigi Tomato Salsa (page 282), made at least 1 hour in advance

Just before serving, stir the croutons, bread, or grissini into the salsa.

Mr. Mink's Panzanella (page 78)

Gigi BLT Salad with Roasted-Tomato Vinaigrette (page 82)

Grilled Steak and Arugula Salad with Parmesan Shavings (page 94)
with *Gigi Lemon Vinaigrette* (page 277)

Enlightened Eggplant Parmesan (page 90)

Gigi Steamed Mussels with Tomatoes and Herbs (page 86)

Watermelon Fennel Salad (page 81)

Gigi Summer Fruit Salad with Zabaglione (page 115)

Garden-Fresh Tomato Basil Soup

MAKES 6 SERVINGS

*Soup is a great opportunity to use up those flavorful but less than perfect tomatoes.
Bruised tomatoes, sometimes called "canners," are fine for this simple
seasonal soup. Use a variety—heirlooms, plums, and cherries are all good.*

2 tablespoons	olive oil
1	medium onion, chopped
12	large tomatoes, cored and chopped
2 cups	chicken or vegetable stock or reduced-sodium broth
1 cup	fresh basil leaves
	Salt and freshly ground black pepper

For creamy tomato basil soup (optional)

1 tablespoon	unsalted butter or olive oil
1 tablespoon	all-purpose flour
1 cup	milk

Heat the olive oil in a soup pot over medium heat. Add the onion and cook until softened, about 5 minutes. Add the tomatoes, stock, and ½ cup of the basil. Season with salt and pepper to taste. Bring to a boil; then lower the heat and simmer for 25 minutes or until the tomatoes are thoroughly mushy. Meanwhile, stack the remaining basil leaves, roll them up tightly, and slice the roll crosswise to make thin ribbons. Set them aside.

Set a food mill or a coarse strainer over a bowl, and work the soup through the mill. Return the soup to the pot. Bring to a boil, add the basil ribbons, and taste for seasoning. Add more salt and pepper if necessary, and serve.

For a creamy tomato basil soup: In a small saucepan, heat the butter or oil over medium heat. Stir in the flour with a wooden spoon and cook, stirring, for 30 seconds. Slowly whisk in the milk. Bring to a boil; then reduce the heat and simmer, stirring, until thickened and creamy, about 5 minutes. Stir into the strained simmering soup, and cook for another 5 minutes. Stir in the basil ribbons, season with salt and pepper as needed, and serve.

VARIATION

Substitute two 24-ounce cans of good-quality canned tomatoes when the fresh ones are done for the season.

LEFTOVERS

Even better the next day. Or toss with pasta and add a sprinkling of Parmesan.

NUTRITION

Loads of vitamin C and lycopene, a potent antioxidant.

ECONOMY $

When in season, fresh juicy tomatoes are quite inexpensive.

Watermelon Fennel Salad

MAKES 4 SERVINGS

This salad provides a refreshing contrast of flavors and textures: crunchy sweet watermelon and fennel; salty, creamy feta; and ever so slightly bitter greens. It is perfect with grilled or seared fish or chicken, or simply on its own as a simple first course. Don't be afraid to add or substitute. Experiment!

2 cups	2-inch chunks seeded watermelon
¼	red onion, very thinly sliced
¼	fennel bulb, thinly sliced
1 tablespoon	chopped fresh mint
1 teaspoon	diced jalapeño pepper
	Grated zest and juice of 1 lime
2 tablespoons	grapeseed oil
	Salt and freshly ground black pepper
4 cups	baby greens
1 cup	crumbled feta

In a mixing bowl, combine the watermelon, onion, fennel, mint, jalapeño, lime zest and juice, and grapeseed oil. Season with salt and pepper to taste, and stir gently. Refrigerate for at least 20 minutes to allow the flavors to meld.

When ready to serve, mound 1 cup of the baby greens on each plate, and divide the watermelon-fennel salad over the greens. Sprinkle the crumbled feta over the salad, and serve immediately.

SERVING SUGGESTION

You can omit the greens and serve the watermelon-feta mixture, chilled, on its own.

VARIATIONS

• Mix it up using a combination of yellow and red watermelon.

• Substitute any young soft cheese for the feta.

NUTRITION

Watermelon gets its vibrant color from lycopene, the same potent antioxidant found in tomatoes. It is also a good source of vitamins A and C and potassium.

Gigi BLT Salad with Roasted-Tomato Vinaigrette

Put bacon on the menu and it sells! Bacon means flavor, and that is certainly true of the Mountain Products Smokehouse variety, which happens to be nitrite-free. In the summer months we serve this salad with a light roasted-tomato vinaigrette; in cooler months we switch over to a creamy goat cheese dressing made with local buttermilk and Lively Run Goat Dairy feta cheese.

Roasted-tomato vinaigrette

¾ cup	extra-virgin olive oil
8	plum tomatoes, cored, halved, and seeded
6	garlic cloves, crushed
5 or 6	thyme sprigs
	Salt
⅓ cup	fresh basil leaves
3 tablespoons	tomato vinegar or sherry vinegar
	Freshly ground black pepper

BLT salad

2	heads Boston or Bibb lettuce, leaves separated, rinsed, and spun dry
3	large ripe beefsteak tomatoes, cut into wedges
8	bacon strips, cooked until crisp

To prepare the roasted plum tomatoes, preheat the oven to 475°F.

Spread ¼ cup of the oil on a rimmed nonstick baking sheet that is large enough to hold the tomatoes in one layer. Place the tomatoes, garlic, and thyme sprigs on the baking sheet, season with salt, and roll the tomato halves to coat them evenly with oil, leaving them round side up. Roast, turning the baking sheet once for even cooking, until the tomatoes are shriveled and slightly charred, 35 to 40 minutes. If any of the garlic overbrowns, remove it.

When the tomatoes are cool enough to handle, slip off the skins. Discard the thyme and store the tomatoes, with the pan liquid, in a covered container in the refrigerator for up to 1 week. You will have double the tomatoes you need to prepare the vinaigrette; enjoy the extras in other salads or with grilled dishes.

To prepare the vinaigrette, place 8 roasted tomato halves, 2 tablespoons of the tomato liquid, the basil, and the vinegar in a food processor, and pulse a few times to blend. Add the remaining ½ cup olive oil and pulse a few more times; the consistency should be slightly chunky. Season with salt and pepper to taste.

To prepare the BLT salad, toss the lettuce and beefsteak tomatoes with the vinaigrette in a large bowl. Arrange on serving plates or in bowls, top each salad with 2 bacon strips, and serve.

VARIATIONS

- Add crumbled cheese (goat, feta, shredded cheddar).
- Substitute your favorite dressing; Gigi Sherry-Shallot Vinaigrette (page 276) would work great.
- Use the roasted tomatoes and/or vinaigrette in other salads or to marinate chicken or mild white fish such as halibut or cod.

LEFTOVERS

The roasted tomatoes can be used in other salads or to accompany or garnish grilled, seared, or roasted fish, poultry, beef, or pork.

NUTRITION

Tomatoes are rich in vitamin C and lycopene, a potent antioxdiant.

ECONOMY $$

Summer Garden Fregola Salad

The Sardinian grain fregola is similar to couscous. Both are made from semolina mixed with water and then rolled into little pellets. Fregola is larger than couscous, about the size of a small pea, and gives off a roasted nutty flavor when toasted. When tossed with seasonal vegetables, it becomes a quick and colorful salad that's both nourishing and flavorful. I use fregola through the seasons, either as a hot dish or cold in a salad (see suggestions opposite).

1½ cups fregola (available in some groceries, in Italian markets, and in gourmet stores)

4 tablespoons extra-virgin olive oil

2 shallots, thinly sliced

1 medium green zucchini, diced

1 medium yellow squash, diced

2 teaspoons fresh thyme leaves

2 cups torn arugula leaves

2 plum or 1 medium tomato, cored and diced

1 tablespoon fresh lemon juice

Salt and freshly ground black pepper

Bring 2 quarts of salted water to a boil in a saucepan. Add the fregola and cook, stirring occasionally, until it is just tender (not mushy), about 12 minutes. Drain well and transfer to a large bowl. Stir in 1 tablespoon of the olive oil and set aside.

Warm 1 tablespoon of the olive oil in a medium skillet over medium heat. Add the shallots and cook until softened, about 2 minutes. Increase the heat to medium-high and stir in the zucchini, yellow squash, and thyme. Cook, tossing or stirring occasionally, about 7 minutes.

Stir the zucchini mixture into the fregola. Gently stir in the arugula and tomatoes, and spoon the salad into a decorative bowl or platter.

To prepare the dressing, whisk together the remaining 2 tablespoons olive oil and the lemon juice, and season with salt and pepper to taste. Add the dressing to the salad, and toss to combine. Let cool and serve at room temperature.

VARIATIONS

- *Spring:* Use fava beans, peas, spring mushrooms, and asparagus.
- *Summer:* Try corn, zucchini, shrimp, and fresh basil; tomatoes, white beans, and chorizo; or cucumbers, tomatoes, fresh basil, and parsley.
- *Fall:* Substitute butternut squash, mushrooms, and sage; or pumpkin and cooking greens (such as chard or kale).
- *Winter*: Use radicchio and mushrooms; or try broccoli rabe, red pepper flakes, and sausage (substitute red wine vinegar for the lemon juice).

LEFTOVERS

Good for another day. Consider stirring leftovers into a brothy seasonal soup. Or make a fregola risotto: reheat with just enough broth to make it soupy, and add some grated Parmesan.

NUTRITION

Fregola has a similar nutrient profile to other pasta. It is enhanced by the fresh seasonal ingredients you "decorate" it with.

ECONOMY $$

Gigi Steamed Mussels with Tomatoes and Herbs

MAKES 2 TO 4 SERVINGS (MAIN COURSE OR APPETIZER)

Whenever Prince Edward Island mussels look fresh and plump, we have them on our dinner specials list. Typically this delicious preparation is featured, but executive chef Wilson Costa has many variations that he enjoys sharing with our guests (see opposite). If I see that they haven't ordered our crispy Tuscan Fries (page 285) to go with the mussels, I'll be around shortly with a small basket.

2 pounds	mussels, preferably Prince Edward Island
3 tablespoons	olive oil
¼ cup	chopped red onion
1	garlic clove, chopped
2 tablespoons	chopped fresh flat-leaf parsley
¼ to ½ teaspoon	red pepper flakes
¼ cup	dry white wine
½ cup	fresh tomato sauce; or 2 plum tomatoes, peeled, seeded, and roughly chopped
	Salt
3 tablespoons	thinly sliced fresh basil leaves
1 tablespoon	unsalted butter
	Freshly ground black pepper

Scrub the mussels, discarding any with broken shells and those whole shells that remain open after tapping them lightly. As you clean them under cold running water, pull off the "beard," the grassy growth at the bottom of the shells.

Heat the olive oil in a large saucepan over medium heat. Add the onion and garlic and cook until they just turn golden, about 1 minute. Add the parsley and red pepper flakes and cook, stirring, for another 30 seconds. Increase the heat to medium-high and add the mussels to the pan. Cook, stirring and turning them, for 1 to 2 minutes. Then add the white wine and cook until it is mostly evaporated, about 1 minute. Add the tomato sauce or tomatoes, season with salt, and cover the pan. Steam, shaking the pan frequently, until the mussels open, 4 to 5 minutes (discard any unopened ones). Remove the mussels one by one, arranging them in serving bowls. Cook the sauce, uncovered, for another 2 to 3 minutes, allowing it to thicken slightly. Then stir in the basil and butter, adjust the seasoning with salt and pepper if necessary, and spoon the sauce over the mussels. Serve steaming hot.

SERVING SUGGESTION

Supply plenty of garlic-rubbed crostini or slices of fresh peasant bread for sopping up the flavorful sauce.

VARIATIONS

• Add chorizo and piquillo peppers when cooking the onion and garlic.
• Add diced bacon or pancetta when sautéing the onion and garlic.
• Omit the tomato sauce (or fresh tomatoes) and basil, and substitute coconut milk, cilantro, lime zest, and green curry paste.

NUTRITION

Mussels are an almost fat-free protein source. A 4-ounce serving (shucked) has less than 100 calories and provides 14 grams of protein.

ECONOMY $$

Sweet and Sour Cod "Saor," Venetian Style

The classic Venetian sarde in saor *consists of fresh sardines layered in a sweet and sour onion, fruit, and pine nut mixture (saor). Traditionally raisins are the fruit used. During summer in the Hudson Valley, fresh currants are available, so why not throw them in too? Currants add to the acidity, so if you're using them, a tablespoon or two more honey may be needed to balance the flavor. I love the classic sardine preparation, but cod is a great Atlantic fish substitution. It's also an easier way to introduce saor to the sardine squeamish.*

Saor

3 tablespoons	unsalted butter
¼ cup	olive oil
2	large red onions, thinly sliced
3	bay leaves
1½ cups	red wine vinegar
½ cup	fresh red currants (optional)
⅓ cup	golden raisins
¼ cup	honey
2 tablespoons	sugar
Pinch	saffron threads
⅓ cup	pine nuts

Cod

¼ cup	olive oil
1½ pounds	cod fillets, cut into 2-inch pieces
	Salt and freshly ground black pepper
½ cup	all-purpose flour

To prepare the *saor,* heat the butter and olive oil in a medium skillet over medium heat until hot and bubbly. Add the onions and bay leaves and cook, stirring often, until the onions are very soft, about 15 minutes; the onions should not brown. Add the vinegar, currants (if using), raisins, honey, sugar, and saffron, and cook until the vinegar is reduced by about half, 2 to 3 minutes. Stir in the pine nuts, and set aside to cool.

To prepare the cod, heat the olive oil in a large sauté pan (preferably nonstick) over medium-high heat. Season the fish with salt and pepper, dredge it in the flour, shaking off any excess, and place the pieces, flesh side down, in the pan. Cook until golden brown, about 3 minutes. Then turn the fish over and cook until it is just cooked through, 3 to 5 minutes. (If necessary, cook the fish in batches to prevent overcrowding, which will limit browning.)

Fill a casserole with alternating layers of cod and the *saor* mixture, ending with the *saor*. Cover and refrigerate, for 1 or 2 days. Serve at room temperature.

SERVING SUGGESTIONS

Serve topped with chopped flat-leaf parsley and garnished with lemon wedges. Pass the crostini or crusty bread.

antibacterial food. They taste pretty good and sweet when they're melted down, too! Cod has moderate levels of protective omega-3s.

ECONOMY $$

Sardines are more economical than cod.

VARIATION

To prepare the traditional version, substitute whole cleaned sardines for the cod.

NUTRITION

Onions contain potent antioxidants and are an anticancer, anti-inflammatory, antiviral, and

Enlightened Eggplant Parmesan

MAKES 4 ENTRÉE OR 8 SIDE SERVINGS

I never understood the appeal of eggplant Parmesan until I traveled in Sicily, where it is all about the eggplant rather than the breading and cheese. I love this version of this dish, since it is closer to the real deal. Young, locally harvested eggplant tends not to be as bitter as the mature variety available in most supermarkets, so you can generally skip the traditional step of salting it in a colander to release water and bitterness.

1¼ cups	fresh bread crumbs
¼ cup	finely grated Grana Padano or Parmesan cheese
4	medium eggplants (about 3 pounds), cut lengthwise into ¼- to ½-inch-thick slices
¼ cup	olive oil, plus extra for the baking sheets and dish
	Salt and freshly ground black pepper
2 cups	Basic Tomato Sauce (page 290), your own homemade sauce, or your favorite commercial brand
1¼ cups	shredded mozzarella cheese
1¼ cups	shaved Grana Padano or Parmesan cheese

Preheat the broiler. Generously grease two baking sheets (preferably nonstick) with olive oil. Lightly oil a 9 x 13 x 2-inch baking dish.

Combine the bread crumbs and grated Grana Padano in a small bowl, and set aside.

Brush both sides of the eggplant slices with the olive oil, and season them with salt and pepper. Arrange them in a single layer on the greased baking sheets and broil until the slices are tender, lightly browned, and softened, about 10 minutes. Remove from the oven and set aside to cool slightly.

Spoon ½ cup of the tomato sauce over the bottom of the oiled baking dish. Layer one third of the eggplant slices over the sauce, overlapping them slightly. Spoon ½ cup of the sauce over the eggplant, spreading it evenly, and sprinkle with ½ cup each of the mozzarella and the shaved Grana Padano. Top the cheese with another third of the eggplant slices, another ½ cup of the sauce, and another ½ cup of each cheese. Top with the remaining eggplant slices, sauce, and cheeses. Cover the dish with aluminum foil, and bake in the middle of the oven until the sauce is bubbling, about 30 minutes. Uncover, sprinkle the bread-crumb mixture over the top, and continue to bake until the crumbs are golden brown, about 10 minutes. Let stand 10 minutes before serving.

SERVING SUGGESTION

Enjoy as an appetizer, side dish, or entrée.

VARIATIONS

- Roast or grill the eggplant instead of broiling it.
- Add fresh basil and/or oregano between the layers.
- Change the flavor by substituting smoked mozzarella for the fresh.

NUTRITION

Eggplant is low in calories and contains anthocyanins, potent antioxidants that also lend eggplant its vibrant purple color.

ECONOMY $

Mediterranean Potato Salad

MAKES 6 TO 8 SERVINGS

There's a time and place for mayonnaise-based salads, but in the heat of the summer,
I like to lighten potato salad with a vinaigrette dressing and the addition of summer-harvest
vegetables and sweet and salty elements such as olives and capers. Enjoy this salad as
an any-day side dish or set it on your buffet when you entertain.

2 pounds	Corola potatoes, or substitute another waxy potato, such as Yukon Gold or baby red
4	oil-packed anchovies, drained and minced
¼ cup	fresh lemon juice
1 tablespoon	Dijon mustard
¾ cup	extra-virgin olive oil
⅓ cup	chopped fresh flat-leaf parsley
Pinch	red pepper flakes
	Salt and freshly ground black pepper
1 pint	cherry tomatoes, halved (quartered if very large)
1	small red onion, thinly sliced
⅓ cup	oil-cured black olives, pitted and halved
2 tablespoons	salt-packed capers, well rinsed and drained

Place the potatoes in a saucepan of salted water and bring to a boil. Reduce the heat to a simmer, and cook until just tender, 15 to 20 minutes, depending on size.

While the potatoes are cooking, prepare the dressing: In a small bowl, combine the anchovies, lemon juice, mustard, and ¼ cup of the olive oil. Whisk to blend, mashing the anchovies into a puree as you mix. Add the remaining ½ cup olive oil, the parsley, and the red pepper flakes, and season with salt and pepper to taste.

Drain and dry the potatoes. While they are still hot, leaving the skins on, cut them into eighths, quarters, or halves, depending on their size (you want a chunk approximately 2 inches wide). Place them in a large bowl. Add the dressing to the bowl, along with the tomatoes, onion, olives, and capers. Stir gently to combine, and serve.

SERVING SUGGESTIONS

Enjoy with all types of grilled meats and a piece of crusty bread, or serve alone atop garden-fresh greens.

VARIATIONS

Add crumbled feta, diced or julienned cucumbers, garbanzo or white beans, good-quality tuna in olive oil, or grilled shrimp.

NUTRITION

Potatoes and tomatoes are rich in vitamin C, and potatoes contain comparable amounts of potassium to bananas and spinach. Olive oil–based vinaigrette is a healthier option than mayonnaise.

ECONOMY $

Grilled Steak and Arugula Salad
with Parmesan Shavings

MAKES 4 TO 6 SERVINGS

Arugula, beef (steak or thinly sliced carpaccio), Parmesan, and lemon are simply buonissimo
*together! It's a marriage of flavors made in heaven (technically Italy). Here I use a
variation of the lemon vinaigrette that I developed for Just Salad, but you can make your own
quick dressing, pouring a bit of fresh lemon juice and olive oil over the arugula leaves
and seasoning lightly with salt and pepper before topping with the cheese shavings.*

Marinated steak

1 cup	fresh flat-leaf parsley leaves
2	garlic cloves
3	tablespoons olive oil
	Salt and freshly ground black pepper
Two	1½-inch-thick New York strip steaks (about 2 pounds)

Salad

12 cups	arugula (about 1 pound)
½ cup	Gigi Lemon Vinaigrette (page 277)
2 cups	thinly shaved Grana Padano or Parmesan cheese (use a sturdy, sharp vegetable peeler to make thin slices)

On a chopping board, coarsely chop the parsley leaves together with the garlic. Transfer the mixture to a small bowl, stir in the olive oil, and season with salt and pepper to taste. Rub the marinade over the steaks and refrigerate, covered, for at least 30 minutes and up to 24 hours.

Set the grill rack about 6 inches from the heat source, oil the rack, and preheat the grill to medium-high.

Scrape any excess marinade off the steaks, and grill for 2 to 3 minutes on each side for medium-rare. (Alternatively, grill the steaks in a hot, well-seasoned ridged grill pan over medium-high heat.) Transfer the steaks to a cutting board and let stand for 5 minutes. Then, holding a sharp knife at a 45-degree angle, cut the steaks across the grain into about 8 slices each.

In a large bowl, toss the arugula with the vinaigrette. Divide the salad among serving plates and sprinkle the cheese shavings over the salad. Arrange the steak slices on top or next to the salad, and serve immediately.

SERVING SUGGESTIONS

Serve with lemon wedges and a medium-bodied Italian red.

VARIATIONS

• Substitute trimmed hangar steaks (about 2-inch-thick cuts) for the New York strip.
• In the winter, fan the steak slices over sautéed or braised cooking greens (such as chard, collard, mustard, spinach); use a basic olive oil/vinegar vinaigrette.

NUTRITION

There is no reason why grass-fed or grass-finished beef without antibiotics and hormones can't fit into a healthy eating plan. Check into local ranchers near you.

ECONOMY $$$

Tomato–Goat Cheese Gratin

MAKES 4 SERVINGS

Summer is supposed to be simple, fresh, and easy. This recipe fits the bill.

2 tablespoons	extra-virgin olive oil, plus extra for the dish
1¼ cups	coarse fresh bread crumbs from crusty bread (or unseasoned dried bread crumbs)
1½ pounds	large tomatoes (about 3), sliced 1 inch thick
	Salt and freshly ground black pepper
1 cup	crumbled goat cheese (4 ounces) (I use Coach Farm)
3 tablespoons	chopped fresh chives
2 tablespoons	freshly grated Grana Padano or Parmesan cheese

Preheat the oven to 450°F. Oil a 9-inch square or oval gratin dish or casserole.

Combine the olive oil and the bread crumbs in a small bowl, and set aside.

Arrange a third of the tomato slices, slightly overlapping, in the prepared gratin dish. Season with salt and pepper to taste, and sprinkle with one-third each of the goat cheese, bread-crumb mixture, and chives. Repeat with two more layers of tomatoes, salt and pepper, and cheese, crumbs, and chives. Sprinkle the Grana Padano over the top.

Bake in the middle of the oven until the gratin is bubbly and the crumbs are golden, 15 to 20 minutes.

VARIATIONS

- Add pitted olives and/or good-quality tuna.
- Substitute your favorite cheese for the goat cheese (such as fresh mozzarella).

LEFTOVERS

Really good rewarmed or at room temperature.

NUTRITION

Fresh, juicy tomatoes are rich in vitamin C and lycopene, a powerful antioxidant.

ECONOMY $

When tomatoes are coming in, people are giving them away. If you don't garden, ask your over-harvest friends for a basket.

Salmon Burgers with Peach Salsa

MAKES 6 TO 8 SERVINGS

I often double this recipe and store the uncooked patties in plastic wrap or self-seal bags in my freezer. They thaw quickly and make for a healthy at-home lunch or in-a-pinch meal when a guest stops by. For entertaining, make 1-ounce burgers and place them on mini-buns.

Peach salsa

2	large or 3 medium ripe peaches, peeled, pitted, and diced
3 tablespoons	thinly sliced scallions (white and light green parts)
1 teaspoon	grated lime zest
1½ tablespoons	fresh lime juice
1 tablespoon	chopped fresh cilantro or flat-leaf parsley
¼	jalapeño pepper, seeded and minced (optional)
Pinch	cayenne pepper or ground cumin (optional)
Pinch	salt

Salmon burgers

2 pounds	salmon, skin removed
1½ tablespoons	Dijon mustard
2 tablespoons	reduced-fat mayonnaise
2 tablespoons	reduced-sodium soy sauce
1 teaspoon	toasted sesame oil
2 tablespoons	snipped fresh chives
	Salt and freshly ground black pepper
1 tablespoon	peanut oil
6 to 8	hamburger buns (optional)

To prepare the peach salsa, combine all the ingredients in a small bowl. Cover, and refrigerate until you're ready to cook the salmon burgers.

Remove any bones from the salmon, then chop it fine by hand or pulse it in a food processor; it should be chunky. Transfer the salmon to a medium bowl and add the mustard, mayonnaise, soy sauce, sesame oil, and chives. Season with salt and pepper to taste, and stir to combine. Form the mixture into 6 to 8 patties, depending on desired size.

Heat the peanut oil in a nonstick skillet over medium heat until it is hot but not smoking. Add the patties and sauté for 4 minutes on each side, or until just cooked through. Transfer the salmon burgers to buns, if using, and top with the peach salsa.

SERVING SUGGESTIONS

- Omit the peach salsa and insert crisp lettuce and farm-fresh tomato slices between the buns.
- Top dressed baby greens with seared salmon burgers.
- Caramelized onions would be a great topper.

VARIATIONS

- *Spanish:* Omit the sesame oil, soy sauce, and chives, and blend diced piquillo peppers and a pinch of saffron into the mayo before adding it to the fish.
- *North African:* Omit the sesame oil, soy sauce, and chives, and add chopped almonds, harissa, ground coriander, and toasted cumin seeds into the mayo.
- *Indian:* Omit the sesame oil, soy sauce, and chives, and add curry powder, turmeric, garam masala, and finely diced dried apricots into the mayo.
- *Tuna burgers*: Substitute a fatty tuna (such as tuna belly) for the salmon.

NUTRITION

This high-protein burger contains less than 2 grams of saturated fat and offers up health-promoting omega-3s.

ECONOMY $$

Tacchino Tonnato

Turkey with Tuna Caper Sauce

MAKES 8 TO 10 SERVINGS

Vitello tonnato is an Italian classic of thinly sliced poached veal with a sauce of pureed tuna, anchovies, capers, lemon, and olive oil. It is served cold and is an elegant meal that can be prepared long before guests arrive. I like preparing it with meats other than veal, such as a farm-fresh turkey breast or pork loin. Several years ago I tested recipes for a slow-cooker cookbook. I was impressed with the results of cooking a whole turkey breast in a slow cooker—very moist and flavorful. If you have a slow cooker, this is the way to go. Otherwise, see the poaching instructions on page 100.

Turkey breast

1	medium onion, quartered
2	medium carrots, sliced
2	celery stalks, halved crosswise and then lengthwise
1 cup	chicken stock, reduced-sodium broth, or water
½ cup	dry white wine
2	bay leaves
1 teaspoon	black peppercorns
1	whole turkey breast (5 to 6 pounds), bone in, skin on, trimmed of excess fat, completely thawed if frozen
	Salt and freshly ground black pepper

Tonnato sauce

12 ounces	imported Italian yellowfin tuna in oil, or two 6-ounce cans oil-packed solid white tuna, drained
1 cup	Gigi Minimal Mayonnaise (page 280) or your favorite brand
8	oil-packed anchovies, drained and chopped
⅓ cup	capers, rinsed
3 tablespoons	fresh lemon juice
½ cup	extra-virgin olive oil
¼ cup	chopped fresh flat-leaf parsley, for garnish
	Lemon slices, for garnish

Lightly grease the inside cooking canister of a 6-quart slow cooker. Place the onion, carrots, and celery in the canister, and stir in the stock, wine, bay leaves, and peppercorns. Season the turkey breast with salt and pepper, and place it in the slow cooker. Cover and cook on low heat for 5 to 6 hours, or until a thermometer inserted in the center of the breast reads 165°F. Transfer the turkey breast to a large plate and let it cool slightly; strain and reserve 1 cup of the cooking liquid. Remove the turkey skin, wrap the turkey breast, and refrigerate until ready to slice and serve.

To prepare the tonnato sauce, combine the tuna, mayonnaise, anchovies, ¼ cup of the capers, the lemon juice, and ½ cup of the reserved turkey cooking liquid in a food processor or blender, and puree until smooth. With the motor running, drizzle the olive oil through the feed tube until the sauce is just emulsified, about 30 seconds. If the mixture is not "saucy" enough, add a bit more of the cooking liquid and pulse to combine. Season to taste with salt and pepper. Transfer the sauce to a bowl, cover, and refrigerate for up to 1 day before you are ready to serve.

To serve, cut the chilled turkey breast on the diagonal into very thin slices, and arrange them, slightly overlapping, on a large platter (or two). Season with salt and pepper, and spread the sauce over each slice. Garnish with the chopped parsley and the remaining capers. Arrange the lemon slices around the platter, and serve.

SERVING SUGGESTIONS

Enjoy the tonnato with a mineral-crisp Italian white such as a Fiano or Falanghina, or a Vermentino from Liguria.

VARIATIONS

- *To poach the turkey breast:* Have your butcher skin, bone, and tightly roll a 5- to 6-pound turkey breast. In a large Dutch oven or saucepan, combine the turkey, onion, carrots, celery, wine, bay leaves, and peppercorns. Add chicken stock or water as needed to cover the meat, and bring to a boil. Reduce the heat to a simmer and cover. Simmer, turning occasionally, until a thermometer placed in the thickest portion of the meat registers 165°F, about 1 hour. When cool, wrap and refrigerate.
- Substitute veal or pork loin or rolled chicken breasts for the turkey.

LEFTOVERS

Serve, cold again, the next day. Use any leftover tonnato sauce to dress pasta (I usually double the sauce recipe to make sure I have enough!).

NUTRITION

A 3-ounce portion of skinless turkey breast contains only 1 gram of fat and 26 grams of protein. Tuna is a good source of protective omega-3s.

ECONOMY $$

Turkey, pork loin, and chicken are economical alternatives to the classic veal preparation.

Lamb Chops with Black Currant BBQ Sauce

MAKES 4 SERVINGS

Black currants are not only delicious; they are also one of nature's most potent antioxidant foods. We buy our currants (red and black) from the Currant Company in Clinton, New York. If you cannot find fresh or frozen black currants, substitute blueberries, which are no nutritional slouch.

Black currant BBQ sauce

1 pint	fresh black currants
¼ cup	raisins
½ cup	packed light brown sugar
½ cup	ketchup
¼ cup	rice vinegar
¼ cup	finely diced shallots
1 tablespoon	Dijon mustard
⅛ to ¼ teaspoon	cayenne pepper
2 tablespoons	unsalted butter
	Salt

Lamb chops

2 tablespoons	olive oil
1½ tablespoons	fresh lemon juice
2	garlic cloves, minced
8	loin lamb chops (2 to 3 ounces each after trimming)
	Freshly ground black pepper

To prepare the BBQ sauce, combine the currants, raisins, ½ cup water, brown sugar, ketchup, rice vinegar, shallots, mustard, and cayenne in a medium saucepan, and stir to combine. Bring to a boil. Then reduce the heat and simmer for 15 minutes, stirring often. Remove from the heat and stir in the butter. Transfer the sauce to a blender or food processor, and puree until smooth. Strain the sauce through a fine-mesh strainer into a bowl, using a rubber spatula to push as much sauce as possible through the mesh. Season the sauce with salt to taste.

To prepare the lamb, combine the olive oil, lemon juice, and garlic in a small bowl. Brush the mixture over the surface of the chops. Cover and refrigerate for at least 15 minutes.

Meanwhile, prepare a medium-hot grill.

Season the chops with salt and pepper, and place them on the hot grill. Cook for 1½ minutes on each side. Then slather on the BBQ sauce and cook for another minute per side for medium-rare, or to the desired doneness. Serve immediately.

SERVING SUGGESTIONS

Enjoy with a simple potato or grain salad and a tossed green salad.

VARIATIONS

Use the currant BBQ sauce on grilled, seared, or roasted salmon; the acidity of the currants works well with the fattiness of the fish. It is also good on venison medallions.

NUTRITION

Lamb is rich in protein, B vitamins, iron, and zinc. Once trimmed, the chops are "lean," meaning they contain less than 4.5 grams of saturated fat and less than 95 milligrams of cholesterol per 3½ ounces.

Best Local Burger

MAKES 4 SERVINGS

Wherever you live, try to find a source of pastured beef from a local farm. There are numerous environmental and health-related reasons to do so, but let's focus on flavor. Grass-fed or grass-finished humanely raised beef is untouchable in its level of quality. For burgers, look for ground chuck or round with 15 percent fat, 20 percent max; more is not better, it just drips into the grill. We buy our ground beef from Northwind Farms, where Richie, Jane, and their son, Russell, put enormous love and care into all their products.

1 tablespoon	olive oil
1	medium onion, minced
2	garlic cloves, minced
1½ pounds	ground locally raised beef (antibiotic- and hormone-free; I suggest 80 to 85 percent lean for moist burgers)
2 tablespoons	Worcestershire sauce
1 tablespoon	Old Bay seasoning (optional)
	Salt and freshly ground black pepper

Heat the olive oil in a medium skillet over medium heat. Add the onion and garlic, and cook until soft and lightly golden, about 7 minutes. Let cool.

In a large bowl, mix the onion and garlic into the beef. Add the Worcestershire and Old Bay, if using, and season with salt and pepper. Form four 6-ounce patties (larger burgers stay moist; if the portion is too large, split them after cooking). Do not mash or press the patties together; simply wet your hands (to prevent the meat from sticking to them), and pat the meat together to ¾- to 1-inch thickness. Use your knuckles to make a dented imprint in the center of each burger to help them cook evenly and prevent the hockey puck look after cooking.

If grilling, place the rack about 5 inches above the heat source. Preheat the grill to medium-high. With the grill covered and the vents open, grill the burgers until they are nicely marked and cooked to your desired doneness (about 8 minutes total for medium-rare).

If pan cooking, heat a nonstick grill pan or cast-iron pan over high heat until it is very hot. Place the burgers on the pan, making sure there is space between them. Cook for 4 to 5 minutes per side for medium-rare, or longer to the desired doneness. Enjoy hot off the pan or grill.

VARIATIONS

- *Summer:* Garnish with sliced beefsteak or heirloom tomatoes, garden cucumber slices, roasted eggplant, or zucchini.
- *Fall/winter:* Try pickled vegetables or caramelized onions.
- *Spring:* Serve with baby lettuces, mâche, watercress, caramelized leeks, or mushrooms.
- *In any season:* Offer great-quality bread or buns, onion slices, avocado, large crunchy lettuce leaves (Bibb, Boston, romaine), and/or locally made cheeses.
- Condiments for any season include locally made ketchups or BBQ sauces, gourmet mustards, tapenades, salsas, and pestos.

NUTRITION

Antibiotic- and hormone-free beef can fit into a healthy diet. It's all about balance.

ECONOMY $$

BBQ Baked Gigandes

MAKES 8 TO 10 SERVINGS

*Don't forget these "Spaghetti Western" beans at your next cookout. Whether for an
informal barbecue or an elegant event, we get requests for these rustic beans
throughout the summer. Make them ahead and bake them the next day.*

6	bacon strips
3 tablespoons	olive oil
1	large onion, chopped
2	celery stalks, chopped
2	small or 1 large green bell pepper, cored, seeded, and diced
2	garlic cloves, minced
3 pounds	cooked Gigi Gigandes (from 1 pound uncooked beans; see page 178), plus 1 cup of the cooking liquid or chicken or vegetable stock or reduced-sodium broth
1½ cups	tomato sauce (homemade, page 290, or store-bought)
⅓ cup	ketchup
¼ cup	pure maple syrup
3 tablespoons	Dijon mustard
1 tablespoon	Worcestershire sauce
2 teaspoons	dried oregano
½ teaspoon	smoked paprika
	Salt and freshly ground black pepper

Preheat the oven to 375°F, and lightly rub a
3-quart casserole with olive oil.

Chop half the bacon; set the other strips
aside. In a large skillet, cook the chopped bacon
in the olive oil over medium heat until the fat is
rendered and the bacon begins to crisp. Drain
off all but a couple of tablespoons of the fat,
and add the onion, celery, bell peppers, and
garlic to the skillet. Cook, tossing or stirring
occasionally, until the vegetables soften, about
8 minutes. Stir in all the remaining ingredients
except the reserved bacon strips, and simmer
for about 15 minutes to blend the flavors.

Transfer the mixture to the prepared
casserole, place it in the oven, and bake for
15 minutes. Then arrange the reserved bacon
strips on top and continue baking until the
mixture is bubbling and the bacon strips are
crisp, about 20 minutes. Serve family-style,
straight from the casserole.

LEFTOVERS

Reheats well.

NUTRITION

Rich in B vitamins, especially folate, and magnesium, potassium, iron, and manganese. Also a good source of fiber, carbs, and protein.

ECONOMY $

Beans are a tasty, filling, and economical combination of complex carbohydrates and protein.

Farm-Fresh Taleggio Creamed Corn

MAKES 6 TO 8 SERVINGS

We buy as much of the local corn harvest as Chuck Mead and Ken Migliorelli will sell to make this creamy Italian take on an American favorite. At Gigi Trattoria, it's served in individual cast-iron crocks, arriving at the table bubbly brown and deliciously fragrant.

6	ears fresh corn
3 tablespoons	olive oil
2	shallots, minced
2	garlic cloves, minced
4 tablespoons	chopped fresh flat-leaf parsley
2 teaspoons	fresh thyme leaves
	Salt and freshly ground black pepper
¼ cup	dry white wine (optional)
2 teaspoons	sugar (optional—taste a kernel of corn to see if it's needed)
1 tablespoon	all-purpose flour
1⅓ cups	milk or half-and-half
3 ounces	Taleggio cheese, cut into small pieces
2 tablespoons	chopped fresh chives
¼ cup	freshly grated Grana Padano or Parmesan cheese (optional)

Slice the kernels from the corncobs; you should have 4 to 5 cups of kernels. Then scrape the cobs with a sharp knife to get all the milk and pulp. Reserve the kernels separately from the milk and pulp.

Heat the olive oil in a large skillet over medium heat. Add the shallots and garlic and cook, stirring, until the shallots soften, 3 to 4 minutes. Increase the heat to medium-high, and stir in the corn kernels, 2 tablespoons of the parsley, and the thyme. Season with salt and pepper to taste. Cook, tossing or stirring often, until the kernels are cooked and lightly browned, about 4 minutes. Add the reserved corn milk and pulp. Stir in the white wine and the sugar, if using, and cook until the liquid has almost completely evaporated, 3 to 4 minutes. Blend the flour with 2 tablespoons water, and stir the mixture into the corn. Then whisk in the milk or half-and-half. Bring the mixture to a simmer and cook, stirring, until thickened, about 3 minutes.

Adjust the seasoning with salt and pepper as needed, and stir in the remaining parsley. Remove the skillet from the heat and stir in the Taleggio and chives. Serve immediately, or transfer the mixture to ovenproof crocks or ramekins, sprinkle the tops with the Grana Padano, and broil under high heat until the tops are bubbly and browned.

VARIATIONS

- Substitute your favorite cheese (goat, Manchego, or even cheddar) for the Taleggio.
- Spice it up with some diced jalapeño or poblano chiles. Add them when you sauté the corn kernels.
- Cream it up by pureeing a third of the corn mixture in a food processor or blender and then stirring it back into the mix.

LEFTOVERS

Before adding the Parmesan topping, this dish reheats well.

NUTRITION

Use milk instead of half-and-half to lower the fat. You can replace the Taleggio with ⅓ cup grated Parmesan to lend big flavor with fewer calories. Corn is rich in vitamins A and C and lutein, a potent antioxidant.

Eggplant Fries

MAKES 4 SERVINGS

The season for freshly harvested eggplant is so short, but so satisfying.
These "fries" appear on our menu when local farms bring us their beauties.

Peanut oil, for deep-frying

3 small to medium eggplants (1½ pounds)

1 cup all-purpose flour

½ teaspoon ground cumin, cayenne
each pepper, and smoked paprika (optional)

Salt

2 eggs, lightly beaten

1½ cups bread crumbs

Pour the oil into a deep-fryer or a large (8-quart) deep Dutch oven to a depth of 5 inches, and heat it to 350°F.

Cut the eggplant into "blocks" about 4 to 5 inches long and 1 inch thick. Season the flour with the spices, if using, and salt. In batches, dredge the eggplant in the flour. Shake off the excess, then dip them in the beaten egg, followed by the bread crumbs. Fry, in batches, until golden and crisp, 5 to 6 minutes. Transfer the fries to a paper towel–lined baking sheet, pat them dry, and season with salt. Serve immediately.

SERVING SUGGESTIONS

Enjoy on their own as a side dish or appetizer, or accompanying just about anything off the grill.

VARIATIONS

• Add fresh herbs such as sage or rosemary to the hot oil (the rosemary can be battered similarly to the eggplant) and serve with the eggplant fries.
• Dust the hot fries with grated Parmesan.

NUTRITION

The deep purple hue of eggplant provides nasunin and other anthocyanins, potent antioxidants.

ECONOMY $

Rosemary Wine Cake with Currants

MAKES 6 TO 8 SERVINGS

*About fifteen years ago I enjoyed a grape-studded wine cake with a glass of Fragolino,
the semi-sweet Italian "strawberry" wine, at a café/bar in Venice. Having a more savory than
sweet palate (just put a cheese plate in front of me), I loved that the cake wasn't overly sweet
and particularly enjoyed the nuances of rosemary and olive oil. I set out to re-create it as soon
as I got home. It took about thirty tries, but here it is, with local currants substituted for the grapes.*

2 cups	all-purpose flour
½ teaspoon	salt
1¼ teaspoons	baking powder
3 tablespoons	unsalted butter, at room temperature
¾ cup	granulated sugar
⅓ cup	extra-virgin olive oil
2	large eggs
1 teaspoon	grated lemon zest
1 teaspoon	pure vanilla extract
¾ cup	sweet red wine, such as Brachetto d'Acqui, Marzemino Dolce, or Fragolino
1 cup	fresh or frozen black currants, thawed
2 teaspoons	finely chopped fresh rosemary leaves
2 tablespoons	coarse sugar
½ cup	crushed walnuts

Preheat the oven to 350°F. Lightly butter a Bundt pan and dust it with flour; tap out the excess.

Sift the flour, salt, and baking powder into a medium bowl. Set aside.

In the bowl of an electric mixer (or in a large bowl, by hand), beat the butter with the granulated sugar and the olive oil until light and creamy. Add the eggs, one at a time, beating after each addition, then add the lemon zest and vanilla. Stir in half of the flour mixture and mix in half of the wine. Repeat with the rest of the flour and the wine, mixing just until smooth. Fold in the currants and rosemary.

Turn the batter into the prepared pan, and use a rubber spatula to spread it evenly. Sprinkle 1 tablespoon of the coarse sugar on top, followed by the nuts, then the rest of the sugar. Bake in the center of the oven for 50 minutes, or until the cake is browned and springy to the touch. Cool partially in the pan on a wire rack. Then invert the cake onto a platter.

SERVING SUGGESTIONS

- Serve the rest of the sweet wine, chilled, with this exceptional cake.
- Serve the cake on its own as an afternoon treat, or with some fresh berries and a dollop of fresh whipped cream for a simple but elegant evening dessert.

VARIATIONS

- Substitute hazelnuts for the walnuts.
- Use grapes in place of the currants.
- Use a white dessert wine, such as Vin Santo, Moscato d'Asti, or Malvasia delle Lipari, in place of the red wine.

LEFTOVERS

Store, covered, at room temperature for 2 to 3 days.

NUTRITION

Currants contain almost double the antioxidants of blueberries.

ECONOMY $$

Blackberry, Raspberry, and Apple
Rustic Fruit Tart

MAKES 6 TO 8 SERVINGS

*Hudson Valley residents and visitors tend to keep it simple and charmingly rustic.
Gigi pastry chef Ashley Kearns gave up on making traditional pies and fancy tarts except around
the holidays; customers prefer this homier tart/galette. We serve mini versions in the bakery
area of Gigi Market, and they often disappear by lunchtime. This mixed-fruit version
exemplifies the crossover of fresh farm ingredients from summer to fall.*

Pastry shell

2 cups	all-purpose flour
½ teaspoon	sugar
Pinch	salt
12 tablespoons	cold unsalted butter (1½ sticks), cut into ½-inch cubes
⅓ cup	fresh orange juice

Filling

1	large or 2 small apples, peeled, cored, and cut into ½-inch chunks or wedges
1 pint	blackberries
1 pint	raspberries
⅓ cup	sugar
2 teaspoons	grated fresh ginger
2 teaspoons	cornstarch
	Grated zest of 1 orange
2	large egg yolks, beaten

To prepare the pastry shell, combine the flour, sugar, and salt in the bowl of a mixer fitted with the paddle attachment. Mix briefly on low speed to combine. Add the cold butter and mix on low speed (setting 2 or 3) until the flour-butter combination resembles gravelly sand—the butter should be the size of garbanzo beans—1 to 2 minutes. Stop the mixer and pour in the orange juice. Mix for 2 to 3 minutes, or just until the dough holds form when you squeeze it together in your hand. Shape the dough into a flattened disk, wrap it in plastic wrap, and refrigerate it for at least 30 minutes. (The dough can be made a few days in advance.)

Preheat the oven to 375°F. Lightly grease a rimless baking sheet.

To prepare the filling, combine all the fruit with the sugar, ginger, cornstarch, and orange zest in a medium mixing bowl. Set aside.

On a lightly floured surface, roll the dough out to form a ¼-inch-thick round. (It is important not to roll the dough too thin, or the fruit will tear it.) Using a paring knife, trim the edges so that you have an approximately 12-inch round. (The remaining dough is perfect to make a mini galette.) Place the round of dough on the prepared baking sheet. Brush a 2-inch perimeter around the edge with some of the beaten egg. Place the fruit in the center of the tart. Starting with the left edge, fold 2 to 3 inches of the dough toward the fruit center, loosely pleating it as you do so. Brush the surface of the fold with beaten egg. Continue to make smaller folds counterclockwise around the tart to complete the circle, brushing each fold with egg as you go. Bake until the shell is deep gold and the fruit is bubbly, 25 to 30 minutes. Let the tart sit for 5 minutes before transferring it to a wire rack to cool. Serve warm or at room temperature.

SERVING SUGGESTIONS

Top the tart with ice cream, gelato, frozen yogurt, or whipped cream.

LEFTOVERS

A delicious and nutritious breakfast with a scoop of low-fat plain or vanilla yogurt.

VARIATIONS

- The key is to have 5 cups of fruit. In summer, peaches and blueberries are a yummy combination, as are apricots and plums (we slightly roast the apricots first to intensify their natural sweetness). In the fall and winter, we move on to apples or pears with nuts and dried fruits such as raisins or cranberries. Strawberry and rhubarb mark the first fruits of spring. Gauge the amount of cornstarch you use on the juiciness of the fruit—2 to 3 teaspoons should do it.
- To make individual tarts, divide the chilled dough into 6 pieces; roll them out to form small ¼-inch-thick rounds, and proceed as above.

NUTRITION

Berries are rich in vitamin C and contain polyphenols such as ellagic acid. These plant protectors are powerful antioxidants and help boost enzymes that dispose of carcinogens.

ECONOMY $

Berries can be costly even when they're in season If there is a pick-your-own farm near you, make a day of it and enjoy lower-priced fruit.

Mead Orchards Chilled Peach Soup

MAKES 4 SERVINGS

Mead Orchard, just north of Gigi Market in Tivoli, New York, is one of the most spectacular and scenic swaths of farmland in the Hudson Valley. Fortunately the Mead family shares it with all of us via their thriving pick-your-own business. When it's time to harvest peaches in late July and August, you'll find our retail cooler at Gigi Market fully stocked. This soup should be made only with perfectly ripe, juicy peaches from close by wherever you call home. Enjoy it after a light summer dinner off the grill on a hot, sultry evening.

5	medium to large ripe peaches, peeled, pitted, and cut into chunks
1 teaspoon	grated lemon zest
Pinch	ground cloves
Pinch	cayenne pepper
½ cup	chilled Prosecco or other chilled dry (brut) white sparkling wine

Place the peaches and ½ cup cold water in a blender, and add the lemon zest, cloves, and cayenne. Puree until smooth. Then, using a rubber spatula, pass the mixture through a sieve into a serving bowl. Cover and chill. When ready to serve, stir in the Prosecco.

SERVING SUGGESTIONS

Ladle the soup from a serving bowl in the center of the table or serve it in individual bowls. Consider topping with a small scoop of vanilla gelato or maple crème fraîche.

VARIATIONS

- Substitute about 5 pounds of ripe plums.
- Omit the Prosecco and substitute a natural sparkling soda or sparkling lemonade.

LEFTOVERS

Makes a great base for a next-day Bellini.

NUTRITION

Peaches are low in calories (less than 40 for a medium one) and high in nutrients, phytochemicals, and antioxidants.

ECONOMY $$

Gigi Summer Fruit Salad with Zabaglione

MAKES 6 TO 8 SERVINGS

Zabaglione, the Italian version of the French sabayon, *adds a touch of creamy elegance and makes fresh seasonal fruit even more of a treat.*

Gigi fruit salad

1 pint	Greig Farm (or your local) blueberries
1 pint	raspberries (red or a mix of yellow and red)
2 cups	sliced peeled peaches (4 to 5 peaches)
	Juice of ½ lemon

Zabaglione

4	large egg yolks
¼ cup	sugar
¼ cup	Marsala wine
½ teaspoon	pure vanilla extract

To prepare the fruit salad, combine all the ingredients in a large mixing bowl. Cover, and chill until ready to serve.

To prepare the zabaglione, combine all the ingredients in the top of a double boiler, off the heat, and beat them together with a wire whisk. Place over steaming (not boiling) water and cook, beating constantly, until thickened to a loose pudding consistency, about 5 minutes. Remove the top of the double boiler from the heat and continue to whisk the zabaglione occasionally while it is cooling.

Portion the fresh fruit salad into glass serving bowls, and spoon the zabaglione over the top. Serve immediately, while the zabaglione is still frothy and light.

VARIATIONS

Add to the zabaglione:
- Grated ginger or autumn spices (such as allspice or a pinch of ground cloves)
- Grated fruit zests and/or pure extracts

Swap seasonal fruits:
- *Fall/winter:* roasted pear or apple slices
- *Spring:* grilled or seared strawberries

NUTRITION

Anthocyanins put the blue in blueberries and beta-carotene contributes to the vibrant orange of peaches. Both are powerful antioxidants.

ECONOMY $$

Fall

Fall is the season of celebration. Piles of decorative gourds from Migliorelli Farm appear in all shapes and sizes, many with knobs all over and fanciful curlicue stems. Wild bittersweet, one of my favorite plants, is loaded with bright orange and yellow berries. I use lots of it to decorate the wood rafters at Gigi Market and the windowsills of Gigi Trattoria. I'm a nut about decorating, and the day after Labor Day is a perfect time to start! Outside my farmhouse door, mums bloom and vines grow wild around the barnboard fencing. The days now are getting a little shorter, the air is crisper, and the villages dotting the Hudson are filled with weekenders visiting farms, hiking, and generally enjoying the spectacular fall foliage.

As someone who champions locally grown food, I think this is the best season to eat locally. The word "harvest" means to gather, and the greatest "gathering" here in the Hudson Valley is during the fall, not the summer. And gather we do. The market is full to overflowing. We're inundated with late-season tomatoes, peppers, and green beans, hard-skinned squashes, pumpkins, kale and mustard greens, broccoli, Brussels sprouts, cauliflower, potatoes, celery root, chard, spinach, sweet potatoes, mushrooms, and a second planting of arugula. Raspberry bushes all over the Valley are heavy with their second growth of fruit. Deep red and swollen with juice, the berries are plentiful enough to use lavishly in desserts, for breakfast, or just to eat out of hand. The cooler September nights have started the fruit on the apple and pear trees ripening. Come October, the market will be piled with boxes of Macouns, Cortlandt, McIntosh, and Red and Green Delicious apples, and Bosc and Bartlett pears. Farmers are working full tilt to clean up their fields, gather everything, and bring it in. It's a busy time.

In the kitchen, my cooking becomes more robust. Grill a chicken? No way. Time to roast it alongside freshly dug potatoes and wedges of fennel. Even salads are a bit more substantial now, with roasted pears and hazelnuts mixed in among the greens. I love to eat stuffed peppers, casseroles, and one-pot meals such as stewed chicken with squash and turnips. Yes, turnips. I've noticed that most people don't like them, but if you've tasted a truly fresh turnip, it's a whole different experience, crisp and sweet. It's time to dig around your kitchen cabinets and haul out the braising pans and slow cookers. Though my slow cooker may be old and frumpy, it makes the best braised dishes, with rich come-hither aromas.

It's been six long months since root vegetables and hard-skinned squashes appeared on our shelves. Gigi Market sits on a working farm, and I've been eyeing the pumpkin patch in the field just behind the back patio, watching all those squashes getting fat and golden in the warm autumn sunshine. Their deep colors and rich flavors and textures keep me going through the fall and winter. Layered dishes are especially satisfying. A mixed vegetable gratin of sweet potatoes, white potatoes, and parsnips with a bit of thickened stock or béchamel, baked until bubbly and brown, is a great one-dish meal, and a root vegetable lasagna with layers of butternut squash, rutabaga, potatoes, and parsnips all bound together with Gruyère is flavorful and fortifying.

All the onions, garlic, and shallots have been pulled, and when eaten fresh, they have a much deeper, truer flavor than you normally get from the supermarket ones. Seared, braised, or roasted beef paired with caramelized onion and shallot jam tastes great. Any leftover jam is a wonderful base for pizza. A cold plate of thinly sliced porchetta and salami and thick rings of local sweet onions makes a great lunch, especially when paired with a cold beer from Chatham Brewery, about an hour north.

For many New Yorkers, the Hudson Valley is synonymous with fruit, especially apples. Brimming with juice, our local apples are snatched up by the bushel by chefs, weekenders, day-trippers, and local folk alike. To my mind, the best way to eat a ripe apple is right out of hand, but they are pretty amazing in pies, cobblers, chutneys, sauces, and salads too. Customers at the market line up for our cider doughnuts, a daily treat that makes good use of the apple onslaught each autumn. Since most of our orchards have "pick your own" programs, city dwellers faithfully return year after year to pick their favorite kinds.

Pears are plentiful too. I love them tossed into salads or included as part of a cheese plate. Pears are versatile, equally at home in both savory and sweet dishes. One of the hands-down-favorite pizzas at Gigi Trattoria is the Bianca, a combination of figs, prosciutto, goat cheese, and thinly sliced pears, roasted in a very hot oven with a sprinkle of salt and pepper, and topped with a few arugula leaves and drizzled with truffle oil. We have regular customers who order it every time they walk through the door.

Braising and roasting concentrate the season's flavors, so I reach for a warmer palette of spices—cinnamon, fennel seed, cumin, and hot chiles—and combine those with the sweet flavors found in fruit, both fresh and dried. If the harvest has been a good one, come September I'm knee-deep in vegetables. By canning some, freezing others, and putting up jar after jar of homemade pickles, I can extend the flavors of summer for a few more months. I also stock up on smoked fish and game that is caught and preserved locally. And of course, there are great local cheeses to enjoy all year long.

Life in the Hudson Valley means the seasons will change. Sweltering summer days slip away, replaced by cool mornings and golden-hued late afternoon sunshine. Now is the time to finally catch up with friends and unwind. Gigi Trattoria stays busy all through the fall, especially on weekends, when our customers congregate in the evening to share a dish of pasta, enjoy a glass of wine, and catch up after the long summer. The holidays are right around the corner, and I'm decorating to my heart's content.

Too soon there will be frost on my farmhouse windows and I'll be curling up in front of the fireplace at night. The trees will be bare and the dark days of winter will be here. Snow on the ground means less fresh produce on the plate. But don't worry—the fall harvest is in, and there will be plenty of great food to keep us all eating happily, and locally, until springtime.

THE FALL HARVEST

Late-Season Vegetables: Tomatoes, Beans, and Peppers

We're down to the last few weeks here, and farmers are picking everything off the tomato and pepper plants and the bean bushes to bring to market. I buy as many late-season tomatoes as possible, some for canning to use during the winter and some to oven-dry and preserve in olive oil. A few green tomatoes are also brought to market, and now's the time to enjoy them fried.

We've talked a lot already about the bounty of tomatoes during the summer. Just remember to choose tomatoes that are deep red and feel heavy for their size. Raw tomatoes are fine for you, but they're even better when cooked. Lycopene is located in the cell wall of the tomato, and cooking releases this compound more completely. That's good news for home gardeners facing a mountain of late-season tomatoes: You can go ahead and start canning them. Tomatoes don't lose any of their nutritional value with high heat processing; canned tomatoes are just as beneficial as fresh ones. Happily, lycopene is best absorbed in the presence of fat: *viva* olive oil! Think about making a basic tomato sauce (page 290), that can be used in myriad different recipes.

You'll also see mature green beans at the market this time of year, the ones that stayed

MONTGOMERY PLACE ORCHARDS

I drive around the Valley all the time, in good weather and bad. While it's usually work-related, on occasion I drive just for the pleasure of it. It's a chance to take a look around. Invariably something beautiful catches my eye, and often it's related to the light, which is just as dramatic as the seasons. On any given day a drive on one of the charming back-country lanes will look different: one day moody and misty, another with dazzling leaves shimmering in the sun. In the autumn, dappled light dances over the slight rise in the road ahead of me, and mounds of copper-colored leaves pile at the foot of the old oaks. Even the river heaving itself upon the rocky-edged shore during a violent summer storm is a sight to witness.

More often than not, I find myself meandering along River Road. I come to Annandale-on-Hudson, a tiny hamlet hugging the water's edge. Following the signs, I often turn off the road and pass down a peaceful half-mile-long allée of trees to arrive at Montgomery Place, an elegant manor house sitting in the middle of over four hundred acres of rolling pasture, orchards, and formal gardens. The house, originally built by Janet Livingston Montgomery in 1802, today is managed by Scenic Hudson, a local conservancy group.

Much of Scenic Hudson's efforts are focused on staying true to the original purpose of Montgomery Place as a working country estate. That includes the orchards, which have been managed by Talea and Doug Fincke for the past twenty-two years. I think there are probably no better people to be entrusted with this particular orchard. Both Talea and Doug are preservationists by temperament, and committed to the health and aesthetic beauty of this place in a way that would greatly please Mrs. Montgomery if she were here to see it. They are apple archivists at heart, with intellects finely attuned to all the different histories, possibilities, and nuances of the fruit they grow. As Talea puts it, "Each apple has a story. You just have to listen."

Over the years Talea and Doug have expanded the orchard to include more than sixty varieties of apples, including the

Esopus Spitzenburg, a favorite of Thomas Jefferson's that was developed in the 1700s right here in the Hudson Valley.

Fruit growing runs in Talea's family. They farmed a thousand acres in Pennsylvania, growing supermarket apples that Talea playfully refers to as "redalicious." She liked farm life, though, and attended the Delaware Valley College of Science and Agriculture after high school. There she met Doug, who grew up in Ulster County. Although he didn't grow up on a farm, Doug said he was surrounded by them and could rarely be found indoors.

After several years of working at orchards in Long Island and Pennsylvania, the Finckes settled on the Montgomery orchards. Their size, location, existing fruit stock, and the handshake arrangement with the conservancy allowed for a good livelihood without having to move toward industrial-style production. Talea treasures that aspect of the operation. As she puts it, "Although he didn't grow up on a farm, Doug was surrounded by them and his childhood was spent outdoors."

The Finckes sell directly to the public via a market stand on Route 9G, just a few minutes from the orchard property. Talea sees her role as an educator, and if you happen to be at her stand, she'll take you on a tasting tour of whatever apples she has that are ready to eat. Since all her apples are fresh, each one has a crisp bite, and the range of flavors goes from simple and sweet to complex and aromatic. During my most recent visit to Montgomery Place Orchards, Talea introduced me to the Cameo apple, a forerunner of the Red Delicious. It's an extremely easy-eating apple, and I thought about buying a few pounds.

"Not so fast," said Talea. "Now try this." She handed me a Black Twig apple, still sweet but with a more interesting flavor.

"You're right," I told her. "I think this one would be a better choice."

Talea shook her head. "Wait a minute," she said. "Try the Ashmead's Kernel." From that first bite, I tasted an apple with a big, deep apple flavor offset by a gently muted sweetness. The idea of that apple paired with some of my favorite cheeses was mouthwatering. Talea says she can tell a lot about a person by the apple they select—even their politics! (That's all I'm going to say about that.)

Talea loves doing tastings, showing off the range of flavors in apples much the way vintners demonstrate wines. That makes sense. Apples are one of the earliest known cultivated fruits, and the difference in flavors among them is enormous. Also, the tradition of turning apples into cider is even older in the United States than turning grapes into wine. By the early 1700s colonists in the Hudson Valley were growing apples almost solely for hard cider, a profitable product.

The tradition of cidering waxed and waned throughout the twentieth century and appears to be on the ascendance these days in the Hudson Valley. Doug Fincke calls cidering the best part of his job. In an old barn, he has set up a traditional apple press and a spotlessly clean fermentation lab, where hard cider ages for a year in gorgeous Italian glass jugs before it's decanted into mason jars bearing the label "Atomic Cider." Doug used to press sweet cider, but regulations in New York require pasteurization or UV treatment, and he thought that made for awful-tasting juice. "When you pasteurize fresh apple juice, it all just tastes like sugar water. Why do that?" he says.

With the hard cider, he experiments with different apples and notes the subtle natural variation among even similar strains of apples, which can make each batch of cider different. During the most violent moments of the fermentation process, Doug sits nearby, watching it all happen. "You know, everything about fruit is seductive," he says. "The perfume of the blossoms in the spring draws you in. You nurture the trees and get to eat nectar-sweet fruit or drink sheer amber-colored cider at the finish. Every phase is pleasurable and astonishing. Living here, spending my life in this orchard, has given me a deeper notion of preservation and a commitment to Mother Nature's beauty and fertility. Not a bad trade-off for a guy who never gets to take a vacation!" I can toast to that.

P.O. Box 24, Annandale-on-Hudson, NY 12590
Orchards: River Road
Farm stand: Route 9G

on the vine a little too long. Don't pass these up. A slow-braised green bean with whole garlic cloves and tomatoes is a delicious treat. Nothing crunchy about those beans; they just melt in the mouth. Take your time and pick beans that are firm, heavy, with a smooth feel and a vibrant green color. They shouldn't have any spots or bruises on them. When you break them in half, you should hear a snap.

Green beans are low in calories and loaded with nutrients. Like tomatoes, they contain plenty of vitamins C, A, and K. Vitamin K helps maintain strong bones by aiding osteocalcin, which anchors calcium in the bone. Green beans also contain magnesium and potassium, which are good for your cardiovascular system, and plenty of fiber to help reduce cholesterol and keep your intestines in good shape.

Along with tomatoes and green beans, bell peppers and hot chiles are harvested toward the end of summer. I love all kinds of spicy food, and I've noticed that the bold flavor and heat of chiles seems to reduce people's tendency to reach for the salt shaker. All peppers are members of the capsicum family and contain capsaicin, an alkaloid concentrated in the seeds and veins of peppers. The big difference between spicy chiles and mild peppers is the level of capsaicin found in each, and this may be why the health benefits of certain chiles are thought to be greater than those of bell peppers. Also, we typically remove the seeds and veins of bell peppers before cooking, whereas many of us toss small chiles into the pot whole. There has been a lot of interesting research, and it seems that high levels of capsaicin can help reduce people's sensitivity to pain. You'll even find capsaicin as an ingredient in some anti-inflammatory arthritis creams and ointments.

Apples and Pears

By October there is a bewildering variety of apples at the market. While the modern ones are all there—including Granny Smith, Delicious, and Rome—a growing number of heirloom apples also show up. The heirlooms don't always look so pretty, but looks are deceiving: their flavor is deeply satisfying. As a general rule of thumb, ripe apples come in two categories: soft or crisp. Soft, sweet apples such as Romes are perfect for cooking and baking, and crisp apples like Macouns are best for eating out of hand or as part of a cheese course.

When apples are in the market, pears aren't far behind. In choosing a pear, find one that feels firm but has a classic pear aroma. Bartletts are, of course, a popular cultivated variety here, but so are Comice, Bosc, and D'Anjou. Firm pears are great for roasting, sautéing, baking, and poaching. If you prefer eating pears out of hand, as I do, place them in a paper bag on the counter and check them every day. That way, you can be sure to eat them at the peak of ripeness.

Both apples and pears are low-calorie foods—about 100 calories for a tennis-ball-size piece of fruit. Eating just one juicy fresh pear with the skin on will put you well on your way to meeting your daily fiber needs, with about 5 grams of fiber—17 percent of the recommended daily intake for adults.

Fiber is the ultimate "something for nothing." You probably already know that eating adequate amounts encourages healthy digestion and reduces cholesterol levels. But recent research also shows that eating more fiber can reduce the risk of coronary heart disease as well as type 2 diabetes. In addition, eating fiber promotes "satiety," which means you feel full longer. That can help you control your appetite and maybe shed a few persistent pounds.

Crucifers

Cruciferous vegetables get their long name from the fact that they all produce four petal flowers in the shape of a cross. This family includes broccoli, cabbage, kale, cauliflower, kohlrabi, radishes, arugula, mustard, turnips, and Brussels sprouts. Because each vegetable is grown by farmers here in all sorts of varieties, my recommendation is to pick the one that you find most beautiful. Odd recommendation, huh? Well, maybe that's because cruciferous vegetables bring out my inner artist. I remember the first time I saw Brussels sprouts on the stalk. I couldn't

believe how charming they looked. I've even been known to use a large green, glossy Savoy cabbage as a table centerpiece.

The truth is that almost all cruciferous vegetables keep pretty well when purchased fresh from the farmers' market and properly stored. Look for creamy white cauliflower with no brown spots and deep green broccoli with rigid stems. Arugula leaves should be fairly small and firm, not wilted; kale leaves should be upright; and kohlrabi and turnips should feel heavy and smooth. Brussels sprouts will be sold on the stem and with the sprouts tightly closed, with no yellow leaves. Buy plenty and let them be a feast for your eyes—at least until your hunger gets the upper hand.

Crucifers contain potent natural chemicals that help the body defend itself against cancer. Broccoli, the most popular, is rich in vitamins A and C and folate, all of which promote good health. It's also a good source of calcium, a mineral critical to bone health, blood pressure control, and possibly colon cancer prevention, which many women (and some men) do not get enough of. Glucosinates, indole-3 carbinol, and isothiocynates—a type of glucosinate—are active phytochemicals, or disease-fighting plant chemicals, found in cruciferous vegetables.

No need to memorize all that. What you need to know is that nutritionists recommend a minimum of four servings of cruciferous vegetables a week. A recent Johns Hopkins University study showed that if you average this amount per week, mortality from any cause declines by 26 percent. So, what is a serving? A mere ½ cup cooked vegetable. Steaming for about 4 or 5 minutes releases most of those handy phytochemicals (microwaving diminishes them), making them more easily absorbed. Steaming also helps retain other nutrients and doesn't add any fat, which allows you to add a light drizzle of extra-virgin olive oil or perhaps a sprinkling of cheese.

Berries

While strawberries have disappeared from the market by this time, loads of other berries are ready to take their place. My favorite is the fall harvest of local raspberries. They come in different colors—yellow, orange, black, and red—and must be handled delicately, since when ripe they are extremely fragile and prone to bruising. It can be hard to tell if you have a good batch in your hand. Ask the farmer if you can taste one, and buy accordingly. Perfect-looking berries are less important. In fact, really ripe berries can be a little misshapen sometimes, so pretty doesn't count for all that much here. Fresh ripe raspberries can be addictive, but at 64 calories a cup, you can happily indulge. Like blueberries, raspberries contain vitamin C and lutein, which helps sharpen your vision. I think that is nature's perfect response to fall's shorter days.

Mushrooms

Cultivated mushrooms appear in market stalls in the spring and fall. You'll find oyster mushrooms, chanterelles, shiitakes, button mushrooms, creminis, and portobellos from a number of local purveyors. The prized morel, which grows wild all over the Valley, is found only in the spring, and even then you'll have to put on your boots and go searching for them in the woods.

The flavor of mushrooms is often called "umami," which is a Japanese word that conveys their near-meat texture and aroma. They're a great choice during the fall when you crave deeper, earthier flavors but want to keep vegetables in the center of your plate. As a health food, mushrooms are a nutrient dynamo! This is partially due to the fact that they absorb soil nutrients easily. Mushrooms can be an excellent source of selenium, a potent antioxidant and cancer fighter. An analysis of seven different kinds of mushrooms—cremini, enoki, maitake, oyster, portobello, shiitake, and everyday white button mushrooms—has shown that they also contain nutrients like copper, potassium, folate, and niacin. Mushrooms contain moderate amounts of protein, a few grams of carbs, almost zero fat, and loads of flavor. With their meaty taste, they can play a key role in enjoying a more plant-based diet.

Mushrooms can be pricey, but remember that a little goes a long way. When shopping, look for mushrooms with taut outer skins, no moldy or dark spots, and firm separate gills. And by all means, mix and match. With so many different kinds available all at once, it's a shame to limit yourself.

Hard-Skinned Squash

A multitude of hard squashes appear in October. These include favorites like butternut and acorn, but there are lots more—including turban squash, Japanese kabocha squash, and one of my favorites, the estimable blue hubbard squash. I like the kabocha and hubbard for their intense flavor and dry flesh, which makes them perfect for gnocchi, tarts, and risotto. While different squashes taste different, they all respond well to steaming, which helps loosen the flesh from the hard exterior. With the exception of smooth, uniformly shaped squashes like butternut, I don't recommend that you peel off the hard skin unless you're doing it as part of your body-building regimen. It's just too easy for that knife to slip. . . . Instead, just chop the squash into wedges or chunks and steam or roast it with a drizzle of olive oil until the flesh is soft but not mushy. Then you can easily remove the skin and cut up cubes of fresh squash as needed.

The big nutritional story on squash is what gives it its glorious color: beta-carotene. Beta-carotene is converted by the body into vitamin A, which helps keep our vision sound and is shown to have cancer-fighting properties. Squash is also an excellent source of vitamin C, potassium, and fiber.

Other Fall Vegetables

There are plenty of other great vegetables that show up in the fall markets, including dark leafy cooking greens, onions and other alliums, potatoes and sweet potatoes, and all sorts of roots such as carrots, beets, radishes, parsnips, celeriac, turnips, rutabaga, and kohlrabi. You'll see them sprinkled throughout the recipes in this chapter, with highlights and tips on how to enjoy them all.

GREAT SEASONAL INGREDIENT

Pumpkin

For most Americans, pumpkins are the two-trick pony of the vegetable world: they appear in pies or on your doorstep. That's about it. Don't get me wrong, I really like pumpkin pie, and my restaurant hosts a pumpkin-carving contest each fall as the witching season descends. But there's a lot more groovy pumpkin love we could all be sharing.

Festive, multifaceted, *and* healthy, pumpkins have it all! Among their many nutritional highlights, their super-high level of beta-carotene, which lends vibrant color, stands out. The body converts beta-carotene, as well as other carotenoids, to vitamin A. Half a cup of canned pumpkin puree provides enough beta-carotene to supply 540 percent of the recommended Daily Value (DV) of vitamin A. It also provides 25 percent of the DV of vitamin K, 10 percent of vitamin C, 4 grams of fiber, and many trace minerals.

Even the pumpkin's seeds are good for you. They can be seasoned (spicy or sweet) and roasted to crunchy perfection. A handful makes a nice snack, and they can also top pies, custards, sauces, and pumpkin-containing starches such as pilafs, polenta, risotto, mashes, and gratins. The seeds provide not only great taste and texture contrast, but also healthy unsaturated fats (omega-3s for one) as well as fiber, iron, zinc, magnesium, and manganese.

Pumpkins come in a wide variety of types, sizes, shapes, and colors (orange, red, white, and blue!). The smaller varieties tend to be sweeter and less mealy. Their protective outer skin can be intimidating for many home cooks, who usually reach for the can when preparing the Thanksgiving pie filling. While 100 percent pure canned pumpkin (not pie filling, which is sweetened and contains spices) is convenient and nutritionally better than fresh (it's concentrated and therefore contains more nutrients and phytochemicals), the puree can limit cooking choices, especially when you want to see the bits of pumpkin flesh in the dish or to toast some seeds for crunchy garnishes or snacks. Generally, the canned version is a quick, tasty, and healthy choice for all recipes that ask for puree. If, however, you wish to start from scratch, do not attempt to peel the skin. Instead, using a sturdy knife, cut the pumpkin into large chunks or wedges. Reserve the seeds, and boil or steam the chunks in lightly salted water until tender, 30 to 40 minutes. Drain off the water, and when the chunks are cool enough to handle, slip off the skin. Using a potato masher or a ricer, puree the pulp.

You can also roast chunks of pumpkin, which helps caramelize the natural sugars and deepens the flavor. Prepared that way, pumpkin puree is a great filling for pasta such as tortellini and ravioli. I enjoy roasted pumpkin in dishes like Maple Pumpkin Polenta (page 176), roasted pumpkin soup, risotto, pumpkin flan with caramelized pumpkin seeds, and chicken, pumpkin, and sage lasagna.

A root cellar is the ideal place to store pumpkins because it's not too cold or too hot and is relatively dry. If you are lucky enough to have a root cellar, by all means use it. Your pumpkins picked in October will last until midwinter. If this is not possible, pumpkins will last about a month in the refrigerator. To increase their storage time, combine 1 tablespoon chlorine bleach with 1 gallon water, and use this to scrub the pumpkins to remove any dirt, which can later become rot or mold and hasten decomposition. Thoroughly dry the washed pumpkins, and then store them.

In the United States, pumpkin picking is an autumn rite of passage. Whether harvesting your own or picking at a farm, look for pumpkins with a healthy green stem and a dull finish; if they're shiny, it's too soon. Again, if the purpose is cooking, smaller tends to be more tender and flavorful.

Pumpkins can be seductive. Just watch a bunch of children in a pumpkin patch. Somehow instructions to "just pick one" are immediately forgotten. I've seen five-year-olds persuasively argue with their parents that a single pumpkin will be lonely, a condition that must be avoided at all costs. My impression is that children require, on average, at least four pumpkins for optimal family (and pumpkin) happiness. A friend's daughter told me she was allowed to pick only two pumpkins for Halloween last year because her parents are "super mean." I believe it.

NORTHWIND FARMS

Richard Biezynski's accent may be straight out of Queens, but his innovative poultry farm has made him a bona fide country farmer and a spokesperson for the sustainable movement in the Hudson Valley. Richie, as he's known here, and his wife, Jane, founded Northwind Farms in the 1980s on 196 acres of rolling hills. They specialize in free-range chicken and standard and heritage turkeys, organic grass-fed beef, ducks, and geese, and fabulous-tasting heirloom pork.

When Richie started the farm he knew he wanted to raise poultry, so he decided to raise a few chickens in a completely natural organic way. Told by other farmers and large poultry producers that it wasn't possible to raise chickens like that, due to disease risk and slim profits, Richie held firm and insisted that it was the only way a piece of chicken was going to be on his plate.

It was a tough learning curve, but pretty soon Richie was raising chickens that were famous all over the Valley. Northwind Farms found itself supplying local grocery stores, restaurants, and people who pulled into the driveway. With business becoming increasingly hectic, Richie thought about quitting and at one point even called all his clients and said, "That's it, I'm done." But no one believed him, and a good thing too, because Richie has a real soft spot for chickens and all sorts of heirloom birds. The phone never stopped ringing: moms whose children could eat his chickens without any allergic reactions, restaurants whose clients demanded his products, and even Balducci's, the legendary specialty retailer, who didn't quite know how to market Richie's more muscular birds and so coined the moniker "free range." The chickens sold like crazy and a potent marketing phrase was born.

Richie is proud to be raising natural food and does his best to practice sustainable agriculture. His fields and his beef are certified organic. He tries to ensure that his chickens and turkeys live a stress-free life, with plenty of fresh air, space to move around, and good food. He even built an on-site slaughtering shed so his birds don't have to undergo a long caged trip to a processing facility, and he is adamant that all farm animals be treated humanely. I'm pleased to note that the humane treatment of animals is something Richie has in common with other natural meat producers in the Valley.

I think the Biezynskis' chickens taste better than anything else on the market. They have a true "bird" flavor, almost wild, with a nice balance between light and dark meat. Their flavor comes through even when a sauce is added, which is practically impossible to find in commercial poultry. Clients and friends say they've never tasted chicken or turkey as good as that from Northwind Farms. And while I can buy less expensive commercially raised natural chicken, pork, and beef, to me it's still factory food, not farm food.

So, Richie continues. He has begun building a healthy herd of heirloom pigs using old breeds like Berkshire, Polish Spot, Yorkshire, and Hampshire. What started as his son Russell's 4-H project in 2000 now represents an ever bigger part of Northwind Farms' business, and Richie expects that raising pigs will be a big part of the farm's future after Russell graduates from college. Lucky for us. At Gigi we buy half or whole pigs to trim down and serve customers. We even use kielbasa and fresh and smoked sausages made on site at the farm.

I believe that the expression "good stewards of the land" aptly describes Northwind Farms.

Supporting local agriculture may be a way of thinking globally and acting locally, but for me, it's all about great taste right next door.

Northwind Farms, 185 Wast Kerley Corners Road, Tivoli, New York 12583
845-757-5591
www.northwindfarmsallnatural.com

Wiltbank Farm Mushroom Ragù

MAKES 8 SERVINGS

We use mushrooms from Wiltbank Farm in Saugerties to prepare this earthy and creamy ragù,
which we toss with our handmade pasta and use to top crispy crostini and polenta canapés.
Substitute the same amounts of any seasonal mushrooms. Be sure to trim the stems on
all mushrooms and even to trim off the underside gills on large mushrooms.

¼ cup	olive oil
½ cup	chopped shallots (about 4 shallots)
2	garlic cloves, minced
2 cups	chopped blue oyster mushrooms (about 6 ounces trimmed, 8 ounces untrimmed)
2 cups	chopped orange oyster mushrooms (about 6 ounces trimmed, 8 ounces untrimmed)
2 cups	chopped shiitake mushrooms (about 6 ounces trimmed, 8 ounces untrimmed)
	Salt and freshly ground black pepper
⅓ cup	dry white wine
¾ cup	heavy cream
1 teaspoon	minced fresh rosemary
½ teaspoon	grated lemon zest
1 cup	grated Fontina cheese
⅓ cup	freshly grated Grana Padano or Parmesan cheese

Heat the oil in the largest skillet you have over medium heat. Add the shallots and garlic and cook until the shallots are translucent and the garlic is just starting to brown, 3 to 4 minutes. Increase the heat to medium-high and add the mushrooms, a little at a time, adding more as they cook down and start to shrink. Season with salt and pepper to taste, and keep stirring until the mushrooms begin to brown, 8 to 10 minutes. Then deglaze the skillet with the white wine, and cook until the liquid has reduced to a few glossy tablespoons, 1 to 2 minutes. Stir in the cream, rosemary, and lemon zest. Remove the skillet from the heat, mix in both cheeses, and taste again for salt and pepper. Serve immediately, or refrigerate the mushroom ragù for a few days and reheat it over a gentle flame with a touch of broth or cream.

SERVING SUGGESTIONS

For crostini, bruschetta, or polenta canapé appetizers: Place a rack approximately 6 inches below the heat source and preheat the broiler. Top the crostini, bruschette, or cold sliced polenta rounds with 1 or 2 tablespoons of mushroom ragù and sprinkle with a little Parmesan cheese. Arrange the crostini in one layer on a rimmed baking sheet. Broil until the tops begin to brown in spots, about 3 minutes. Watch closely so the crostini don't burn or scorch. Transfer to a serving platter, and serve warm.

VARIATIONS

I like to use whatever seasonal herbs I can snip from my garden plot. Sage can take the place of rosemary quite successfully. In the springtime I even substitute tarragon, which adds a lovely anise flavor and pairs well with the mushrooms.

LEFTOVERS

This ragù holds very well in the refrigerator for 2 to 3 days. I love it mixed into scrambled eggs, used as an omelet filling, stirred into risotto, or even topping a pizza. You're limited only by your imagination. This is even great spooned into a roasted sweet potato—a treat for the eyes and the stomach. Yum.

NUTRITION

Mushrooms are an excellent source of selenium, a cancer-fighting powerhouse, plus lots of great minerals such as copper.

ECONOMY $$

Wild mushrooms are expensive, but combining button mushrooms with a few wild mushrooms can reduce the cost considerably while still resulting in a great dish.

Gigi Fresh Ricotta and Tuscan Kale Tartlets

MAKES 24 TARTLETS

Gigi Market is the home of our catering operations. These tartlets, prepared with Gigi's own fresh ricotta (made with Hudson Valley Fresh milk) and Hearty Roots Farm's Tuscan kale (a dark cabbage with tall, slender leaves), are among our clients' favorites for hors d'oeuvres. Our tart crust recipe is quick and easy, but to save time, you could purchase a good-quality puff pastry or prebaked tartlet shells.

Tartlet shells

2 cups	all-purpose flour
¼ teaspoon	salt
1 cup	cold unsalted butter (2 sticks), cut into ½-inch cubes
4 tablespoons	ice-cold water

Filling

4 ounces	Tuscan kale or regular kale leaves
3 tablespoons	olive oil
1 cup	minced Spanish onion (about 1 medium)
1 cup	half-and-half
4	large egg yolks
¼ to ½ teaspoon	salt
⅛ teaspoon	freshly ground black pepper
4 ounces	Gigi Homemade Fresh Ricotta (page 288) or your favorite brand

Prepare the tartlet shells: Combine the flour and salt in a food processor, and pulse a few times to mix. Add the butter and the cold water, and pulse until moist clumps form. Gather the dough, and shape it into a 6-inch-long log. Cover it in plastic wrap and refrigerate it for at least 1 hour and up to 1 day.

Cut the log into twenty-four ¼-inch-thick rounds. Press 1 round into each cup of a nonstick 24-cup mini muffin pan (1-ounce cups); the dough should come three-quarters of the way up the sides. Freeze for 30 minutes.

Meanwhile, preheat the oven to 375°F.

Arrange the kale leaves in a stack and roll it up to form a long "cigar." Cut the "cigar" crosswise into very thin slices, forming thin ribbons, or chiffonade. Set aside.

Line the tartlet shells with aluminum foil and fill them with pie weights or raw beans. Bake until the sides are set and the edges are lightly golden, about 12 minutes. Remove the pan from the oven and remove the foil and weights. Reduce the oven temperature to 350°F.

Prepare the filling: Heat the olive oil in a large skillet over medium heat. Add the onion and cook, stirring, for 2 to 3 minutes. Add the kale and cook until it has wilted and the water from the greens has evaporated, 4 to 5 minutes. Remove from the heat.

In a medium bowl, whisk the half-and-half, egg yolks, salt, and pepper together. Mix in the ricotta; then add the kale mixture.

Spoon the filling into the shells. Bake until the filling is set and the crust edges are golden, about 15 minutes.

Let the tartlets cool for 5 minutes in the pans. Then, using a small knife, cut around the tartlets to loosen them. Turn out the tartlets and arrange them on a platter. Serve warm or at room temperature. (The tartlets can be made 1 day ahead: Cool, cover, and refrigerate them in the pan. Rewarm, uncovered, in a 350°F oven for 12 minutes.)

VARIATIONS

- Make these tartlets really easy and rustic: Instead of using a mini muffin tin, roll the dough to fit a 13 x 9 x 2-inch baking pan, reaching 1 inch up the sides of the pan (you may have a little extra dough; gather and freeze it for another occasion). Blind bake (page 133), then pour in the filling and bake until puffy and golden. When cool, cut into small squares.
- Substitute your favorite cooking green, such as collards or chard, for the kale.
- Add diced roasted red bell peppers for color and a pinch of cayenne for a bit of heat.

LEFTOVERS

These tartlets are great reheated.

NUTRITION

Kale has the number one ORAC rating (antioxidant capacity) among vegetables.

ECONOMY $

Rustic Onion Tart

MAKES 1 TART: 4 LUNCH SERVINGS OR 6 TO 8 APPETIZER SERVINGS

The success of this recipe rests on using the freshest produce available; we use local Hearty Roots Farm's fresh-picked onions instead of those from the supermarket, which may have lost texture and flavor from being held in cold storage for too long. This recipe is for a tart, but the onion confit alone is worth making to use as a bruschetta topping, or simply to stir into stews or soups. Actually, this confit is the base of a classic French onion soup—just add beef broth. The pastry dough could be used as the crust for a quiche or tart.

Onion confit

1 tablespoon	unsalted butter
3 tablespoons	olive oil
3	large onions (about 1½ pounds), thinly sliced
2	bay leaves
	Salt and freshly ground black pepper
¾ cup	chicken or vegetable stock or reduced-sodium broth
3	thyme sprigs, leaves removed and stems discarded

Dough

1 cup	all-purpose or pastry flour
¼ teaspoon	kosher salt
5 tablespoons	cold unsalted butter, cut into ½-inch pieces
4 tablespoons	ice-cold water, or more if needed

Garnish

10	pitted picholine or Niçoise olives
1 tablespoon	finely chopped fresh marjoram or thyme
1 tablespoon	extra-virgin olive oil

To make the confit, heat the butter and oil in a large deep skillet over medium heat. When the butter has melted and is frothy, add the onions and the bay leaves, and season with salt and pepper. Reduce the heat to low and cook, stirring often, until the onions are soft but not browned, about 30 minutes. Add the stock and cook, stirring occasionally, until the liquid has completely evaporated and the onions are very soft and deeply caramelized, 30 to 35 minutes; stir in the thyme leaves during the last 5 minutes of cooking.

While the onions are cooking, prepare the dough: In a large bowl, stir together the flour and salt. Using a pastry blender or two knives, cut in the butter until pea-size balls form. Add the cold water a little at a time while stirring with a fork, until the dough comes together; if necessary, add more water, a few drops at a time (avoid overworking the dough, or it will be tough). Form the dough into a disk, wrap it in plastic wrap, and refrigerate until cold, about 15 minutes.

Remove the onions from the heat, and discard the bay leaves. Preheat the oven to 400°F. Lightly grease a baking sheet with butter or olive oil cooking spray.

On a lightly floured work surface, roll out the dough to form a ¼-inch-thick round that is 10 to 12 inches in diameter. Place the dough on the prepared baking sheet and prick it in several places with a fork. Mound the onion confit in the center of the dough, leaving a 1½-inch border. Scatter the olives and marjoram over the onion confit, sprinkle with salt, and drizzle with the olive oil. Fold the edge of the tart up over the confit to hold in the filling while creating a rustic shape. Bake the tart until the crust is golden brown, 20 to 25 minutes. Let it cool on the baking sheet for 5 to 10 minutes before cutting into slices and serving.

SERVING SUGGESTION

Serve the tart with soup, or with a salad tossed with a red wine, sherry, or balsamic vinaigrette.

VARIATIONS

- Make small tarts by dividing the dough into four pieces and rolling out four rounds.
- Top the onions with assorted grilled seasonal vegetables and a sprinkling of a local cheese, such as mozzarella or goat cheese.
- Add sliced or diced cooked potatoes and chorizo for a Spanish touch. Sprinkle the top with grated Manchego cheese.

LEFTOVERS

Serve at room temperature or reheat in a 375°F oven or grill.

NUTRITION

Until recently we measured an ingredient's health power only by its vitamin and mineral content. The last two decades of research highlighting substances in foods called phytochemicals (natural plant chemicals) has changed the playing field. Onions are not only the base layer of flavor for many dishes (in this recipe their deliciousness is at the forefront), but they contain powerful antioxidants, such as flavenoids like quercetin. Antioxidants protect against many chronic diseases, including heart disease and cancer. Studies have shown that consumption of onions may prevent gastric ulcers by preventing growth of the ulcer-forming microorganism *Helicobacter pylori*.

ECONOMY $

Onions, which are very inexpensive, are the star and the meat of this recipe.

Butternut and Pear Soup

MAKES 6 SERVINGS

I love returning to hot soup when the air gets chilly in the early fall. I'll grab some butternut squash from my garden and some pears from nearby Montgomery Place Orchards to make this soup, which showcases the flavors of autumn. Garam masala adds a little warm spice to the slightly sweet squash and pears.

1 tablespoon	olive oil
1 tablespoon	unsalted butter
1	medium onion, chopped
2	bay leaves
1	large butternut squash, peeled, seeded, and cut into 2-inch chunks
¼ teaspoon	garam masala (see Note)
¼ teaspoon	cayenne pepper
2	ripe pears, peeled, cored, and cubed
½ cup	dry white wine (optional)
5 cups	vegetable or chicken stock or reduced-sodium broth
1	medium potato, peeled and roughly cubed
	Salt
⅓ cup	half-and-half (optional)

Note: Garam masala is a seasoning blend that can include up to twelve spices, often including black pepper, cinnamon, cloves, coriander, cumin, cardamom, fennel, mace, and nutmeg. It is used in Indian cooking and is available in many supermarkets and specialty stores.

In a large heavy-bottomed pot or Dutch oven, heat the oil and butter over medium heat. Add the onion and bay leaves and cook, stirring often, until the onion is soft, about 5 minutes. Increase the heat to medium-high and add the squash, garam masala, and cayenne. Cook, stirring occasionally, for 8 minutes or until the vegetables begin to brown. Add the pears and cook for another 2 minutes. Add the wine, if using, and cook until it is almost completely reduced, 1 to 2 minutes. Add the stock and the potato, and season with salt to taste. Bring the mixture to a boil. Then reduce the heat and simmer until the squash and potatoes are very soft, 25 to 30 minutes. Remove the bay leaves. Puree the soup, in batches, in a food processor or blender. Return the soup to the saucepan, stir in the half-and-half (if using), and bring to a simmer. Add more salt if necessary, and serve piping hot.

VARIATIONS

- Add the heel of a chunk of Parmesan when you simmer the soup. Remove it with tongs before serving.
- Top each serving with a drizzle of extra-virgin olive oil and some grated Parmesan or shredded New York State cheddar.
- Add dried ancho or fresh poblano chiles to the soup as it cooks; remove before pureeing.
- Stir in curry powder and turmeric to taste.
- Substitute apples for the pears.

LEFTOVERS

This soup is great reheated.

NUTRITION

Butternut squash is a beta-carotene (vitamin A) titan and contains beta-cryptoxanthin, which may prevent lung cancer. Both butternut squash and pears are high in fiber.

ECONOMY $

Butternut squash and pears are quite inexpensive and at top quality during the fall.

Gigi Autumn Mushroom Soup

MAKES 6 SERVINGS

A mixture of Wiltbank Farm oyster and shiitake mushrooms is the base for this heavenly fall soup.
We salt the onions to remove excess liquid and bitterness, and then rinse them thoroughly.
The sweet onions contrast beautifully with the earthy mushrooms.

1¾ pounds	Spanish onions (about 2 large)
¼ cup	kosher salt
3 tablespoons	olive oil
12 ounces	fresh oyster mushrooms, tough stems removed, caps sliced
12 ounces	fresh shiitake mushrooms, stems removed, caps sliced
	Salt and freshly ground black pepper
2 tablespoons	chopped fresh flat-leaf parsley
⅓ cup	dry white wine
2 tablespoons	unsalted butter
2	medium potatoes, peeled and cubed
¼ cup	chopped celery leaves
7 cups	chicken or beef stock, reduced-sodium broth, or water
	Extra-virgin olive oil, for drizzling (optional)

Peel and thinly slice the onions (a mandoline on its finest setting will produce uniform thin slices). Spread the onions in a colander and sprinkle the kosher salt evenly over the top; use your hands to mix. Set aside for 2 hours.

Rinse the onions thoroughly, squeeze out the excess water, and pat them dry with a clean kitchen towel or between sheets of paper towels.

Heat the olive oil in a medium skillet over medium-high heat. Add the mushrooms, season with salt and pepper, and cook, stirring often, until they are lightly browned, about 5 minutes. Add the parsley and cook for another minute. Then add the wine and cook until it has almost completely evaporated, 1 to 2 minutes. Remove the skillet from the heat and set aside.

In a medium saucepan, melt the butter over medium heat. Add the onions, increase the heat to medium-high, and cook, stirring often, for 2 to 3 minutes. Add the potatoes and celery leaves, and cook for another 2 to 3 minutes. Stir in the mushrooms and their juice. Cook, stirring frequently, for 3 to 4 minutes to blend the flavors. Add the stock and bring the mixture to a boil. Then reduce the heat and simmer, uncovered, for 1 hour, or until the mushrooms, onions, and potatoes are quite soft. Let cool slightly.

Transfer the soup, in batches, to a food processor or blender and pulse eight to ten times to puree, leaving small visible bits of mushroom. Rinse the saucepan, and return the soup to the pan. Heat to a simmer. Add more salt if necessary (it will likely require little, if any, because of the salted onions). Divide the soup among warmed soup bowls, drizzle with extra-virgin olive oil if desired, and serve immediately.

VARIATIONS

Substitute whatever good-quality mushrooms you have available; large ones will need the gill side cleaned.

LEFTOVERS

This soup is great reheated.

NUTRITION

In addition to being loaded with minerals, mushrooms contain beta-glucan, which helps stimulate the immune system. Shiitakes also contain all eight essential amino acids (rare for a plant food) as well as linoleic acid, an essential fatty acid.

ECONOMY $$

Yellow Split Pea and Wild Rice Soup

MAKES 8 SERVINGS

I love to make this heartwarming soup ahead (it freezes well) because the flavor develops over time. Simply reheat it slowly and enjoy on a cold wintry day. The sweet yellow split peas break apart as they cook, resulting in a creamy texture without the addition of dairy or fat. Smoky paprika yields a meaty flavor that replaces the traditional ham bone and counters the slightly sweet notes. You can find smoked paprika in the spice section of the supermarket. The greens, kale or Swiss chard in this case, are added at the end of the cooking time to preserve their color, texture, and nutrients.

2 tablespoons	olive oil
1	medium onion, chopped
2	medium carrots, chopped
2	celery stalks, chopped
1 pound	dried yellow split peas
1	garlic clove, minced
1 teaspoon	smoked or regular sweet paprika
5 cups	vegetable or chicken stock or reduced-sodium broth
2	medium potatoes, peeled and cut into ½-inch cubes
1	bay leaf
½ cup	wild rice
½ cup	barley
4 cups	chopped kale or Swiss chard leaves
	Salt and freshly ground black pepper

Heat the oil in a large saucepan over medium heat and add the onion, carrots, and celery. Cook, stirring occasionally, until softened, about 5 minutes. Add the split peas and garlic and cook, stirring, for 1 minute. Stir in the paprika and cook, stirring constantly, for 1 minute. Then add the stock, 5 cups water, the potatoes, and the bay leaf. Bring to a boil and then reduce the heat. Simmer, stirring occasionally, until the split peas have broken down and are creamy, about 25 minutes.

Add the wild rice and barley, and simmer until just tender, about 35 minutes. Stir in the kale or chard and cook for 1 minute more. Season the soup with salt and pepper to taste, ladle it into bowls, and serve hot.

SERVING SUGGESTIONS

Perfect as a first course, or serve as a main course with crusty bread and a salad.

VARIATIONS

• To add protein, top with crumbled crisp-cooked bacon or pancetta and serve with freshly grated Parmesan; or stir in some leftover shredded or cubed cooked ham, turkey, or chicken.
• For Indian flavors, substitute cumin and/or curry powder for the smoked paprika.
• Substitute spinach for the kale.

NUTRITION

Rich in protein, fiber, unrefined carbohydrate, B vitamins (especially folate), and minerals

(calcium, iron, and zinc), split peas deliver a nutritional wallop. This soup, spiked with whole grains and dark leafy greens, provides more than 50 percent of the recommended Daily Value (DV) for fiber and presents a complete protein package in one dish.

ECONOMY $

Legumes are inexpensive substitutes for meat; a 1-pound bag can make eight portions and generally costs less than $1, which helps us to enjoy a more economical plant-based diet.

Gigi Barbina Salad (page 146)

Veal Chop Saltimbocca: *pounded veal chop stuffed with prosciutto, parmesan, and sage* (page 158)

Harvest Stuffed Peppers (page 156)

Root Vegetable Gratin (page 170)

Gigi Broccoli Rabe (page 168)

Gigi Affogato (page 188)

Just Salad Immunity Bowl

MAKES 4 SERVINGS

*I signed on as the chef/partner for Just Salad shortly after the founders and principals,
Nick Kenner and Rob Crespi, raised the money to open the first Just Salad store in New York City.
My task was to develop, design, and implement delicious, health-balanced dressings, toppings,
and salads using fresh ingredients in a fast food venue. A tall order! The Immunity Bowl was
my jumping-off point. It offers great flavors, colors, and textures, and ingredients that
support the immune system and contain loads of antioxidants. It's a bestseller.
Earlier this year we opened our fifth Manhattan location.*

*Just Salads are designed to be one-bowl meals. The portion sizes can
be scaled back to be an appetizer or side-dish portion.*

1½ cups	roasted diced butternut squash (recipe follows)
1⅓ cups	cooked wheat berries (recipe follows)
12 cups	mesclun (about 1 pound) (mixed baby greens)
1⅓ cups	diced peeled cucumbers
¾ cup	dried cranberries

¾ cup	Gigi Lemon Vinaigrette (page 277)
12 ounces	roasted marinated salmon (recipe follows)

In a large mixing bowl, toss all the ingredients except the salmon with the lemon vinaigrette. Divide the salad among four serving plates, and top with the flaked salmon. Serve immediately.

VARIATIONS

• Top the salad with a small (3-ounce) pan-seared piece of salmon fillet instead of the roasted salmon.

• Substitute golden raisins, pomegranate seeds, or dried cherries or blueberries for the cranberries.

• Add roasted mushrooms and/or asparagus.

A mix of omega-3-rich protein, whole grains, and antioxidant-rich vegetables and dried fruit. Loaded with vitamins, minerals, fiber, phytochemicals, and *flavor*.

Pan-seared or oven-roasted chicken breast can add protein and is less expensive than salmon.

Roasted Butternut Squash

1	small butternut squash
1 tablespoon	olive oil
	Salt and freshly ground black pepper

Preheat the oven to 400°F.

Peel and halve the butternut squash, and remove the seeds. Cut the halves into ½-inch pieces and transfer them to a bowl. Drizzle the olive oil over the squash, season with salt and pepper, and toss to mix. Spread the squash in a single layer on a baking sheet, and roast until tender and golden on the edges, about 20 minutes. Let cool before adding to the salad.

Roasted Marinated Salmon

1½ tablespoons	olive oil
1 tablespoon	tamari or soy sauce
1 teaspoon	toasted sesame oil
One	1-pound salmon fillet (in one or two pieces)
	Salt and freshly ground black pepper

In a medium bowl, combine the olive oil, tamari, and sesame oil. Place the salmon in the bowl and turn the fillet(s) to coat evenly. Marinate, covered and refrigerated, for at least 15 minutes and up to 24 hours. Preheat the oven to 425°F.

Place the salmon, skin side down, on a baking sheet, and season it with salt and pepper. Roast until just cooked through, about 12 minutes. Let cool. Lift the flesh from the skin and discard the skin. Using your hands, flake the meat into large chunks.

Wheat Berries

> 1 cup   wheat berries
> ½ teaspoon   salt

Place the wheat berries and the salt in a small saucepan, and add 2 cups water. Bring to a boil. Then reduce the heat, cover the pan, and simmer until the wheat berries are tender (they will still be chewy), about 1¼ hours. (Alternatively, combine the ingredients in a pressure cooker and cook on high heat, adjusting to maintain the pressure, for 45 minutes.) Let the wheat berries cool before adding to the salad.

Gigi Barbina Salad

MAKES 4 SERVINGS

The Barbina is the most popular salad at Gigi Trattoria. Almost every ingredient is purchased locally, including baby greens from Sky Farm and Coach Farm goat cheese. We follow the seasons for the choice of ingredients (see the variations opposite). The vegetables are always roasted to heighten their natural sweetness and concentrate their flavors. (All the prep work can be done in advance; toss the salad with the vinaigrette just before serving.) Our generous portions encourage guests to enjoy this salad as a main dish or to split one as an appetizer.

⅓ cup	crushed walnuts
4	medium beets (2 to 3 inches in diameter), preferably a mix of red and gold, stems trimmed to 1 inch
10 ounces	mixed seasonal mushrooms
2 tablespoons	olive oil
	Salt and freshly ground black pepper
3 cups	diced peeled butternut squash
12 cups	mesclun (16 ounces) (mixed baby greens)
⅓ to ½ cup	Gigi Sherry-Shallot Vinaigrette (page 276)
4 ounces	goat cheese, crumbled, at room temperature

Preheat the oven to 375°F.

In a small, heavy, dry skillet, toast the walnuts over medium heat, stirring once or twice, until fragrant and slightly browned, 3 to 4 minutes. Set aside.

Wrap the beets tightly in aluminum foil (red and gold separately) and roast them in the middle of the oven until fork-tender, 45 to 60 minutes, depending on their size. Let the beets rest in the foil for 15 minutes. Then carefully open the foil, letting any residual steam escape, and transfer the beets to a cutting board. With a small sharp knife, cut off the stems and peel the beets. Cut the beets into "rustic" bite-size pieces. Reserve yellow and red beet pieces separately.

Increase the oven temperature to 450°F.

Using a moist kitchen or paper towel, wipe the mushrooms clean; remove any tough portion of the stems. Halve or quarter any large mushrooms. Place the mushrooms in a single layer in a small baking dish. Drizzle with 1 tablespoon of the olive oil, season with salt and pepper to taste, and toss to combine. Roast for 10 to 12 minutes, until the juices are nearly evaporated and the edges of the mushrooms are beginning to brown. Remove the dish from the oven and turn the mushrooms with a spatula. Continue roasting until the mushrooms are uniformly browned and all the liquid has evaporated, 5 to 7 minutes longer. Set aside to cool.

While the mushrooms are roasting, place the butternut squash in a baking pan that is just large enough to hold it in one layer.

Drizzle with the remaining 1 tablespoon olive oil, season with salt, and toss to combine. Roast until the squash can be pierced easily and is lightly browned, 15 to 20 minutes. Set aside to cool.

Divide the beets, butternut squash, and mushrooms among four salad plates. In a large mixing bowl, combine the greens with the vinaigrette, and toss to combine. Place a neat mound of the salad in the center of the vegetables. Scatter the goat cheese over the salads, and sprinkle with the toasted walnuts. Serve immediately.

VARIATIONS

- *Fall/winter:* Add pomegranate seeds and/or substitute roasted sweet potatoes for the butternut squash.
- *Spring:* Substitute roasted snap or snow peas or asparagus for the butternut squash.
- *Summer:* Enjoy roasted green or wax beans in place of the butternut squash.
- Use your favorite grated or crumbled cheese instead of the goat cheese.

NUTRITION

The naturally vibrant colors tell you all you need to know: an antioxidant powerhouse.

ECONOMY $$

LEFTOVERS

Dress only as much salad as you need and enjoy the rest the next day.

Celery Root Salad

MAKES 8 SERVINGS

This classic céleri rémoulade *is a refreshing counterpoint to warm fall side dishes. I love the crisp texture of the apple when combined with the celery root and the creamy herb dressing. We purchase our celery root from nearby Migliorelli Farm. Ken Migliorelli grows one of the most diverse samplings of vegetables here in the Hudson Valley.*

⅓ cup	walnut halves
	Salt
½ cup	mayonnaise, reduced-fat mayonnaise, or sour cream
2 tablespoons	Dijon mustard
2 tablespoons	fresh lemon juice
2 tablespoons	finely chopped shallots
2 tablespoons	finely chopped cornichons
1 tablespoon	chopped fresh tarragon
½	green apple, peeled, cored, and julienned
1½ pounds	celery root (about 1 medium)
	Freshly ground black pepper

In a small, heavy, dry skillet, toast the walnut halves over medium heat, stirring occasionally, until fragrant and golden brown, 3 to 5 minutes. Immediately transfer the walnuts to a plate to stop the cooking, and season them with salt to taste.

In a medium bowl, whisk together the mayonnaise, mustard, lemon juice, shallots, cornichons, and tarragon until well combined. Fold in the apple.

Celery root's knobby exterior can present a challenge to peel. To create a flat, stable surface, trim off enough of the stringy root end to expose the smooth, cream-colored interior. Peel away the remaining outside of the celery root. Stand the root on its trimmed end and cut it into ¼-inch-thick slices, and then cut those into thin matchsticks; or coarsely grate the root on a box grater. Fold the celery root into the mayonnaise mixture, and season with salt and pepper. Spoon the salad into a serving bowl, and top with the toasted walnuts.

For lunch, spoon the salad onto a bed of lettuce as part of a composed salad with boiled new potatoes and green beans.

VARIATIONS

- To add protein, stir in chopped smoked salmon and chopped fresh dill.
- Fold in chopped peppery arugula or a few handfuls of thinly sliced Napa cabbage.

NUTRITION

Long underestimated as a nutrition powerhouse, celery root is packed with phytochemicals (naturally occurring "protectors" in plants) such as phthalides and the flavenoids quercetin, apigenin, and luteolin. Big words, big flavors. Together they provide antioxidant and anti-inflammatory protection.

ECONOMY $

This vegetable may be ugly, knotty, and gnarled, but it sure is tasty, economical, and versatile. A pound and a half of celery root, at approximately $1.50 a pound, can make a soup, puree, or salad that serves eight.

Mixed-Grain Risotto with Bok Choy, Radicchio, and Mushrooms

MAKES 6 TO 8 SERVINGS

*Why not serve a bit of creamy whole-grain goodness as a main course or side dish?
Whole grains are toasty and delicious and make for a satisfying "risotto." This recipe
can be made in any season by substituting the vegetables of the harvest.*

2 tablespoons	olive oil
⅓ cup	diced onion
3 cups	thinly sliced shiitake mushroom caps (about 8 ounces)
2	heads baby bok choy, halved, cored, and thinly sliced
1	small head radicchio, halved, cored, and thinly sliced
½ cup	pearl barley
½ cup	brown rice
½ cup	wild rice
¼ cup	dry white wine
6 cups	chicken or vegetable stock or reduced-sodium broth
½ cup	freshly grated Grana Padano or Parmesan cheese
3 tablespoons	chopped fresh flat-leaf parsley
	Salt and freshly ground black pepper

Heat the olive oil in a medium saucepan over medium-high heat. Add the onion and cook, stirring, until softened, 2 to 3 minutes. Add the mushrooms and cook, stirring often, until lightly browned, about 5 minutes. Stir in the bok choy and half of the radicchio, and cook, stirring occasionally, until the vegetables are aromatic and softened, about 5 minutes. Add the barley and both rices, and cook for another 2 minutes.

Pour in the wine and cook until the liquid is reduced to about a tablespoon, about 1 minute. Add the stock, partially cover the pan, and cook, stirring occasionally, until the risotto is thick and slightly soupy and the grains are tender, 50 to 55 minutes. During the last 5 minutes of cooking, stir in the remaining radicchio.

Remove the pan from the heat, stir in the Grana Padano and parsley, and season with salt and pepper to taste. Serve immediately.

- Instead of the barley and rices, use 1½ cups of a whole-grain mix. Excellent-quality whole-grain mixes are readily available in supermarkets and gourmet stores.
- Add bite-size pieces of chicken, pork, sausage, or beef. If the meat is raw, sear it after you cook the mushrooms; if cooked, add it with the bok choy and radicchio.
- *Spring*: Substitute peas and asparagus segments for the radicchio and bok choy, adding them, along with some watercress or spinach leaves, during the last 5 minutes of cooking the rice.
- *Summer*: Substitute zucchini and/or yellow squash, tomatoes, and fresh basil for the radicchio, bok choy, and mushrooms. Sauté separately until tender but still firm, and stir in during the last 5 minutes of cooking.
- *Winter*: Add cubed harvest squash (acorn, butternut, or other), halved Brussels sprouts, or dried fruit such as chopped apricots, golden raisins, cranberries, or cherries to the mixture when you add the bok choy.

LEFTOVERS

To make whole-grain risotto cakes, chill the risotto until it is firm, shape it into patties, and pan-fry in a skillet with a bit of olive oil.

NUTRITION

Whole grains contain the germ, the nutrient-rich core of the grain. Unlike refined grains, in which the germ has been discarded, whole grains are rich in vitamins (E, thiamin, folate, B_6), minerals (zinc, iron, magnesium, phosphorus, and potassium), and protective phytochemicals.

Butternut, Apple, and Fontina Risotto with Toasted Rosemary Walnuts

MAKES 4 ENTRÉE OR 6 APPETIZER SERVINGS

How could risotto be more Hudson Valley Mediterranean? By adding fall apples, butternut squash, and fine Italian cheeses (Fontina and Parmigiano-Reggiano). The toasted rosemary walnuts add nutty goodness plus a little crunch.

Toasted rosemary walnuts

1 tablespoon	olive oil
2 teaspoons	chopped fresh rosemary
⅓ cup	lightly crushed walnuts
	Salt

Risotto

2 quarts	chicken or vegetable stock or reduced-sodium broth
2 tablespoons	olive oil
2 tablespoons	unsalted butter
1	small onion, minced
2 cups	Carnaroli rice
½ cup	dry white wine
1½ cups	diced peeled butternut squash (small dice)
1 cup	finely diced peeled apple
1 cup	diced Fontina cheese

⅓ cup	freshly grated Grana Padano or Parmesan cheese
	Salt

To prepare the toasted rosemary walnuts, heat the olive oil in a small skillet over medium heat. Add the rosemary and walnuts and cook, tossing or stirring, until the nuts smell toasty, 1 to 2 minutes. Lightly season the walnuts with salt. Set aside in the skillet.

To make the risotto, bring the stock to a simmer in a medium saucepan over medium heat. Keep it at a low simmer.

Heat the olive oil and 1 tablespoon of the butter in a heavy 5- or 6-quart saucepan over medium heat. Add the onion and cook, stirring, until very soft but not browned, about 2 minutes. Using a wooden spoon, stir the rice into the onions. "Toast" the rice, stirring constantly, until it looks chalky and you can see a white dot in the center of each grain. Stir in the wine. When the rice has absorbed the liquid, add the butternut squash and 2 cups of the simmering stock. Stir until the liquid is almost completely absorbed. Continue adding stock, ½ cup at a time, stirring after each addition and allowing the rice to absorb the liquid before adding more. This should take 15 to 17 minutes altogether.

Add the apple and taste a grain of rice. It should have a slight resistance to the bite. If it seems too hard, add a little more stock and continue cooking for another 1 to 2 minutes. Remove the pan from the heat. Place the skillet containing the walnuts on medium heat just to warm them.

Stir the Fontina, Grana Padano, and remaining 1 tablespoon butter into the risotto. Season with salt to taste. Whip with the wooden spoon to bring out the creaminess of the rice and to incorporate all the ingredients. Divide the risotto among serving plates, and top each serving with a spoonful of the toasted rosemary walnuts.

VARIATIONS

Risotto lends itself to innumerable seasonal preparations. Use last night's veggies to prepare tonight's dinner.

LEFTOVERS

Pack leftover risotto into a parchment paper–lined pan so it is about 2 inches thick. Place a sheet of parchment paper on top and chill for at least 4 hours or overnight. Cut 2- or 4-inch disks (appetizer or side-dish size) of risotto and cook them over medium heat in a bit of olive oil or butter in a nonstick pan until golden, crispy, and heated through.

NUTRITION

The combination of apples, butternut squash, walnuts, and rosemary provides a plethora of nutrients and phytochemicals.

ECONOMY $

Risotto is a rich and satisfying yet economical meal.

Baked Macaroni and Cheese with Cauliflower and Chard

MAKES 6 ENTRÉE OR 8 SIDE SERVINGS

With an "enlightened" béchamel cheese sauce and spiked with vegetables, this is a delicious and healthier version of the American classic. The cauliflower melts as it cooks, leaving a creamy texture, and the chard adds flavor, color, and nutrients.

	Kosher salt
8 ounces	dried short pasta, such as fusilli, elbows, campanelle, or cavatappi
Small florets	cut from about 1 pound cauliflower
6 cups	Enlightened Béchamel (page 281)
1½ cups	shredded local sharp cheddar cheese
½ cup	shredded smoked cheddar (2 ounces) or smoked Gouda cheese
2 cups	chopped cooked green Swiss chard (see page 264), or 2 cups frozen chard, thawed and drained
⅓ cup	unseasoned dried bread crumbs (homemade or packaged)
⅓ cup	freshly grated Grana Padano or Parmesan cheese

Preheat the oven to 375°F. Butter a 12- to 14-inch round or a 13 x 9-inch rectangular baking dish.

Bring a large pot of water to a boil and season it with kosher salt, add the pasta and cook until al dente, following the package directions (usually 8 to 12 minutes), adding the cauliflower florets during the last 3 minutes of cooking. Drain the pasta and cauliflower, and transfer to a large bowl.

Pour the béchamel into the bowl, add the shredded cheeses and chard, and stir to combine. Transfer the mixture to the prepared baking dish. In a small bowl, combine the bread crumbs and the Grana Padano. Scatter the bread-crumb mixture evenly over the macaroni, and bake until golden and bubbly, about 25 minutes. Serve immediately.

- Substitute 2 cups peas or other cooked vegetables, such as quartered Brussels sprouts, for the chard.
- Substitute whatever cheese suits you, including reduced-fat, but do not use fat-free cheese, because it won't melt.
- Add bite-size pieces of cooked chicken.
- Mix Dijon or spicy mustard into the béchamel.

LEFTOVERS

Great reheated in a microwave.

NUTRITION

This dish is lower in fat than the classic mac 'n' cheese. Cauliflower and chard are both members of the cancer-fighting brassica family of vegetables.

ECONOMY $$

Harvest Stuffed Peppers

MAKES 4 ENTRÉE OR 8 APPETIZER SERVINGS

Peppers are abundant at summer's end in the Hudson Valley, which allows me to put my foot down: I make this dish only when I can get fresh-picked peppers. If they do not come from my garden, then I'll select some from a local grower. Wherever you live, think about making peppers a star component of the meal when they're newly harvested. The aroma, flavor, and texture is vastly different from the typical supermarket variety; those huge bell peppers can serve as a holding vessel for the stuffing but don't really contribute to the flavor of the dish. Small to medium farm-fresh peppers tend to have much thinner walls. This means the pepper is cooked, wilted and fork-ready, when the stuffing is still moist and the top golden-crusted. I like a North African style of spice mix and a whole-grain stuffing, with or without pork sausage, but this dish is very versatile (see the variations opposite).

9	medium green bell peppers (or yellow, red, or a mixture)
8 ounces	sausage, crumbled
1 tablespoon	olive oil
1	small onion, diced
½ teaspoon	ground cumin
¼ teaspoon	garam masala (see Note, page 137)
¼ teaspoon	ground cinnamon
⅓ cup	dried currants or cranberries
¼ cup	chopped dried apricots
¼ cup	white wine or water
4 cups	cooked wild rice or whole-grain rice blend
4 ounces	soft goat cheese, crumbled
	Salt and freshly ground black pepper
3 tablespoons	freshly grated Grana Padano or Parmesan cheese

Preheat the oven to 375°F. Lightly oil a baking dish that is just large enough to hold 8 peppers in a single layer.

Remove the stem and slice the top off of each bell pepper. Remove and discard the seeds. Set 8 of the peppers aside. Chop the remaining pepper along with the tops of the others. Reserve the whole and chopped peppers separately.

Place the sausage and the olive oil in a medium nonstick skillet and cook over medium-high heat until lightly browned, 4 to 5 minutes. Add the onion, chopped peppers, and spices and cook, stirring often, until the onion is soft, about 3 minutes. Add the dried fruit and cook for 1 minute. Then stir in the white wine or water. Transfer the mixture to a large bowl and stir in the cooked rice. Fold in the goat cheese, and season with salt and pepper to taste. Stuff the peppers with the filling, and place them in the prepared baking dish. Cover with aluminum foil, using enough foil to create a tent, so that the edges can be sealed but the top does not touch the tops of the peppers. Bake for 40 minutes.

Remove the foil and sprinkle the tops of the peppers with the Grana Padano. Bake for 10 minutes more, or until the tops are lightly browned and the peppers are tender. Serve immediately.

VARIATIONS

- Substitute ground beef or lamb for the sausage.
- Use other cooked whole grains, such as brown rice, barley, bulgur, or quinoa, in place of the wild rice.
- Add mushrooms, peas, or leftover cooked vegetables.
- *Vegetarian*: Omit the sausage and add 3 cups sliced mushrooms (about 10 ounces) to the vegetables.
- *Italian-style stuffed peppers*: Omit the spices and dried fruit, and add zucchini, diced tomato, and fresh oregano and basil. Substitute Parmesan, mozzarella, or ricotta for the goat cheese. Top with tomato sauce and sprinkle with Parmesan during the last 10 minutes of cooking.
- *Mexican*: Substitute poblano peppers for the bell peppers, chile powder for the garam marsala, and queso blanco for the goat cheese.

LEFTOVERS

The peppers reheat well. The filling can also stuff mushrooms and poultry, such as Cornish hens.

NUTRITION

Wild rice provides ample folate (and other B vitamins), vitamin E, iron, vitamin K, fiber, and protein. It has more protein, four times as much vitamin E, and six times as much folate as brown rice.

Peppers are an excellent source of vitamins A and C, both powerful antioxidants. They are also a very good source of potassium. If you delay harvesting peppers on the plant until they mature from green to red (or purple), they'll have ten times the vitamin A and double the vitamin C.

ECONOMY $$

Wild rice typically costs more than other varieties. Its cooking time is very similar to brown rice, so to economize, mix them or use all brown rice.

Veal Chop Saltimbocca

Pounded Veal Chop Stuffed with Prosciutto, Parmesan, and Sage

MAKES 4 TO 6 SERVINGS

This is chef Wilson Costa's version of the Roman classic. Rather than using veal cutlets, he leaves the bone on the chop, which makes for a dramatic presentation. Our guests enjoyed this dish during our 2008–2009 New Year's celebration and have been requesting it ever since. We serve it with a pan sauce (see variations), polenta or mashed potatoes and roasted vegetables in the winter. In the spring sautéed asparagus and ramps or Spring Trifolati (page 48) works well. Broccoli rabe (see page 168) works year-round.

Four	10-ounce veal chops, bones cleaned
	Salt and freshly ground black pepper
8 ounces	thinly sliced prosciutto
4 ounces	shaved Parmesan cheese
24	fresh sage leaves
2 tablespoons	unsalted butter, cut into small cubes

Preheat the oven to 325°F.

Using a kitchen mallet, pound the meat on the veal chops between two large pieces of plastic wrap until each chop is about 5 or 6 inches in diameter and about ¼ inch thick. Lightly season the chops with salt and pepper, and arrange a slightly overlapping layer of prosciutto over the meat. Top the prosciutto with a layer of Parmesan shavings and 6 sage leaves per chop. Pick up the far outer edge of the meat (opposite the bone) and fold it ¼ inch toward the bone. Then take the left side (closest to the bone) and fold it halfway in. Pull in the right side so that it overlaps and creates a long cylinder. Stand the bone up and tie the meat together with kitchen string. Place the veal chops in a roasting pan that is just large enough to hold them in one layer, season with salt and pepper, and dot with the butter. Roast, basting often with the pan juices, until the veal is just cooked and lightly browned, 20 to 25 minutes. (Veal is very lean, so be careful not to overcook it.)

Serve immediately, presenting the chops whole or in ½-inch-thick slices draped over the bone.

VARIATIONS

- *Optional sauce:* For a quick pan sauce, transfer the veal chops to a platter and tent with foil to keep warm. Stir some julienned shallots into the roasting pan and roast at 325°F for 5 minutes. Add a splash of white wine, a splash of lemon juice, and some veal stock, stirring to deglaze the flavorful bits on the bottom of the pan. Return the pan to the oven and cook until the sauce is reduced slightly, 4 to 5 minutes. Pour the pan sauce over the veal.
- Substitute coppa or salami for the prosciutto.

NUTRITION

Veal is a very lean protein source, and the chop can be replaced by another lean and more economical option: pork.

ECONOMY $$$

Harvest Pork Chops

MAKES 4 SERVINGS

This recipe is prepared with apple butter, which lends a concentrated flavor and a creamy finish to the sauce. Fruit butters, such as apple, pear, and pumpkin, are fat-free spreads that offer the intense flavor of the fruit. I select mine from the shelves of Gigi Market, where we retail local fruit butters from Grey Mouse Farm and Beth's Farm Kitchen. They can be purchased in some supermarkets and gourmet stores.

1 tablespoon	olive oil
4	pork chops (8 ounces each, 1½ to 2 inches thick), trimmed of fat
	Salt and freshly ground black pepper
½ cup	apple butter
½ cup	chicken stock or reduced-sodium broth
2 tablespoons	Dijon mustard
2	apples, peeled, cored, and quartered
1	medium onion, thinly sliced
2 tablespoons	white wine vinegar

Heat the olive oil in a large nonstick skillet over medium-high heat. Season the pork chops with salt and pepper, and sauté until they are browned, 3 to 4 minutes per side. Transfer the chops to a plate. Do not wash the skillet.

In a small bowl, whisk together the apple butter, stock, and mustard. Set aside.

Add the apple quarters and onion slices to the skillet used to brown the chops. Cook, tossing or stirring, until golden and softened, 5 to 7 minutes. Deglaze the skillet with the vinegar. When the vinegar cooks off, pour in the apple butter mixture, and stir gently to blend. Return the pork chops and any released juices to the skillet. Cover and simmer for 8 to 10 minutes, until the chops are just slightly pink in the center.

To serve, place a chop on each plate and top with a generous spoonful of the apple sauce.

Enjoy with mashed potatoes, Herb Spaetzle (page 249), polenta, or roasted potatoes or vegetables. A glass of slightly spicy Riesling would round out the meal.

• Substitute pears and pear butter for the apples and apple butter.
• Use boneless chicken breasts or thighs instead of the pork.

The trimmed pork chops are relatively lean, and pork is one of the best sources of the B vitamin thiamin. Apples are a good source of fiber and provide abundant amounts of quercetin, a powerful antioxidant that also has anti-inflammatory properties.

This dish is best enjoyed immediately, but you can reheat it on the stovetop or in a microwave.

Northwind Farms Autumn Brasato

MAKES 4 SERVINGS

A brasato is a stew of meat and vegetables that is enjoyed during the chilly months in Italy. This autumn-spiced stew will take the chill out of the raw days. During the late fall and early winter Northwind Farms no longer has the poussin (baby chicken) that I enjoy throughout the rest of the year, but they do have larger roasters that are perfect for braising.

2 tablespoons	olive oil
1 tablespoon	unsalted butter
One	5- to 6-pound roasting chicken, cut into 8 pieces
	Salt and freshly ground black pepper
2 ounces	pancetta or bacon, diced
3	shallots, chopped
2	celery stalks, chopped
1	garlic clove, crushed
1 tablespoon	chopped fresh flat-leaf parsley
½ cup	dry white wine
¼ teaspoon	ground cinnamon
¼ teaspoon	ground cloves
Up to 5 cups	chicken stock or reduced-sodium broth
⅓ cup	half-and-half

Heat the oil and butter in a large Dutch oven or braising pan over medium-high heat. Season the chicken pieces with salt and pepper, and add them to the hot pan. Sear the chicken until the pieces are evenly browned, about 8 minutes; then transfer them to a plate. Drain most of the fat from the pan, add the pancetta, and return the pan to medium heat. Cook, stirring occasionally, until the fat is rendered, 2 to 3 minutes. Then add the shallots, celery, garlic, and parsley. Cook, stirring often, until the vegetables soften, about 5 minutes. Add the wine, cinnamon, and cloves, stirring to deglaze the bottom of the pan. When the wine is almost completely reduced, return the browned chicken to the pan along with any released juices. Add just enough of the chicken stock to cover the chicken. Bring the mixture to a boil, reduce the heat, and simmer, uncovered, until the chicken is cooked and can be pulled easily from the bone, and the pan juices have reduced, about 1¼ hours.

Transfer the chicken to a plate and cover loosely with foil to keep warm. Puree the pan juices until smooth with a handheld blender, or in a blender or food processor. Stir in the half-and-half, and add salt and pepper as needed. Simmer for 5 minutes, or until warmed through. Serve piping hot over the chicken.

SERVING SUGGESTIONS

Serve the chicken over rice, couscous, mashed potatoes, or polenta (Maple Pumpkin Polenta, page 176, is perfect for this dish), and smother with the sauce.

VARIATIONS

- Omit the half-and-half and thicken the sauce with a teaspoon or two of cornstarch mixed with water stirred in before adding the chicken and stock to the pan.
- Add dried fruit or diced fresh apples or pears when simmering the pureed sauce.
- Mix in chopped cooking greens (kale, collards, spinach, or chard) when simmering the pureed sauce.

LEFTOVERS

Great reheated the next day.

NUTRITION

Turn this high-protein dish into a complete balanced meal by serving it over whole grains such as polenta or whole grain couscous.

ECONOMY $$

Mashed Potato-Rutabaga-Turnip Gratin

MAKES 8 SERVINGS

*One of my smaller life goals is to get more people turned on to the culinary
pleasures of rutabagas and turnips. This dish recently did the trick with a friend who
enjoyed the merits of a day of recipe testing at my home. Thirty-something
years of hating both vegetables went out the window...*

1	small rutabaga (12 ounces), peeled and cut into large dice
3	medium potatoes (1¼ pounds), peeled and quartered
2	medium-large turnips (12 ounces), peeled and quartered
¾ cup	freshly grated Grana Padano or Parmesan cheese
2 tablespoons	olive oil
¾ teaspoon	salt
1 teaspoon	chopped fresh thyme leaves
¼ teaspoon	ground nutmeg
¼ teaspoon	cayenne pepper

Bring a large pot of salted water to a boil. Add the rutabaga and cook for 20 minutes. Add the potatoes and turnips and cook for another 20 to 25 minutes, until all the vegetables are easily pierced with the tip of a paring knife.

While the vegetables are cooking, preheat the oven to 400°F and grease a 2-quart casserole dish with butter or cooking spray.

Drain the vegetables, and while they are still hot, carefully press them through a ricer into a large bowl (the gratin is "fluffy" when riced). Add ½ cup of the Grana Padano (leaving enough to dust the top) and all the remaining ingredients; stir to incorporate. Transfer the mixture to the prepared casserole. Sprinkle the top with the remaining ¼ cup Grana Padano, and bake until heated through and the top is browned, about 20 minutes. Serve hot.

SERVING SUGGESTIONS

Serve immediately; or prepare the casserole in advance, refrigerate it, and then bake it 1 hour before the meal.

LEFTOVERS

This dish reheats well in the microwave.

NUTRITION

Potatoes are rich in vitamin C and have more potassium per serving than a banana. Turnips and rutabagas are members of the cancer-fighting Cruciferae family of vegetables.

ECONOMY $

Rosemary-Roasted Brussels Sprouts, Baby Carrots, and Cipollini Onions

MAKES 6 SERVINGS

These oven-caramelized fall vegetables will convert die-hard Brussels sprout foes into instant supporters. This easy side dish can be made in advance and offers a colorful and delicious preparation for the holiday table or for autumn and winter meals.

1 pound	seasonal baby carrots, scrubbed and trimmed (see Note)
1 pound	Brussels sprouts, ends trimmed, halved
6	cipollini onions, peeled and halved
3	garlic cloves, crushed
2	rosemary sprigs
2 tablespoons	olive oil
	Salt and freshly ground black pepper

Note: If you cannot find seasonal baby carrots, substitute 3 medium carrots, peeled and then sliced on the diagonal into ¼-inch-thick pieces. Do not substitute the turned carrots sometimes marketed as "baby carrots" in the supermarket— they are tough and woody.

Preheat the oven to 375°F.

Combine the carrots, Brussels sprouts, onions, garlic, rosemary, and olive oil on a rimmed baking sheet that is large enough to hold them in a single layer. Stir to combine and to coat the vegetables with the oil. Roast in the upper third of the oven, stirring once halfway through the roasting, until the vegetables are golden and tender, about 30 minutes. Use the tip of a sharp paring knife to test the doneness of the base of a Brussels sprout and the thickest point in a carrot; it should insert easily. If the vegetables are well browned but not tender enough, tent them with foil and continue cooking.

Season the vegetables with salt and pepper as soon as they come out of the oven. Discard the rosemary sprigs, and enjoy hot or at room temperature.

- Substitute 3 medium red or white onions cut into 8 wedges each (root end left intact) for the cipollini onions.
- Add chopped roasted chestnuts and/or bits of crisp-cooked pancetta or bacon.
- When they're hot out of the oven, glaze the roasted vegetables with some maple syrup spiked with cayenne.

LEFTOVERS

Great reheated in the microwave or in the oven at low temperature.

NUTRITION

Brussels sprouts belong in the protective Cruciferae vegetable family (which includes broccoli, cabbage, cauliflower, kale, mustard greens, and so on). For optimal health, we should eat a serving per day of one of these tasty and versatile vegetables.

ECONOMY $

Gigi Broccoli Rabe

MAKES 4 TO 6 SERVINGS

This is an every-season side dish at Gigi Trattoria. We also use this as the base for our broccoli rabe pesto, to fill stuffed pasta, and to top our popular Skizza Rustica (page 29).

	Kosher salt
2 pounds	broccoli rabe, trimmed, tough stalks peeled
¼ cup	extra-virgin olive oil, plus additional for drizzling
2 or 3	garlic cloves, thinly sliced
¼ to ½	jalapeño pepper, seeded and minced, or ½ teaspoon red pepper flakes
	Salt and freshly ground black pepper
1	lemon, cut into 4 to 6 wedges

Bring 3 quarts of water to a boil and season it generously with kosher salt. While the water is heating, fill a large bowl with ice and water.

Cook the broccoli rabe in the boiling water for about 5 minutes, until tender. Drain, and transfer it to the bowl of ice water to stop the cooking and keep the color bright. Drain, and pat dry. (The broccoli rabe can be cooked to this point up to 2 days in advance. Store it in a plastic storage bag in the refrigerator.)

Heat the olive oil in a large heavy skillet over moderately high heat. Add the garlic and jalapeño or red pepper flakes, and sauté, stirring, until fragrant, 30 to 45 seconds. When the garlic is just beginning to brown, add the broccoli rabe and sauté, tossing or turning it with tongs, until tender, about 2 minutes. Season with salt and pepper to taste, and serve with the lemon wedges alongside.

SERVING SUGGESTIONS

Try the broccoli rabe with a drizzle of olive oil, topped with shaved or grated Parmesan, with grilled sausages or over polenta.

VARIATIONS

• Add 2 or 3 anchovy fillets when sautéing the garlic. Mash them into a puree with the back of a wooden spoon.

- Top with toasted chopped or sliced almonds or toasted pine nuts or shavings of Parmesan.
- Puree the broccoli rabe with olive oil, Parmesan, pine nuts, salt, and pepper to make a broccoli rabe pesto. Serve it tossed with pasta, spread on a sandwich, or stirred into a dip.

LEFTOVERS

- Enjoy warmed or at room temperature.
- Chop and stir into risotto or pasta.
- Add to an omelet, frittata, or soup.

NUTRITION

Broccoli rabe contains flavenoids, sulforaphane, and indoles, all disease fighters. It is also rich in vitamins A and C.

ECONOMY $$

Root Vegetable Gratin

MAKES 8 TO 10 SERVINGS

I started preparing this dish for guests about ten years ago, and now I cannot entertain in the fall or winter without a request for it. I'm happy to comply. Root Vegetable Gratin is now a selection on the holiday and winter catering menus at Gigi Market.

1 tablespoon	unsalted butter, at room temperature
6 cups	Classic Béchamel (page 281)
2	small smoked chiles, such as anchos or dried smoked jalapeños
3	medium russet potatoes (about 3 pounds), peeled and sliced into ⅛-inch-thick rounds
1½ cups	fresh or canned roasted red bell peppers, cut into strips
	Salt and freshly ground black pepper
4 cups	shredded sharp cheddar cheese
1	medium sweet potato (8 ounces), peeled and sliced into ⅛-inch-thick rounds
1	small or ½ large rutabaga (about 12 ounces), peeled and sliced into ⅛-inch-thick rounds

Preheat the oven to 350°F. Grease a 12- to 14-inch round baking dish or a 13 x 9-inch rectangular baking dish with the butter.

Pour the béchamel into a saucepan and bring it to a simmer over low heat. Remove the pan from the heat, add the whole dried chiles, and steep for about 10 minutes. Remove and discard the chiles.

Arrange half of the russet potato slices in a single layer on the bottom of the prepared baking dish. Top with a third of the red pepper strips. Season with salt and pepper to taste. Spread 1½ cups of the béchamel evenly over the potatoes and red pepper strips. Sprinkle with 1 cup of the cheddar. Arrange the sweet potato slices on top, slightly overlapping, in a spiral pattern. Season with salt and pepper, and top with another third of the red pepper strips. Again top with 1½ cups béchamel followed by 1 cup cheddar. Add the slices of rutabaga, slightly overlapping in a spiral pattern, and strew with the remaining red pepper strips. Add

1½ cups béchamel followed by 1 cup cheddar. For the final layer, arrange the remaining slices of russet potato on top, slightly overlapping, in a spiral pattern. Season with salt and pepper. Spread the remaining 1½ cups béchamel and 1 cup cheddar on top.

Cover the dish with aluminum foil and bake for 1¼ hours. Remove the foil and bake until the top of the gratin is bubbly and nicely browned, about 20 minutes. A knife inserted in the center of the gratin should easily pierce the fully cooked, soft root vegetables. Serve piping hot.

SERVING SUGGESTION

This is great right out of the oven, but it's also good reheated the next day.

VARIATIONS

• To lighten this dish, use Enlightened Béchamel (page 281); or make a cornstarch/water slurry, stir it into chicken broth, and simmer until it achieves a béchamel-like consistency.

• Omit the chiles and/or roasted red bell pepper.
• Substitute turnips for the rutabaga.

NUTRITION

Roasted red pepper strips add flavor, color between the layers, and lots of vitamin C.

ECONOMY $$

Red Chard with Onions, Pancetta, and Raisins

This vegetable side dish can be prepared with red or green Swiss chard, collards, kale, or turnip greens. The slight bitterness of the greens is balanced by the sweetness of the onions and raisins, and it all contrasts well with the saltiness of the pancetta.

2 bunches	chard red Swiss (about 2 pounds)
3 tablespoons	olive oil
1	medium onion, thinly sliced
2 ounces	pancetta, diced (optional)
¼ cup	golden raisins
¼ cup	chicken stock, reduced-sodium broth, or water
	Salt and freshly ground black pepper

Separate the chard leaves from the stems. Rinse the stems and chop them into ½-inch pieces; set aside. Tear the leaves into large pieces, wash them thoroughly, and spin or pat dry; set aside.

Heat the olive oil in a large skillet over medium heat. Add the onion and pancetta and cook, stirring frequently, until the onion is quite soft and slightly browned, about 7 minutes. Add the chard stems and cook for 2 to 3 minutes. Stir in the raisins and cook for another 2 to 3 minutes. Add the chicken stock, cover the skillet, and simmer until the stems have softened, 5 to 7 minutes. Add the chard leaves, season lightly with salt and pepper, and stir to combine. Cover the skillet and braise for 3 to 4 minutes. When the chard leaves are wilted and most of the liquid has evaporated, it is done. Serve hot or at room temperature.

VARIATIONS

• Cook the onions slowly, over low heat, allowing them to express their sweetness.

• Substitute bacon for the pancetta.
• Add a pinch of smoked paprika for a hint of smokiness.

- Heat it up with some minced jalapeño or red pepper flakes.

LEFTOVERS

- The chard is great stirred into risotto or tossed with pasta.
- Add it to soups, stews, omelets, or frittatas.

NUTRITION

Chard is related to beets. It is off the charts in its content of vitamins A (beta- and alpha-carotene) and C, as well as potassium, lutein, and zeaxanthin.

ECONOMY $

Warm Fingerling Potato Salad with Gorgonzola Dolce and Grainy Mustard Sauce

MAKES 8 SERVINGS

RSK Farm in Saugerties provides us with the most amazing potatoes. My favorite varieties include their Corolas, Adirondack Blues, and fingerlings. This combination of young potatoes and sweet and pungent Gorgonzola can warm up any fall or winter evening. Gorgonzola dolce is a younger and milder version of aged Gorgonzola. It is soft and spreadable and adds ample flavor without being overwhelming.

⅓ cup	walnut halves
1¾ pounds	fingerling or baby Red Bliss potatoes, halved lengthwise
½ cup	farm-fresh sour cream (see Note)
2 tablespoons	grainy mustard
3 ounces	Gorgonzola dolce, crumbled
2 tablespoons	white wine vinegar
	Salt and freshly ground black pepper
3 cups	loosely packed baby arugula or baby spinach

Note: I realized that I had never tasted sour cream until I tried farm-fresh sour cream from Boice Brothers Dairy in Kingston, New York. Try to get the fresh stuff, if possible.

Toast the walnuts in a small skillet over medium heat until they are fragrant, 3 to 4 minutes, shaking the pan for even cooking. Set aside.

Bring a large pot of salted water to a boil. Add the potatoes and cook until tender, 15 to 20 minutes, depending on their size.

While the potatoes are cooking, prepare the dressing. In a large bowl, combine the sour cream, mustard, Gorgonzola, and vinegar. Stir, and season with salt and pepper to taste.

Drain the potatoes and transfer them to the bowl containing the dressing. Fold gently to combine, and add more salt and pepper if necessary. Add the arugula or spinach and fold the ingredients together again. Top with the walnuts, and serve.

Serve warm with roast duck, pork, chicken, or beef.

VARIATIONS

- Add cooked sausage, kielbasa, or chicken.
- Top with small bits of crisp-cooked pancetta or bacon.
- Fold in watercress (stems removed) in the spring.

LEFTOVERS

Best enjoyed immediately, but good for up to 2 days

NUTRITION

No doubt this is a bit on the rich side, but it has fewer calories and fat than a mayo-based potato salad. If you want to reduce the fat further, substitute low-fat sour cream.

ECONOMY $$

Maple Pumpkin Polenta

MAKES 4 SERVINGS

This is among the most popular side dishes at Gigi Trattoria during the fall and winter months. The addition of pumpkin and maple syrup adds a seasonal and festive hue to polenta. We buy ground cornmeal from Wild Hive Farm in nearby Clinton Corners, but any coarse-grain cornmeal can substitute. Enjoy the slightly sweet notes balanced by a little spice from the cayenne pepper.

1½ teaspoons	kosher salt
1 tablespoon	extra-virgin olive oil
1¼ cups	ground yellow cornmeal
1½ cups	pumpkin puree (fresh or 100-percent-natural canned pumpkin)
⅓ cup	pure maple syrup
¼ teaspoon	cayenne pepper
½ cup	freshly grated Grana Padano or Parmesan cheese
1 tablespoon	unsalted butter
	Salt and freshly ground black pepper, to taste

Bring 4 cups of water to a boil in a medium saucepan. Add the kosher salt and the olive oil, reduce the heat to a simmer, and gradually whisk in the cornmeal, a small amount at a time to prevent clumping. Reduce the heat to low and cook, stirring often, until the polenta is tender and is pulling away from the sides of the pan, about 25 minutes. Stir in the pumpkin puree, maple syrup, and cayenne, and cook for another minute or two. Then remove the pan from the heat and stir in the Grana Padano and the butter. Add salt and pepper, if needed. Serve warm.

SERVING SUGGESTION

This dish accompanies our braised lamb shank and autumn roasted vegetables (page 262) at Gigi Trattoria. Just about any meaty stew or braise would be a good accompaniment.

VARIATIONS

• Serve topped with stewed or braised vegetables or as a creamy bed for curried or stir-fried vegetables.

• Pour the hot polenta into a 13 x 9 x 2-inch baking dish and let it cool to room temperature;

then cover and refrigerate for at least 30 minutes. Cut the chilled polenta into squares or rounds using a 2-inch cookie cutter. Drizzle with olive oil, and grill or sear in a nonstick pan. Top with Wiltbank Farm Mushroom Ragù (page 131).

LEFTOVERS

It's difficult to reheat polenta to a creamy mash, so it's best to smooth it into a baking pan and make polenta fritters (see variation above).

NUTRITION

Polenta (cornmeal) is a whole grain. The pumpkin contributes enough beta-carotene to supply about 25 percent of your daily requirement of vitamin A.

ECONOMY $

A fairly economical and substantial side dish.

Gigi Gigandes

Giant White Beans with Rosemary

MAKES 8 TO 10 SERVINGS

Gigi customers often request this recipe, which is easy to prepare at home. We serve these soupy, creamy beans in crocks with bits of rosemary mixed in. After a long night at the restaurant, I often forgo the main dish and select all sides: these "meaty" beans, a bit of broccoli rabe (page 168), and some seasonal roasted vegetables (page 262).

1 pound	dried "gigandes," Italian Corona beans, or large dried lima beans
2	celery stalks, halved
1	carrot, halved
1	medium onion, halved
2 or 3	garlic cloves
3	bay leaves
2 tablespoons	extra-virgin olive oil
3	rosemary sprigs, leaves removed and stems discarded
¾ cup	freshly grated Grana Padano or Parmesan cheese
	Salt and freshly ground black pepper

Place the beans in a bowl and add cold water to cover by at least 2 inches. Soak for 12 to 14 hours.

Drain the beans, place them in a heavy-bottomed pot, and add water to cover by 4 inches. Add the celery, carrot, onion, garlic, and bay leaves, and bring to boil. Reduce the heat and simmer until the beans are tender, about 2 hours. Allow the beans to cool in their cooking liquid. Then drain, reserving ¾ cup of the cooking liquid.

When you're ready to serve the beans, heat the olive oil in a large skillet over medium-high heat. Add the rosemary and cook until fragrant, about 1 minute. Add the beans and the reserved cooking liquid. Cook, stirring often, until soupy and heated through, 5 minutes. Remove the skillet from the heat, add the Grana Padano, and toss to combine. Season with salt and pepper to taste, and serve.

Serve the beans as a side dish in small crocks, as we do at Gigi, or mix the beans into pasta dishes or soups. These beans are often served underneath our Northwind Farm baby roasted chicken.

VARIATIONS

- Prepare them "spaghetti western" style—see the BBQ Baked Gigandes on page 105.
- Puree into a great-tasting bean dip, or add broth and blend to turn into a soup.

NUTRITION

Beans are rich in B vitamins, especially folate, as well as magnesium, potassium, iron, and manganese. They're also a good source of fiber, carbs, and protein.

ECONOMY $

Beans are a tasty, economical, and filling combination of complex carbohydrates and protein.

LEFTOVERS

Yes, please.

Green Beans in Warm Dijon Vinaigrette

While green beans are available in markets almost year-round, they taste best and are least expensive from summer through early fall. We select ours from nearby Migliorelli Farm, and we always buy extra so we can pickle them for our antipasto plates.

¼ cup	olive oil
2 tablespoons	red wine vinegar
2 tablespoons	minced shallots
2 teaspoons	Dijon mustard
1 teaspoon	chopped fresh thyme leaves
¼ teaspoon	salt, plus more as needed
⅓ cup	paper-thin-sliced red onion
1½ pounds	thin green beans, trimmed, cut in half on the diagonal
2 tablespoons	chopped fresh flat-leaf parsley
	Freshly ground black pepper

To make the vinaigrette, whisk the oil, vinegar, shallots, mustard, thyme, and the ¼ teaspoon salt in a small bowl. Stir in the onion and set aside.

Fill a large bowl with ice and water. Bring a large pot of salted water to a boil. Add the green beans and cook until crisp-tender, about 5 minutes. Drain, and transfer to the bowl of ice water to cool. Then drain well. (The vinaigrette and the green beans can be prepared 1 day ahead. Cover separately and chill.)

Heat the vinaigrette in a large skillet over medium heat until warm. Add the beans, toss to combine, and cook until heated through and coated with the vinaigrette, about 5 minutes. Add the parsley and toss to coat. Season with salt and pepper to taste. Transfer the beans to a bowl, and serve.

SERVING SUGGESTIONS

Enjoy with oven- or pan-roasted chicken or pork or seared beef tenderloins.

VARIATIONS

• Add 1 cup of fresh or frozen peas when heating the beans in the vinaigrette.

- Add 1 cup diagonally sliced carrots to the boiling water with the green beans.
- Spice it up with a pinch of cayenne or some harissa stirred into the vinaigrette. Add some smokiness with a bit of smoked paprika.
- Substitute blanched broad beans or roasted asparagus spears for the green beans.

LEFTOVERS

Enjoy reheated.

NUTRITION

Green beans are a good source of vitamin A because they contain many carotenoid precursors, including beta-carotene. They also contain healthy amounts of dietary fiber, potassium, vitamin K, folate, calcium, and iron.

ECONOMY $

Grandma Lauck's Pumpkin Bars

MAKES 8 TO 10 SERVINGS

My friend Derek Lauck faithfully makes his grandmother Audrey Lauck's pumpkin bars for the whole Gigi staff every Thanksgiving. This deliciously light and creamy pumpkin custard can be baked as bars in a 13 x 9-inch pan or as a pie/tart in a 9-inch springform pan or a 10-inch round ceramic dish. Instead of buying the spices separately, you can substitute 2 teaspoons pumpkin pie spice. Grandma Lauck's tip: to enhance the filling flavor, combine the ingredients a day ahead, cover, and keep chilled; then proceed with the recipe.

Crust

½ cup	quick-cooking oatmeal, such as Quick Quaker Oats
1 cup	all-purpose flour
½ cup	packed light brown sugar
8 tablespoons	unsalted butter (1 stick), melted
Pinch	salt

Filling

One	16-ounce can pumpkin puree
One	12-ounce can evaporated milk
6	large eggs
¾ cup	granulated sugar
½ teaspoon	salt
1 teaspoon	ground cinnamon
½ teaspoon	ground ginger
½ teaspoon	ground cloves
⅛ teaspoon	ground allspice

Preheat the oven to 350°F.

Stir all the crust ingredients together in a medium bowl, and press the dough over the bottom of a 13 x 9-inch baking dish. Bake in the middle of the oven until the crust is set and pale gold, about 15 minutes. Transfer the dish to a wire rack and let it cool slightly. Leave the oven on.

While the crust is cooling, whisk all the filling ingredients together in a bowl until smooth. Pour the mixture into the crust and bake in the middle of the oven until the filling is just set, 35 to 40 minutes. Transfer to a wire rack and allow to cool completely.

Cut into bars with a serrated knife.

SERVING SUGGESTIONS

Top each bar with whipped cream flavored with vanilla extract and a pinch of powdered sugar and cinnamon. Also consider adding a shot of brandy or rum to the whipped cream.

VARIATION

Use fresh instead of canned pumpkin. Simply cut an unpeeled pumpkin into large wedges or chunks, and use a spoon to remove the strings and seeds. Cook the chunks in lightly salted boiling water until fork-tender, 30 to 40 minutes, and drain. When cool enough to handle, slip off the skins and use a potato masher, ricer, or food processor to puree the pulp.

NUTRITION

Among other antioxidants, pumpkin has a super-high level of beta-carotene, which the body converts to vitamin A. Half a cup of canned pumpkin provides enough beta-carotene to supply 540 percent of the daily requirement of vitamin A.

ECONOMY $

Fresh or canned pumpkin costs less than $1 per pound.

Apple Sour Cream Coffee Cake

MAKES 8 TO 10 SERVINGS

This is another great way to use up the bushels upon bushels of apples we begin to see in the fall. It makes for a great morning treat, served warm with a cup of coffee. To make things easy for the shopper headed home with a large bag of apples, we sell our streusel topping at Gigi Market.

Coffee cake

2 cups	all-purpose flour
1¼ cups	granulated sugar
4 teaspoons	ground cinnamon
2 teaspoons	baking powder
2	large eggs
¾ cup	milk
¼ cup	sour cream
8 tablespoons	unsalted butter (1 stick), melted
2	medium apples (Gala, Honeygold, and/or Empire work well), cored, peeled, and cut into small dice (about 2 cups)

Streusel topping

⅓ cup	firmly packed light brown sugar
⅓ cup	granulated sugar
12 tablespoons	cold unsalted butter (1½ sticks), cut into tiny pieces
1½ teaspoons	ground cinnamon
1 teaspoon	salt
½ teaspoon	vanilla extract
2 cups	bread flour

Preheat the oven to 350°F. Butter and dust a Bundt pan with flour; set aside.

Mix the flour, 1 cup of the sugar, 1 teaspoon of the cinnamon, and the baking powder in a large bowl. In a separate bowl, mix the eggs, milk, sour cream, and butter until well blended. Stir the wet mixture into the dry mixture until well incorporated (I do this by hand, but you can use a standing mixer—just don't overmix).

Pour half of the batter into the prepared pan, and use a spatula to spread it out evenly.

In another bowl, mix the apples, the remaining ¼ cup sugar, and the remaining 3 teaspoons cinnamon. Spread three quarters (about 1½ cups) of the apple mixture over the batter. Cover the apple layer with the remaining batter.

To make the streusel topping, put all the streusel ingredients into a mixer fitted with the paddle attachment. Mix on low speed for 5 to 7 minutes, until it really comes together and the butter is well incorporated. The topping should feel moldable when squeezed in your hands.

Scatter the remaining apple mixture over the batter, followed by the streusel topping.

Bake in the center of the oven until a toothpick inserted into the center of the cake comes out clean, 70 to 75 minutes.

Transfer the pan to a wire rack and allow the cake to cool completely. If the cake pan was well floured, you should be able to tip the cooled cake out of the pan. Otherwise just cut it into portions right in the pan and enjoy.

SERVING SUGGESTIONS

Well wrapped, this coffee cake can hold for a week and a half in the fridge, or for 4 days on the counter. It tastes best when served at room temperature or warmed up in the oven. Enjoy it any time of the day. For more of a dessert effect, top it with zabaglione (see page 115).

VARIATIONS

• Skip the sour cream and replace it with vanilla or plain whole-milk yogurt.
• Instead of the apples, substitute 2 cups berries, 1 cup pitted fresh cherries, or 2 medium bananas, either pureed and mixed into the batter, or sliced and laid in the center, or chopped into the streusel.
• Omit the fruit completely and add a brown sugar/melted butter smear between the two layers of batter.

NUTRITION

Apples are loaded with flavenoids, particularly quercetin, a powerful antioxidant, natural antihistamine, and anti-inflammatory. Research shows that quercetin may help to prevent cancer, especially prostate cancer.

ECONOMY $

Gigi Cider Doughnuts

MAKES 75 DOUGHNUT HOLES OR ABOUT 24 DOUGHNUTS

*Greig Farm, home to Gigi Market, has a long tradition of agritourism. For many years
the Greig family operated the market space where we now reside. While they did not run a café,
as we now do, they did offer local products such as cider and Mother Greig's cider doughnuts,
which had people driving from all over every fall. Gigi pastry chef Ashley Kearns has
revived the tradition with these doughnut holes, and the brown baggies fly out
of the store during apple and pumpkin picking time.*

4 cups	all-purpose flour, plus extra for dusting
1 cup	sugar
½ teaspoon	baking soda
2 teaspoons	baking powder
1 teaspoon	salt
1½ teaspoons	ground nutmeg
1 teaspoon	ground cinnamon
1 cup	apple cider (see Note)
¼ cup	vanilla or plain whole-milk yogurt
2	large eggs
1	large egg yolk
½ cup	whole milk
4 tablespoons	unsalted butter (½ stick), melted
4 quarts	peanut oil or solid vegetable shortening, for frying

*Note: Apple cider is not apple juice! Cider is
ground up and strained apples. Apple juice is just
that, the squeezed juice from apples, and it's often
watered down. Cider is preferable for this recipe.
It has a much richer flavor, a thicker texture, and
a better mouth feel.*

Put all the dry ingredients into the bowl
of a mixer fitted with the paddle attachment.

In a small saucepan, boil the apple cider
until it is reduced to about 2 tablespoons
of syrup, about 10 minutes. In a separate
bowl, mix the yogurt, eggs, egg yolk, and
milk until well combined. Add the melted
butter and the reduced apple syrup, and
mix well.

Add the wet ingredients to the dry
ingredients and mix on low speed until well
combined. The batter should look like a
cross between cookie dough and pie dough.
Transfer the dough to a well-floured surface

and form it into a ball. Sprinkle some additional flour on top. Using a rolling pin, roll out the dough until it is ¼ to ½ inch thick. Cut the dough into holes or doughnut shapes with a doughnut cutter.

In a Dutch oven or a deep-fryer, heat the oil to 375°F (a candy thermometer will help here if you're cooking the doughnuts on the stovetop). Fry the doughnuts, in batches, for 2 to 3 minutes on each side, until they are a dark golden brown. Watch your oil temperature closely, adding doughnuts only when it is at 375°F. Rushing will result in a greasy doughnut.

When the doughnuts are cooked, put them on a wire rack to allow the oil to drip off.

SERVING SUGGESTION

When they are still slightly warm, toss the doughnuts with granulated sugar or confectioners' sugar.

VARIATIONS

- *For plain doughnuts:* Eliminate the cider and reduce the flour to 3⅓ cups.
- *For cinnamon doughnuts:* Toss slightly warm doughnuts in cinnamon-sugar.
- *For filled doughnuts:* Consider piping pastry cream or jelly into the doughnut holes.

- Substitute ¾ cup buttermilk for the milk/yogurt combination. The doughnuts will be a touch more sour.
- *To make ahead:* The dough can be cut into holes or doughnut shapes and then refrigerated for 2 days or frozen for up to 6 months. You can fry the doughnut holes while they are still frozen; let the dough defrost for larger doughnuts.

ECONOMY $

Gigi Affogato

MAKES 1 SERVING

When I recently read that the affogato, a traditional treat in bar/cafés throughout Italy and on the Gigi menu since we opened, was going to be the savior of Starbucks, I had to laugh. I would have done that R and D! Seriously, Italians have had this right for a long time—it's a simple and delicious indulgence in between or ending a meal.

1 teaspoon	chopped hazelnuts
3	small scoops hazelnut or vanilla gelato
1 double shot	hot brewed espresso
1 scoop	whipped cream
Dash	cocoa powder
2	Gigi Biscotti (optional, page 271)

Toast the hazelnuts in a small dry skillet over medium heat until lightly brown and fragrant, about 2 minutes.

Scoop the gelato into a 10-ounce clear parfait glass or mug. Pour the hot espresso over the gelato. Top with the whipped cream, a dash of cocoa powder, and the toasted hazelnuts. Place the biscotti into the gelato or serve on a side plate.

Roasting a Farm-Fresh Turkey

Farm-fresh turkeys generally roast more quickly than the water-filled agribusiness turkeys. We proudly purchase and prep Tivoli's Northwind Farms birds during the holiday season. Our customers can purchase them fresh, brined, or cooked to perfect juicy doneness—Gigi Market is open until noon on Thanksgiving Day for customers to pick up turkeys and all the trimmings.

A farm-fresh turkey can be stored in a very cold environment (28° to 34°F) for up to a week in advance of cooking. Have thermometers on hand for refrigeration and for testing the final doneness of the Thanksgiving centerpiece.

To cook your farm-fresh turkey, first be sure your bird is completely thawed. A frozen turkey should be thawed in the refrigerator at a temperature of 40°F or lower; this can take a couple of days. Rinse the bird and the giblets under cold running water. Preheat the oven to 325°F (a hotter oven can dry out your turkey; a lower temperature risks prolonged time in the "danger zone," the temperature range in which bacteria multiply most quickly). Truss the legs together and tuck the wing tips back under the shoulders of the bird. If you plan to stuff the turkey, do so now, immediately before putting the turkey into the oven. Generously season the turkey and place it, breast side up, on a flat wire rack in a 2½- to 3-inch-deep roasting pan. Pour ½ cup water into the pan.

For turkeys up to 20 pounds, roast for 15 minutes a pound—an 18-pound bird should roast for about 4½ hours. Roast larger birds for 12 minutes a pound. A stuffed turkey may require an extra buffer of 30 minutes.

Take the temperature of both the bird and the stuffing. Oven temperatures vary, as do farm-fresh turkeys, so begin checking for doneness about 30 minutes before the turkey is expected to be done.

If your bird has reached the desired golden brown but is not yet done, place a tent of foil over the turkey. This prevents over-browning and drying.

Testing for doneness:

- Temperature: Deep in the breast should be 160° to 165°F. The thigh temperature should register at 180° to 185°F.
- Knife test: Insert a paring knife into the breast and thigh. When the juices run clear—not at all pink—the turkey is cooked.
- Leg separation: When the turkey is adequately cooked, the leg will easily separate from the bird with a light tug.

When the turkey is done, let it sit at room temperature for 15 to 30 minutes before carving. This makes for juicier meat and easier and more attractive carving. Farm-fresh turkeys may be lightly pink toward the bone—this is totally normal.

Refrigerate leftovers no more than 2 hours after removing the turkey from the oven. Wrapped tightly in aluminum foil or freezer-grade plastic, the roasted meat can be frozen.

How many will your turkey feed?

6 pounds=4 to 6 people

8 pounds=6 to 8 people

12 pounds=8 to 10 people

15 pounds=10 to 12 people

18 pounds=12 to 15 people

22 pounds=15+ people

Leftovers: For next-day sandwiches, smear 2 tablespoons of reduced-fat cream cheese (it's easier if it's softened) on one slice of toasted whole-grain or Pepperidge Farm white bread. Spread 2 tablespoons cranberry chutney, sauce, or relish on another toasted bread slice. Fill the sandwich with thinly sliced leftover turkey (about 2 ounces), a couple of slices of cheddar cheese (about 1 ounce), some apple slices, and a handful of trimmed watercress or baby spinach.

Winter

It can be hard to pinpoint the start of winter. One day I'll grab a warmer jacket when I take my Labrador, Gabbi, out for a romp in the fields and be glad to find a pair of gloves in the pocket. Or suddenly I'm craving a mug of Gigi's hot chocolate as an afternoon pick-me-up. At the restaurant, Wilson Costa, the executive chef, has changed the menu to feature soul-warming dishes such as braised lamb shanks with maple pumpkin polenta, Fontina mac and cheese with speck, or a classic lasagna Bolognese. Yep, all signs point to winter.

To be honest, this season is the hardest one for me. The Valley has a well-earned reputation for harsh, unpredictable winters. The temperature can go from chilly to blistering cold and then suddenly turn balmy for a day or two, with steady rain followed by lots and lots of mud. Now muck boots rather than strappy sandals are the fashionable footwear of choice. The sky stays gray and overcast for seemingly weeks on end, and icy winds blow across the empty fields, leaving my face and hands chapped. It feels endless. Sometimes, though, when I least expect it, that perfect winter day shows up: cold and clear, with a vivid sunset casting a patina of gold, orange, and fuchsia against the smudged blue outlines of the Catskill mountain range in the distance. It's an awe-inspiring view.

While winter officially starts on December 21, just about everyone here agrees that January 2 marks the beginning of the long "hunkering-down" days. Knowing that the toughest months are ahead of them, my friends and neighbors always celebrate the holidays with gusto. Come December everyone is in a festive, if rushed, mood. The summer crowds have thinned, but there are still plenty of shoppers ducking into boutiques throughout quaintly decorated Rhinebeck for their Christmas shopping. Gigi Trattoria is a hub of feverish activity, with party after party booked through the New Year.

This is a busy catering time as well, with local holiday get-togethers and tree trimming parties in full swing. There are black-tie-and-cocktail-dress galas held at the opulent "robber baron" homes that line River Road, and more casual jeans-and-a-sweater parties held at warmly lit clapboard farmhouses and stone cottages throughout the Valley. I host my annual Christmas cocktail party for seventy or so friends and favorite customers. I stock the bar with homemade vin brûlée (a great Italian mulled wine), my eye-opening eggnog, and of course bottle after bottle of Champagne and red wine. The buffet includes plenty of *baccalà mantecato* and North American caviar from Hansen, a treasured Hudson Valley importer. Both taste great with a glass of bubbly. The tree is decorated, the fires are laid and lit, candles are glowing in every window, and I've lined the entrance to the front door with lanterns. It looks so pretty. Before long the house is filled to the brim, noisy, and not a little chaotic, and I'm having a great time celebrating the season, toasting the end of another good year.

During the days leading up to Christmas, Gigi Market is packed with shoppers eager to stock up on special holiday treats. Bags of spiced and candied walnuts, hazelnuts, and almonds are ready to enjoy as a cocktail nibble or as part of a cheese board or salad. We make loads of brittles and white and dark chocolate bark, ginger cookies, molasses cookies, panettone, and pandoro. Gift baskets hold an assortment of treats, including our own blend of hot chocolate, a super-thick concoction that tastes like pure

melted chocolate in a mug. The last of the season's apples are cut and baked into pies, and the last of our frozen summer berries are turned into scones, muffins, and turnovers. Pears, too, become part of our daily pastry offerings. The wonderful floral shop down the road, Grandiflora, supplies the market with garlands that we drape over the wooden beams. The smell and look of them, along with the beautiful gift baskets and pandoro boxes, make the market feel festive but still natural.

Derek, a great friend and de facto "little brother," always helps me cut down Christmas trees at a local farm and drag them back to my home and to the market. We have heated discussions (really heated!) over the right tree, but I have to admit, he always picks an absolute beauty. Plus, he'll never let me live down the time I went with another friend instead of him. We cut down a tree double the size of my ten-foot ceilings! We dragged that big boy down a hill, strapped it onto my truck, and shoved it through my front door. I'll never forget the look on Derek's face when he saw what we had done.

Before we start decorating the trees, Derek and I raid the refrigerator case for some Hudson Valley Fresh milk to mix up another batch of eggnog. It provides tremendous artistic inspiration! With the home tree decorated, we head to Gigi Market to do the same. Before long, the market looks its absolute best. The tree is glowing, the rafters are swagged with garlands, and the shelves are loaded with festive goodies. A few of our customers inquire whether they can throw a party in the middle of it all, and why not? I can't think of a more nostalgic place than a renovated (heated!) nineteenth-century barn. It's a great space to celebrate the holidays.

Too quickly, Christmas and New Year's arrive with gifts and good wishes . . . and then are gone. The part-time residents and their guests depart. The Valley gets quieter, the roads emptier, and the tempo of life is more andante than allegro. Winter settles in. The restaurant and market slow down, but I still find ways to keep busy. My staff and I look at new programs and new products we can promote, and I plot out all the things I want to accomplish in the upcoming busy seasons. I spend time testing new recipes, writing, planning my spring garden, and trying not to eat too much. I also try to hop on a plane to Italy. There, I brush up on the language, eat local dishes, drink great wine, and generally get inspired with ideas to translate into my Hudson Valley Mediterranean style. I don't run from one city to the next, but stay in one place to get a feel for the local food culture, its ingredients, and its soulful traditions. My life in Italy revolves around the quest for the next meal. What a luxury! I return home energized and ready for spring.

Dinner parties help keep winter moving along. Entertaining now is low-key and simple. I'll invite maybe ten people over and start something cooking in the oven. A traditional goulash, peposa, or a crown roast

of local pork served with a root vegetable gratin (page 170) is a comforting, warm-you-up meal. With some great local cheeses and nuts set out beforehand, a salad, and a couple bottles of wine, all the makings of a great evening are in place. I even host a "Who Cares About the Super Bowl?" party every year. As the only football fanatic among all my friends, I'll never get invited to a Super Bowl party unless I throw it myself! I stock up on wine, lay out a sandwich board with roasted Northwind Farms turkey and ham, cheeses, an assortment of breads, pickles, chutneys, and spreads, and welcome a crowd. Some enjoy the football, some enjoy the food, some enjoy the wine, and everyone has a great time.

As an advocate for local and seasonal eating, I believe great winter meals are no harder to pull off than great summer meals. The menu just shifts once again to the foods that are local and abundant. Right now there are beautiful handmade cheeses, including Coach Farm goat cheeses, our own freshly made ricotta using Hudson Valley Fresh milk, firm Hawthorne Valley cheddars that are flavored with horseradish or dill and sometimes smoked, and delicate French-style raw milk cheeses such as Barat, Ouray, and Toussaint from Sprout Creek Farm. Wiltbank Farm still cultivates oyster and shiitake mushrooms. Winter endive and radicchio make an appearance, and all sorts of root vegetables are ready to be turned into gratins, soups, or stews. Pickled and preserved vegetables can be enjoyed with hearty winter fare like choucroute garni (see page 52), along with chutneys or mostarda. The variety of relishes, preserves, jams, and jellies from Grey Mouse Farm and Beth's Farm Kitchen reminds us of the flavors of summer and autumn. I dip into my own caches of preserved and dried fruits for both sweet and savory dishes.

I love to simmer pastured local beef into a rich Bolognese to pair with homemade gnocchi, fresh fettucine, and Gigi-made ricotta. It's one of our most popular dishes at Gigi Trattoria during the winter, and with good reason. Duck and venison are once again on the menu, along with heirloom turkeys and Berkshire pork. Tomatoes canned during the height of summer remind me of their grower, Mr. Mink. After early fall, we won't see him again until he stops by in midwinter with his seed catalogs. At least I can still enjoy his handiwork.

And then there are potatoes, a winter mainstay. New York is one of the country's large potato-producing states, and almost all smaller farmers here add potatoes to their harvest. The deep topsoil around the mid-Hudson makes for a near-perfect potato patch, and the variety planted is astonishing. RSK Farm in Prattsville has fingerlings with romantic names like Blush, Adirondack Blue, and Corola. Also locally available is the All Blue potato (which stays blue throughout, even after cooking), as well as the Chieftain, Yukon Gold, Kennebec, Green Mountain,

Austrian Crescent, La Ratte, Rose Finn, Katahdin, and the German Butterball.

When it comes to potatoes, my Irish side comes out. I'm a potato fanatic. Baked—sure. Sautéed—more, please. Roasted—delish. Mashed with plenty of locally made butter—yes, yes, and yes. Fried? Oh, how I love thee! At the market our Gigi-made RSK potato chips are sliced paper-thin and fried with fresh herbs. It's hard to keep them on the shelves.

To round out my eating options during the winter, I visit the increasing number of winter farmers' markets. More and more local farmers are growing vegetables in hoop houses during the winter. It's not ideal for delicate vegetables, but at around 50°F root vegetables and hardy greens can thrive. I also buy from Winter Sun Farms, a company in New Paltz that distributes locally grown and flash-frozen summer produce during the winter months. For me this is another option for high-quality, local, organic, and sustainable produce, albeit nonseasonal, and it is a way for local farmers to reduce waste and increase revenue from their harvest. I can support that.

Winter belongs to all our local food artisans. Beer craftsmen like Brewery Ommegang, a Belgian-style brewery in Cooperstown, and Chatham Brewery are creating sought-after beers in a variety of styles. Bread artisan Dan Leader's company Bread Alone in Boiceville and Our Daily Bread in Chatham turn out beautiful and varied loaves every day. Ray Tousey's honey is available now, and by late winter Uncle Neilie's and Fitting Creek Farm's maple syrup will begin to make an appearance. And while egg production has slowed a little this time of year, I still get gorgeous fresh eggs delivered from Feather Ridge Farm and Awesome Farm to meet my needs. There's plenty of great organic beef and lamb from Grazin' Angus Acres, Fleisher's Meats, Northwind Farms, and Herondale Farm to add to the pots of chili, soups, and stews that follow one after the other in a constant stream of warming one-dish dinners.

And so the days pass. Slowly at first, and then with quickening speed, the season slips forward. Hudson Valley winters can seem austere, but if you look closely you see that nature thrives here under extreme conditions. Even now the Hudson is a river of life. A snowy hike out to Poet's Walk in Red Hook yields evidence of whitetail deer tracks. Look up and you can spy bald eagles flying low toward the Kingston–Rhinecliff bridge. The Esopus Creek above the dam at Saugerties is good for winter fishing, with rich schools of yellow perch, bluegill, black crappie, and pumpkinseed fish, along with the occasional huge striped bass. On the river you can spy harbor seals and other marine mammals dining on the bounty of fish, especially in late winter. Since the Hudson is both river and estuary, the presence of seals reminds me of our connection to the open sea. Waterfowl are abundant. Along the river and in bays

and ponds you can see greater scaups, hooded mergansers, coots, gadwalls, mallards, black ducks, ring-necked ducks, American widgeons, Canada geese, brants, swans, and ruddy ducks. In the air red-tailed hawks and turkey vultures ride the winds. On clear nights I drive home from work guided by moonlight scattered over winding roads and snowy pastures. In bed I hear screech owls communicating with each other and I wonder if they, like me, are waiting for spring.

A gray area between the fall and winter sections of this book naturally exists, because there are many crossover ingredients during these two seasons, especially in different growing areas. I classify each ingredient in the season most typical for the Hudson Valley, but most vegetables mentioned in fall or winter are available and work well in cooking during either season.

THE WINTER HARVEST

Root Vegetables

Winter is the season when root vegetables get some well-deserved love and attention. With favorable climate and growing conditions here in the Hudson Valley, the harvest of root vegetables each fall can be impressive. At Gigi Market, we highlight a local grower, Hearty Roots Community Farm, for bringing us their beautiful organic specimens to enjoy and to share with our customers. Another local grower, Migliorelli Farm, has been bringing roots and greens to local and New York City markets for years.

What exactly is a root vegetable? Well, I think of root vegetables as plants with hard but edible roots. In the Valley that includes common vegetables like carrots, turnips, rutabagas, kohlrabi, beets, and parsnips, and some less common ones too, such as salsify and scorzonera, or black salsify.

From a culinary standpoint, the brilliance of these vegetables lies in their long-lasting nature and variety of flavors. Properly stored, they can provide meals for months without losing significant flavor or nutrients. Some can even stay on the ground during the winter, for picking just when you need them. The flavor of root vegetables can range from delicate to brawny to peppery, so the cook has plenty of options for creating interesting meals and keeping mealtime doldrums away.

Root vegetables are invaluable for providing good nutrition during the winter when little else is growing. They contain no fat, are low in calories, and can be an excellent source of protein and complex carbohydrates. As the "storage bin" for a plant's nutrients, roots are powerhouses of vitamins and phytonutrients. The phytonutrients are associated with the color of the vegetable, and the more intense a vegetable's color, the more phytonutrients it contains. So, those intensely red beets? Chock-full of healthy antioxidants.

Consider the carrot. Nowadays, carrots come in a myriad of colors from pale yellow to deep purple. There is even a two-toned variety called Purple Haze that is purple on the outside and orange on the inside. No matter what the color, carrots are a healthy and tasty winter mainstay whether served raw, steamed, roasted, or mashed in soup.

Carrot sales nationwide jump after the holidays, when New Year's resolutions become a top priority. One of carrots' fat-fighting features is their respectable fiber content. This helps fill you up and may help lower blood cholesterol levels too.

Carrots contain carotenoids, a class of natural fat-soluble pigments found principally in plants to aid photosynthesis. When we eat carrots, their primary carotenoid, beta-carotene, converts to vitamin A in our bodies. Beta-carotene is just one of more than five hundred carotenoids (lycopene in tomatoes is another) that help prevent cancer and heart disease; they all play an important role in human health by acting as biological antioxidants, protecting cells and tissues from the damaging effect of free radicals. Carotenoids set up molecular roadblocks, restricting the access of free radicals to other molecules and thus limiting harm to your body's healthy tissue. All colorful fruits and vegetables are packed with all sorts of carotenoids. In many cases, these compounds are more easily absorbed by the body when cooked in a little fat—so pass the olive oil!

Turnips, rutabagas, parsnips, and kohlrabi are what I call "low glow" veggies. People's faces don't typically light up when they're served a side order of mashed turnips. But I blame that mostly on industrial food production, which delivers spongy turnips, oddly waxed and mealy rutabagas, and bendable parsnips to the produce section bins. A good turnip has a crisp texture, with a mellow, slightly sweet flavor when eaten raw. Larger late-winter turnips may be more pungent, especially when they've been stored improperly, so I try to use early ones because I like their flavor best. The rutabaga, which is related to the turnip, also has a crisp texture, but its denser flesh takes slightly longer to cook. The rutabaga has a touch of natural sweetness (more than a cabbage, less than a carrot) and is great with some of the same spices you use with sweet potatoes. These terrifically versatile roots can be boiled, drizzled with olive oil and salt and roasted, sautéed, pureed, and incorporated into lots of different gratins, stews, and soups.

Kohlrabi is, I suppose, the least known common root vegetable. It has a round light-green root ball with stems sprouting from its body, giving it an odd satellite-like appearance. Kohlrabi hasn't always lured Americans to the table, and to this day it is still more popular in Europe than here. That's a shame. Kohlrabi is delicious raw or cooked and has a sweet, mild flavor, similar to broccoli stems or the inner heart of cabbage.

When buying turnips, rutabagas, parsnips, or kohlrabi, take care to select small to medium roots that feel heavier than you would expect. They should have good color and feel firm—no bruises, soft spots, or signs of shriveling. And remember, all of these vegetables are loaded with "healthy" carbohydrates, nutrients, and protective phytochemicals. Plus, they are rich in flavor and easy on the wallet. What more do you need to know?

Well, maybe you aren't ready to dive right into a plate of parsnips. Not to worry. Start with something a little more familiar, like beets. When you hold an uncooked beet in your hand, it's hard to believe such a rough looking root is such a sweet, tender vegetable. Beets are harvested in the late fall, and I tend to eat them a lot during the early winter. I love their versatility. You can enjoy them as salads, pickled, roasted, and even raw. In fact our most popular salad at Gigi is the Barbina (page 146), which includes beets, Sky Farm's baby greens mix, roasted mushrooms, crumbled Coach Farm goat cheese, and toasted walnuts, all tossed with our sherry-shallot vinaigrette. All those earthy ingredients play beautifully off of one another.

While we all ate the classic red beet growing up, there are now other colors, ranging from gold to purple to striped (in the case of Chioggia beets). Serving a variety of colorful beets makes for a more visually satisfying dish. Beets are naturally sweet, easy to cook and serve, and have health benefits ranging from protection against cancer (especially colon cancer) and heart disease to lowering blood pressure and, if consumed during pregnancy, to delivering enough B vitamin folate to enhance normal tissue growth in developing babies. Beets are also a good source of dietary fiber, vitamin C, magnesium, iron, copper, and phosphorus.

Farmers' markets will have an interesting selection of beets for sale. Choose small or medium-size beets that are firm and have a smooth skin and rich color. Small early beets may be so tender that peeling won't be needed after they are cooked. This is good news, especially when buying organic, since most nutrients in root vegetables are found close to the skin. Avoid beets that have spots, bruises, or soft, wet areas, all of which indicate spoilage. Beets also shouldn't be shriveled or have a flabby root tip. Store them unwashed in the vegetable bin in your refrigerator, where they can stay fresh for 2 to 4 weeks. Unfortunately, you can't freeze raw beets since they become unappealingly mushy as they thaw. Instead, freeze them after cooking. They'll retain their flavor and texture with no problem.

Sweet potatoes suffer from more than their fair share of linguistic confusion, but you need to remember only this: in the United States we grow sweet potatoes. They can be the moist-fleshed, orange-colored root vegetable we all love to eat at Thanksgiving, or they can be a lighter-colored, dry, starchy root tuber. But they are both sweet potatoes. Yams—true yams—aren't even related to sweet potatoes, and you find them mostly in Latin American or Caribbean grocery stores,

sometimes labeled *boniato* or *batata*. Their culinary uses and cooking methods are very similar to those of a sweet potato, which adds to the confusion.

While most of the sweet potato plant is edible, we just eat the tuber. The intensity of the sweet potato's yellow or orange flesh color is directly correlated with how much beta-carotene it contains. The beta-carotene in orange-fleshed sweet potatoes delivers vitamin A in a more accessible form than that found in dark green leafy vegetables. If you run across purple-fleshed sweet potatoes (and you do see them occasionally at the farmers' market), snap them up. They have the highest antioxidant activity among sweet potatoes—even higher than that of a blueberry! Interestingly, the sweet potato skin contains the bulk of its total nutrients and fiber. The skin is great to eat—just be sure to wash it well before cooking.

With lots of vitamins A and C and heart-healthy potassium, sweet potatoes are like a low-calorie candy, with about 100 calories per medium potato. They're also considered an anti-inflammatory food because of the presence of quercetin and chlorogenic acid, both potent anti-inflammatory compounds. This is good news for people who suffer from diseases like asthma, Alzheimer's, chronic allergies, digestive disorders such as Crohn's, hormonal imbalances, and osteoporosis. As for their glycemic load (their ability to raise blood sugar), even a diabetic or prediabetic can enjoy sweet potatoes if their blood sugar levels are managed with diet, exercise, and in some cases, medicine.

Choose sweet potatoes that are firm and without cracks, bruises, or soft spots. Don't buy any found in the refrigerator case, since cold temperatures give sweet potatoes an "off" flavor. If you can't eat them right away, you can store them in a cool, dark, well-ventilated place. Sweet potatoes can last for up to 6 months in fine condition in a root cellar, but most people choose to store them, loosely piled in a basket, in the basement or in a cool cupboard for about a week to 10 days. If you purchase organically grown sweet potatoes, you can eat the entire tuber—flesh and skin. But be careful if you buy conventionally grown ones, since sometimes the skin is treated with dye or wax.

Sweet potatoes are a winter staple for me. I like them mashed and in soups, stews, gratins, biscuits, breads, pies, or just roasted whole, split, and served with a pat of butter or a drizzle of olive oil. A slice of sweet potato pie is a great breakfast treat the morning after Thanksgiving, especially with a cup of dark coffee. For that matter, when I'm on the run, I'll throw a cold baked sweet potato into my snack box.

Winter Greens

Not everything green is eaten during the spring and summer. In fact, there are some greens that are planted here in late summer and harvested when the snow covers the ground. These include most members of the chicory family, such as endive and radicchio, some hardy chards, collards, kales, and tatsoi, which keep producing until quite late in the season, and all types of cabbages, harvested in the late fall and kept through the winter. There is also mizuna and other members of the mustard family, and winter-hardy arugulas. These brassicas and chicories (arugula, endive, escarole, and radicchio) thrive when the temperature drops and develop peppery, spicy flavors from growing in chilly weather.

The brassica family of plants hosts a large group of diverse vegetables: flowers (cauliflower, broccoli, broccoli rabe), roots (rutabagas, turnips), stems and leaves (cabbage, collard greens, Brussels sprouts, chard, kale, mustard, spinach, watercress). A number of health organizations recommend eating at least three servings of brassica vegetables per week. Not only will you get a good dose of vitamins A and C, but you'll also get a class of phytochemicals called isothiocyanates, which are responsible for that slightly sulfurous smell some winter greens have. They help boost your immune system, have antiviral and antibacterial properties, and are thought to help fight certain cancers.

All the winter greens have a place in a healthy diet. For example, radicchio's red color is a good indicator that it is a nutrient-rich plant, and tests show that it is equal to blueberries and spinach in antioxidants, which provide protection against cellular damage. This is great news, since radicchio bridges the seasons between fall berries and spring lettuce and spinach.

Cabbages, surprisingly, contain significant amounts of vitamin C, calcium, and potassium. No wonder Americans didn't suffer from vitamin C deficiency in winter before oranges could be shipped up by train from Florida—they relied on cabbage and sauerkraut (which is really nothing more than shredded cabbage and salt) to keep them healthy. As for dark leafy greens, a recent study conducted by Spanish researchers indicated that a daily serving might cut the risk of lung cancer by 50 percent.

I enjoy greens in my winter cooking. Their culinary use is limited only by my imagination. Radicchio and endive can be eaten raw in salads or mixed into dishes such as risotto or lasagna. Every once in a while during winter, a cold contrast on the plate is a nice thing. Gigi chef Wilson Costa makes a marinated radicchio slaw that tops hot caramelized wedges of acorn squash. Just before serving, he drizzles aged balsamic vinegar on top. As for other greens, I like them added as part of a stir-fry or a winter pasta salad, mixed into a breakfast omelet, or added to soups and stews for their color and peppery bite. Chard isn't usually eaten raw, but I love it cooked in olive oil with garlic, red pepper flakes, and a pinch of salt. It's a great side dish or addition when tossed into hot pasta with some cooked Italian sausages

or Spanish chorizo and cooked white beans. Cooked Swiss chard, or any other leftover braised greens (collard, kale, or spinach), can be stirred into a next-day frittata or risotto or can fill a tart shell before the custard is added (see Gigi Fresh Ricotta and Tuscan Kale Tartlets on page 133).

Cabbages, either your classic green cabbage or the leafier Savoy cabbage, are both grown in abundance, and I'll bet they've been in cultivation since the original Dutch settlers established farms here some four hundred years ago. The growing conditions are perfect. One of my favorite winter dishes is a hearty northern Italian dish called Pizzoccheri alla Valtellinese (page 227), which is buckwheat pasta combined with long-simmered Savoy cabbage and melted Fontina. It's rich and warming, just the thing after a full day of downhill skiing, sledding, ice skating, or hell, even snow shoveling!

I especially love red cabbage, as much for its flavor as its beauty. It's great with beef and pork dishes throughout the winter. A favorite dinner that is as colorful as it is delicious is roasted rack of pork (page 246) paired with a root vegetable gratin (page 170) and braised red cabbage studded with local apples. I cooked this for my fortieth birthday celebration with a bunch of friends. It all turned out so well, even I was impressed!

When greens are picked fresh, their stems are taut, their leaves have a high gloss, and in the case of cabbage, they feel surprisingly heavy for their size. Wan, limp greens with slightly shriveled leaves are better left in the bin. Experiment with all types and look around for interesting ones you've never tried before. The one I really love is called cavolo nero, or Lacinato kale. It's a member of the kale family with thin, straight, tender leaves, and it has a tangy flavor at first bite followed by an ever so slightly sweet aftertaste. Hearty Roots Farm provides Gigi with a steady supply from summer through late fall and during a brief period in the spring. You can braise or boil cavolo nero, but it is also tasty sautéed in olive oil with thinly sliced onions and garlic, and seasoned simply with salt and pepper. Serve it hot as a side dish or at room temperature as a crostini topping, or better yet as part of a winter antipasto plate Just add some chunks of Grana Padano or Parmigiano-Reggiano, a semi-firm Manchego, a soft Gorgonzola dolce, Brie, or even fresh ricotta (page 288), olives, a bit of salami, and hearty bread and you may decide to skip the main course altogether.

Dried Fruit

With its rich tradition of orchards and fruit production, the Hudson Valley has found ways to preserve its harvest to last throughout the year. Beth's Farm Kitchen and Grey Mouse Farm are just two local businesses that dry fruit in addition to making wonderful jams and jellies from fresh-picked fruit. That is great news for the winter chef, because the sweet tartness in dried fruit can be used across the menu from starters to dessert. I love stocking up in late fall, with dried apples, peaches, nectarines, apricots, blueberries, pears, prunes, and raisins all sharing space in my pantry. It's all local, available at either the farmers' market or directly from the farmers themselves.

I enjoy eating dried apples out of hand, or sprinkling dried blueberries into yogurt or my morning hot cereal, but I really love cooking with dried fruit. Some of my favorite dishes that incorporate fruit are Harvest Stuffed Peppers (page 156), Sweet 'n' Sour Chicken Liver Mousse (page 212), and all types of grain salads, where dried fruit pairs so well with barley, fregola, or wild rice. A handful of dried fruit tossed in during cooking increases the flavor and complexity of braised dishes. The tongue senses flavors that are sweet and salty and rich all at once. Dried fruit can also balance out the heavier, sometimes gamier, foods of winter. Added to whole-grain pilafs, it adds a sweet counterpoint to the grain's nutty flavor. When dried stone fruit is soaked in brandy or Calvados, it can become a decadent dessert, especially when incorporated into puddings, cakes, tarts, or pies.

Dried fruit consumption has been relatively steady among Americans. That is due, in part, to the increased choice of granola bars, trail mix, and breakfast cereals containing dried fruit, coupled with a greater awareness of just how important all fruit is

Freeze-Dried Harvest

Freeze-drying—the removal of water from inside a food—is an interesting technique for preserving fruit, vegetables, and even grains. Unlike air-drying (which is what turns a grape into a raisin or a plum into a prune), this elegant process pulls water out, leaving the fruit or vegetable both light and fully fortified at a cellular level—in other words, all of the water-soluble vitamins, nutrients, and phytochemicals remain in the cell walls. What you're left with is crisp, crunchy fruits or vegetables that can be eaten as snacks, sprinkled on cereals and salads, and offered as appetizers. Nutritionally, freeze-dried food may have higher ORAC levels than traditionally dried food. ORAC (oxygen radical absorbance capacity) is a measure of the level of antioxidants in a food. The link between the high antioxidant levels of fruits and vegetables and the health benefits of diets high in fresh fruits and vegetables may help us further understand how a good diet may slow down the rate at which our bodies age. Currently only about 2 percent of all dried fruits are freeze-dried nationally, but I think this method could have great implications for Hudson Valley farmers. Freeze-drying is an energy-intensive process, but there may be future alternative energy sources that can make that process more efficient. Imagine harvesting local fruit at its peak and then freeze-drying that flavor and nutrition to enjoy all year long! This concept has immense potential for farmers because it would smooth out the naturally variable harvests from year to year, and for consumers because they could enjoy a nutritionally whole source of summer and fall fruits without needing to buy produce shipped in from great distances. It seems like a technology perfectly suited for our Hudson Valley growers.

for maintaining good health. Plus, it's easy to enjoy—you just open up the bag and eat. Along with being high in fiber, complex carbohydrates, vitamins, minerals, and phytochemicals, dried fruit is extremely tasty, especially when you crave something sweet.

Dried fruit doesn't provide the full nutritional value of fresh fruit (freeze-drying is another matter—see above). Some nutrition is lost in drying and processing. But it still has its place, especially during winter, when our choices are limited. All that goodness, though, comes with one little caveat: watch how much you eat. Dried fruit is packed with calories. It takes about 5 pounds of fresh fruit to make 1 pound of dried fruit, and none of the calories dissipate in the drying process. So keep servings small, to about a quarter of a cup. Not very much, but still enough to give you a quick boost of energy and a smile.

Citrus

Well, I'm certainly not going to claim that lemons grow in the Hudson Valley! They don't, of course, but I've included them in this winter section because they have a long culinary tradition here. Citrus shows up in chutneys served with local cheeses, in compotes for desserts, as an ingredient in fish dishes, and in cocktails. Its flavorful zest flavors our marinades and dressings and studs my Orange-Cranberry-Crusted Leg of Lamb (page 244). I find that a little citrus cleans, clarifies, and elevates the flavors of most dishes.

It is exciting to see how many different kinds of citrus are available during the winter. It's no longer just lemons, limes, oranges, and grapefruit. Now you see delicate Meyer lemons, small mild Mexican limes, and Valencia oranges. Satsuma tangerines are for sale along with clementines, packed in their handsome wooden boxes. Beautiful blood oranges appear, including the very dark Moro orange and the lighter Tarocco. Both make

sexy and mysterious-looking martinis. The Ruby Red, a Cosmopolitan made with freshly squeezed red grapefruit in place of cranberry juice, is a winter favorite on the Gigi cocktail list. Tiny kumquats and limequats add an exotic note to meat dishes or can be transformed into a new kind of marmalade.

Let's face it, the sunny flavor of citrus gives food (and life) a boost during the dark days of winter. Its bright acidity perks up long-simmered dishes and soups. For example, I like to add a touch of grated lemon or orange zest to a butternut squash soup. It somehow brings the round sweetness of the squash into clearer focus. Citrus also pairs well with warmer spices like cumin, curry, ginger, and turmeric and with all kinds of dried fruit. Often rich cuts of meat can be paired successfully with citrus. A New Year's dish we created at the restaurant paired homemade ricotta gnocchi with braised lamb, olives, and preserved lemon. What a great combination of flavors.

The U.S. orange industry has done a wonderful job teaching us that the flesh of citrus fruits packs a significant vitamin C punch. But the fragrant skin, or zest, shouldn't be overlooked. It contains powerful compounds called limonoids. Limonene, a protective plant substance, is considered an anticarcinogen and gives a boost to toxin-fighting enzymes in the body. More than twenty epidemiological studies have shown a positive relationship between the consumption of citrus and protection against many types of cancer. Another limonoid called limonin seems to be able to reduce cholesterol, and some promising studies are ongoing.

But, health benefits aside, the zests of citrus add concentrated flavor to food and can pick up most salads, pastas, risottos, soups, stews, or even simply a cup of tea.

Potatoes

There are certain plants that change the world. Think of cotton and rice, for example. Their cultivation transformed early society in the United States, entrenched the institution of slavery, created worldwide trading links, and helped fuel the growth of wealth in Britain and America.

The story of potatoes is just as revolutionary. Consumed in the Andes for thousands of years, the potato was carried by the Spanish to Europe in the sixteenth century. Now European farmers could grow a plant that flourished even in relatively poor soil and produced a food with four times more carbohydrates than grain. This was a boon to hungry populations that until then had relied solely on wheat and other grasses to deliver needed calories. In fact, historians have linked the planting and consumption of potatoes with a spurt in European population growth.

The potato has continued its spread around the globe and is grown in more countries today than any other crop except corn. Developing countries account for more than half of the world's potato harvest, with China as the largest grower of potatoes worldwide. Interestingly, the potato is not a globally traded commodity, but is almost exclusively a locally grown food. Prices are determined by local production costs, not international commodity board speculation. In this respect, potatoes are a "secure" food that can help low-income farmers and vulnerable consumers ride out world food supply ups and downs.

Potatoes are easy to grow, are rich in carbohydrates for energy, and have the highest protein content (around 2.1 percent by weight) of all root/tuber crops, with an amino-acid pattern well matched to human needs. A single medium potato contains about half the recommended daily intake of vitamin C and more potassium than a banana. They are also a great source of fiber. Like sweet potatoes, potatoes will deliver more nutrients if the skin is consumed. So if you're eating the skin, buy organic and just wash them well before cooking.

The plethora of potato varieties that we grow and enjoy here in the Hudson Valley is nothing compared to the more than five thousand varieties still grown in the Andes. Imagine all the potatoes we *norteños* have yet to taste! Still, I don't feel too deprived. Potatoes are a great local product, and I like them best when eaten soon after they've been dug up. When fresh, they bring forth their own distinctive flavors to savor. I eat them throughout the winter, heedless of those who preach a low-carb lifestyle. To be frank, I'm suspicious of any diet that derides a whole category of foods. As a nutritionist, I've never found that to be a sound approach to health. You actually do need carbohydrates in your diet: they help regulate body temperature and keep you warm, they sustain you through long days of work, and they provide balance to your diet. I love that over the last few years, the Macy's Thanksgiving Day parade has proudly floated a giant Mr. Potato Head. So long, low-carb nonsense! In fact the food and agriculture sector of the United Nations adopted a resolution in 2005 to focus world attention on the importance of the potato, and the General Assembly declared 2008 the International Year of the Potato. *Bravi!* My Irish-Italian eyes are smiling!

HEARTY ROOTS COMMUNITY FARM

What a stroke of luck to have Benjamin Shute and Miriam Latzer's farm, Hearty Roots, right behind Gigi Market in Red Hook. The farm provides organic vegetables for our market for most of the year, allowing us to get our hands on some of the best-grown veggies in the Valley. Hearty Roots exists primarily as a CSA farm—a community-supported agricultural endeavor, which sells its produce directly to members who pay for their "harvest shares" in advance of the growing year. As a CSA member, you have literally bought the farm! Our market and several other farmers' markets in the Hudson Valley and Brooklyn also get some of the Hearty Roots bounty, and we make good use of every drop.

I love the farm and its beautiful vegetables, but I especially love Ben and Miriam's progressive approach to creating healthy farms and communities around the issue of food and wellness. Right up my alley! As a CSA, the farm develops strong links to the communities it serves, but it goes even further by hosting several events each year— like their annual onion planting party in May, which relies solely on volunteers to get over 16,000 fragile onion slips planted in a single day. Who comes to plant? Well, mostly their shareholders, friends, and families who will eat their work in July, but also members of the local growing community who simply like to spend time outdoors and enjoy the old-fashioned camaraderie of planting. That there is never a shortage of volunteers speaks volumes about Miriam and Ben's ability to make people enthused about farming and about supporting local farms in the Valley.

Miriam and Ben changed all my preconceived ideas about your "typical" Hudson Valley farmer. They are young, highly educated, very enthusiastic, and on a mission. Miriam, a Vassar and Rutgers graduate and former urban planner, and Ben, an Amherst grad and nonprofit activist, may once and for all redefine what it means to be a farmer in the twenty-first century. Their knowledge base is broad, their perspective is global, and their aim is to change the way we feed ourselves and protect the land. Ben would describe his career path as more Venn diagram than straight line. His early professional life revolved around issues such as food security, hunger, social justice, and the environment.

Orange-Cranberry-Crusted Leg of Lamb (page 244)

Lavender Pork Rib End Roast (page 246)

Winter Pasta Salad with Chicken, Mushrooms, and Radicchio (page 236)

Biscuit-Topped Chicken and Root Vegetable Stew (page 242)

Gigi Cioccolata Calda (page 273)

Now with Hearty Roots he has a closer, feet-on-the-ground understanding of the complexities, opportunities, and connections involved in growing and distributing food.

Ben is an enthusiastic spokesperson for creating a "green collar" movement to bring young people back to the land and to create social dialogue and commitment between consumers and growers. Land like ours in the Hudson Valley can be terrifically productive and can safely feed many people. Ben's goal is to create a new public awareness about the advantages of cultivated land and to move the intellectual discussion regarding land trusts, long-term agricultural land leases, and public productive landscapes from talk to reality. His partner, Miriam, is in agreement. "As a farmer along the Hudson, you often feel in crisis mode. We're so close to New York City and there is always development pressure. We have a lot of great land for growing here, but unfortunately it isn't in the hands of the growers. And once the parking lot cement is poured, you'll never get that land back."

Farmers like Ben and Miriam know a good fight when they see one. They've shaped Hearty Roots into a low-carbon-footprint farm practicing sustainable, organic agriculture, right down to their Allis Chalmers tractor, converted to electric. They participate on the local agriculture and open space committees to advocate for green space and sensible development planning; they lecture to audiences in the city and around the state about the CSA model; and they encourage farmers to rethink their planting mix, moving from low-value crops, such as hay, to higher value crops like vegetables.

Their unquenchable enthusiasm and commitment shows in the field. Each spring, boxes of beautiful arugula, baby lettuces and turnips, beets, bok choy, broccoli, kale, radicchio, radishes, spinach, and sugar snap peas stock the market. By summer, the fields are loaded with beans, cucumbers, tomatoes, eggplants, fennel, melons, greens, onions, and chiles, and in fall there are all those gorgeous root vegetables that I love. I'm not alone. Hearty Roots has doubled its plantings in each of the last few seasons and still can't keep up with demand from customers.

Miriam and Ben work with the good-natured demeanor of people who love what they do. Each week their newsletter shows up in my e-mail, letting me and their shareholders know what's happening and what's being harvested. That way we can quickly adapt and update our menus to take advantage of their fresh produce. Plus, it's great reading.

Hearty Roots Community Farm, P.O. Box 277, Tivoli, New York 12583

www.heartyroots.com

Hudson Valley Fresh Eggnog

MAKES 5 CUPS (10 SERVINGS)

Hudson Valley Fresh is a consortium of dairy farms initiated and run by my friend Sam Simon, a retired orthopedic surgeon who grew up on a dairy farm. Sam runs this nonprofit dairy cooperative just like one of his former operating rooms: with incredible standards of quality and cleanliness. In the 1970s, there were 275 dairies in Dutchess County, the highest number of dairy farms in New York State—and now there are only 26. His efforts have helped keep local farmers that remain in business. Hudson Valley Fresh ensures a fair price for milk that meets their high standards, which not only saves farms but also means preventing the loss of the land to development. Since the inception of Hudson Valley Fresh more than 5,000 acres of open land have been preserved. This certainly sounds like sustainable agriculture to me. I'm not a huge fan of overly sweetened, thick eggnog, so I skip the traditional cream and blend whole milk and half-and-half and cut the usual number of egg yolks from 8 to 6. If you prefer a more classic eggnog, add back the 2 yolks and up the sugar by ⅓ cup.

2 cups	whole milk
2 cups	half-and-half
¾ cup	sugar
1 teaspoon	pure vanilla extract
1 teaspoon	freshly grated nutmeg
½ teaspoon	ground cloves
Pinch	salt
6	large egg yolks
1 cup	of your favorite spirits, such as dark rum, bourbon, or whiskey

Set a medium metal bowl into a larger bowl filled with ice and water. Set aside.

In a medium saucepan, whisk together the milk, half-and-half, sugar, vanilla, nutmeg, cloves, and salt. Heat over medium heat, whisking or stirring often, until steaming; do not allow the mixture to boil. Place the egg yolks in a small bowl and whisk in about ½ cup of the hot milk mixture. While whisking, pour the yolk mixture back into the hot milk. Cook over medium-low heat, stirring constantly, until the mixture thickens, about 5 minutes. Do not let it simmer or boil.

Strain the mixture through a sieve into the bowl set in the ice bath, and let it cool completely. Refrigerate, with a piece of plastic wrap placed directly over the surface to prevent a "skin" from forming, until chilled and ready to use. Just before serving, stir in the spirits.

SERVING SUGGESTION

Serve in small clear glasses, with a light sprinkle of additional freshly grated nutmeg on top.

VARIATIONS

• Adjust the amount of spirits to your level of "festivity."
• Turn this into the base for eggnog ice cream by using a total of 8 egg yolks and a bit more sugar.

LEFTOVERS

Good for 2 or 3 days, refrigerated.

NUTRITION

Well . . . how about calcium? This is a once- or twice-a-year indulgence.

ECONOMY $

Candied Spiced Nuts

MAKES 2¾ CUPS

I love these crunchy, slightly sweet and spicy nuts sprinkled over salads and dotting cheese plates, but they're especially good by the handful with your favorite aperitivo. They don't stay on the shelves long at Gigi Market.

1	large egg white
8 ounces	walnut halves
8 ounces	almonds
½ cup	sugar, preferably superfine
1 tablespoon	ground cinnamon
1 teaspoon	ground ginger
1 teaspoon	salt
½ teaspoon	ground coriander
Pinch	cayenne pepper

Preheat the oven to 250°F.

In a medium bowl, whisk the egg white and 1 tablespoon water together until frothy. Add the nuts and stir to coat them completely. Transfer the nuts to a strainer or sieve and allow them to drain for about 5 minutes.

Combine the sugar, cinnamon, ginger, salt, coriander, and cayenne in a large plastic bag and shake vigorously to blend. Add half of the nuts and shake to coat them thoroughly. Remove the nuts and place them in a large baking pan. Repeat with the remaining nuts and add them to the baking pan. Shake the pan slightly to distribute the nuts evenly. Bake for 15 minutes.

Stir the nuts gently, smoothing them back into a single layer. Lower the oven temperature to 200°F and bake until the nuts are caramelized and crisp, about 45 minutes. Midway through baking, rotate the pan to ensure even browning.

Allow the nuts to cool completely. Store in an airtight container at room temperature for up to 2 weeks.

VARIATIONS

- *Savory candied nuts*: Change your spices to black pepper and cayenne, and cut the sugar in half.
- *Sweet and simple:* Don't add any spices at all, and don't let the nuts color. Stop the cooking when the nuts are crunchy and the sugar has crystallized. I especially like this approach for walnuts—it takes away some of their bitterness.

LEFTOVERS

A great way to use those last leftover nuts is to grind them up and add them to a short dough, like a pie crust, to provide some extra crunch. Leftover nuts can also be used as a garnish on tarts or ice cream sundaes.

NUTRITION

Researchers at the Harvard School of Public Health found that women who reported eating nuts at least five times per week reduced their risk of type 2 diabetes by almost 30 percent compared to those who rarely or never ate nuts. As long as you control total calories, eating a handful of nuts daily may help prevent weight gain and possibly promote weight loss (the fat, protein, and fiber in nuts help you feel full longer, so you may eat less during the day).

ECONOMY $

Sweet 'n' Sour Chicken Liver Mousse

MAKES ABOUT 3 CUPS

This mousse has converted those who adamantly declared their aversion to chicken livers. The dried fruit and citrus freshen the rich gaminess of the chicken livers. I get my little livers from Northwind Farms. If you purchase local chickens, ask for the supplier to set aside a couple of pounds; otherwise, get all-natural livers from your supermarket. Make the mousse up to 2 days ahead; the flavors will only get better.

⅓ cup plus 1 tablespoon	extra-virgin olive oil
1 ounce	pancetta or bacon, diced
1	medium shallot, chopped
2 tablespoons	golden raisins or dried cherries
¼ teaspoon	garam masala (see Note, page 137)
2 pounds	chicken livers, cleaned
	Salt and freshly ground black pepper
2 tablespoons	sherry vinegar
1 tablespoon	fresh orange juice
1 tablespoon	pure maple syrup
	Grated zest of 1 lemon

Heat the 1 tablespoon olive oil in a large skillet over medium heat. Add the pancetta and shallot, and cook, stirring often, until fat is rendered from the pancetta and it is slightly browned, 3 to 4 minutes. Add the raisins and garam masala and stir. Increase the heat to medium-high, season the chicken livers with salt and pepper, and add them to the skillet (they should fit in one layer; do not crowd). Cook, turning the livers with tongs once or twice, until they are firm but still slightly pink inside, about 5 minutes, depending on the size. Add the vinegar, orange juice, and maple syrup and cook until slightly reduced, about 1 minute. Remove from the heat and let cool slightly.

Transfer the mixture to a food processor, add the lemon zest, and pulse a few times to blend. With the motor running, pour in the remaining ⅓ cup olive oil in a steady stream. Season the mousse with salt and pepper to taste. Refrigerate until cooled and thickened, about 2 hours.

Transfer the mousse to a serving bowl and allow it to warm slightly at room temperature before serving.

Spread on toasts or crostini. Or transfer to a terrine mold, pack down, cover with plastic wrap, and refrigerate for at least an hour; serve sliced. This dish looks best with a garnish; try pomegranate seeds.

LEFTOVERS

Use in a *salsa peverada*, a classic sauce from the Veneto region of Italy. Typically the mousse is stirred into hot cooked borlotti beans, melting into a luscious sauce.

NUTRITION

Chicken livers are rich in protein, vitamin A, iron, and B vitamins, especially B_{12} and folate. A little goes a long way for flavor and nutrition.

ECONOMY $

Chicken livers are an inexpensive protein source.

Gigi Zuppa di Contadina (Farmer's Soup)

MAKES 8 TO 10 SERVINGS

*We serve this minestrone all year long, adding whatever vegetables come in from the
local farms. The recipe below is our "base"—sometimes it also includes kale
or other cooking greens and butternut squash. Follow the seasons
where you live, adding farm-fresh vegetables.*

¼ cup	olive oil
4	celery stalks, thinly sliced
2	medium carrots, diced
1	large onion, diced
½ cup	chopped fresh flat-leaf parsley
	Salt and freshly ground black pepper
4	parsnips, peeled and diced
3	medium potatoes, peeled and cut into 2-inch cubes
2	bay leaves
1	rosemary sprig
1 pound	Gigi Mixed Contadina Minestra; or 8 ounces dried cannellini beans, 8 ounces dried cranberry beans, 1 tablespoon dried parsley, 1 teaspoon dried oregano, and ¼ teaspoon red pepper flakes
4 quarts	water, vegetable or chicken stock, or reduced-sodium broth

Heat the olive oil in a large saucepan or a
soup pot over medium heat. Add the celery,
carrots, onion, and ¼ cup of the fresh parsley,
and season with salt and pepper to taste.
Cook, stirring often, until the onion softens,
about 5 minutes. Add the parsnips, potatoes,
bay leaves, and rosemary and cook, stirring
often, for about 10 minutes. Then stir in the
bean mix, add the water, stock, or broth and
bring to a boil. Reduce the heat and cook at
a low boil until the beans are very tender and
the soup has thickened, 1½ to 2 hours.

Remove the bay leaves and rosemary,
add the remaining ¼ cup fresh parsley, and
season the soup with salt to taste. Serve
piping hot.

Drizzle with extra-virgin olive oil and top with a sprinkle of grated Parmesan. Serve with crusty bread or crostini.

VARIATIONS

- *Spring:* Omit the parsnips, and add peas and asparagus tips during the last 5 minutes of cooking.
- *Summer:* Omit the parsnips and add sliced summer squash during the last 20 minutes of cooking, and/or diced tomatoes and fresh basil just before serving.
- *Fall/winter:* Add diced rutabaga and/or turnips when adding the potatoes and parsnips, and/or add diced butternut squash and cooking greens during the last 20 minutes of cooking.

LEFTOVERS

Enjoy for up to 3 days.

NUTRITION

This soup is low-calorie and satisfying, and it's loaded with fiber and antioxidants from the beans and vegetables.

ECONOMY $

It isn't called Farmer's Soup for nothing!

Fava, Barley, and Kale Soup

*Sweet, nutty dried fava beans provide a terrific contrast to slightly bitter kale.
Try all types of kale, such as green, purple, or black (Tuscan), or substitute collard or
mustard greens. This soup is even better reheated. It also freezes well, so consider making
a big batch and storing it in small containers for a quick, tasty meal on a busy day.
Beans and barley will continue to absorb liquid and soften even after they're
fully cooked, and this soup thickens considerably when it cools,
so add a little stock or water to thin it slightly when reheating.*

2 tablespoons	olive oil
1	celery stalk, chopped
1	onion, chopped
2½ cups	dried split fava beans (about 12 ounces) available in gourmet markets and some supermarkets
2	garlic cloves, thinly sliced
¼ teaspoon	red pepper flakes
10 cups	chicken or vegetable stock, or reduced-sodium broth
1	bay leaf
½ cup	pearl barley
¾ pound	roughly chopped kale leaves (about 8 cups)
	Salt and freshly ground black pepper

Heat the olive oil in a large saucepan over medium heat. Add the celery and onion and cook, stirring often, until softened, about 5 minutes. Add the fava beans, garlic, and red pepper flakes and cook, stirring often, for another 2 to 3 minutes. Add the stock and bay leaf, and bring to a boil. Reduce the heat and simmer, stirring occasionally, for 40 minutes. Add the barley and cook for another 40 minutes. By now the fava beans should have broken apart, making the soup quite creamy.

Finally, add the kale and cook for 5 minutes. Remove the bay leaf, add salt and pepper to taste, and serve.

- Drizzle each serving with extra-virgin olive oil. Top with shaved or grated Parmesan.
- Make it a full meal with some crusty bread and a hunk of New York State (or Vermont or Wisconsin) cheddar.

VARIATIONS

- Substitute wild rice for the barley.
- Swap any cooking green for the kale.
- Use dried white beans or limas instead of the fava beans.
- Hulled barley, which contains the outer bran layer, is the most nutritious. If you can find it, substitute it for the pearl barley. It takes longer to cook, so add it when you add the stock.

LEFTOVERS

Cool, cover, and refrigerate for up to 3 days. Delicious reheated.

NUTRITION

Chock-full of three "super foods"—dark cooking greens, legumes, and whole grains.

Hudson Valley Onion Soup

I make this soup only when I can get sweet farm-fresh onions, which have a better texture and are far sweeter than the typical supermarket varieties. Prepare this recipe in full, or stop after reducing the Marsala: the cooked onions make a delicious addition to cooked pasta or as a topping for pizza (or Gigi Skizza) or bruschetta with a sprinkling of crumbled goat cheese or grated Parmesan.

8	medium local white onions (about 3 pounds), halved and thinly sliced lengthwise
2 tablespoons	unsalted butter
2 tablespoons	olive oil, plus more for brushing
¼ cup	roughly chopped fresh flat-leaf parsley
½ cup	Marsala wine
10 cups	beef or chicken stock or reduced-sodium broth
2	bay leaves
2 teaspoons	chopped fresh thyme
1 teaspoon	chopped fresh rosemary
	Salt
Twelve	¼-inch-thick baguette slices
4 ounces	Grana Padano, Parmesan, or Pecorino, cut into 12 thin slices

Place the onions in a large heavy-bottomed saucepan with the butter and the olive oil. Cook over medium-low heat, stirring often, until the onions have broken down and have a deep, rich hue, 35 to 40 minutes. Add the parsley and cook for 1 minute. Add the Marsala, stirring to deglaze the bottom of the pan, and cook until the liquid is reduced by two thirds, about 1 minute. Stir in the stock, bay leaves, thyme, and rosemary, and season lightly with salt. Bring to a boil. Then reduce the heat and simmer, uncovered, until the soup has reduced by almost half, about 1 hour. Adjust the seasoning with more salt, if necessary, and discard the bay leaves.

Just before serving, prepare the cheesy baguette rounds: Arrange a rack 5 to 6 inches below the heat source and preheat the broiler.

Place the baguette slices on a baking sheet, spray or brush them with olive oil, and then top each one with a slice of the cheese. Broil until the cheese is melted, bubbly, and lightly browned.

Ladle the soup into bowls and add 2 or 3 baguette rounds to each bowl; ladle extra soup on top to soften them. Enjoy immediately.

VARIATIONS

- *Egg-drop style*: For a thicker, less brothy soup, temper a beaten egg with some of the hot broth in a small mixing bowl; whisk to combine. With the finished soup at a boil, stir the egg into the soup. Then remove from the heat and serve.
- *For sweeter onions*: Thinly slice the onions with a mandoline on its finest setting. Spread the onions in a colander and sprinkle ½ cup kosher salt evenly over them; use your hands to mix. Set aside for 2 hours. Then rinse the onions thoroughly, squeeze out the excess water, and pat dry with a clean kitchen towel or between sheets of paper towels. Proceed with the recipe.

NUTRITION

Onions are relatively unknown as a nutrition "super food"—they contain powerful antioxidants, such as quercetin, which blunts the risk of heart disease and cancer. They also have antibiotic, antiviral, and anti inflammatory properties. Among their collections of health-promoting compounds are thiosulfinates, sulfoxides, and sulfides (think of their great smell!).

ECONOMY $

LEFTOVERS

As long as the baguette rounds have not been added, this makes a great next day meal.

Jayne Keyes–Approved Hudson Valley Cajun Gumbo

Among her many other life accomplishments, Jayne Keyes is the Hudson Valley's hostess extraordinaire. Count yourself lucky to be a guest at one of her dinner parties. Even the lowest-key evening has every hint of elegance; it's all in the details. Jayne's Louisiana roots came in handy when I was trying to create a Hudson Valley gumbo. When I brought up the subject, like a good southern woman, Jayne said, "It's all in the roux." I'm very proud that this recipe, which draws inspiration from our local farms, has her tested seal of approval.

In the late 1800s, a large number of Sicilian immigrants settled in southern Louisiana. They left distinct influences on Creole cooking, including the use of garlic and "red gravies"—brown roux with tomato paste. If you wish to make this gumbo Mediterranean-style, "fry" ¼ cup of tomato paste in the roux after it has darkened.

12 ounces	Northwind Farms pork sausages, crumbled or cut into ¼-inch-thick slices
4 tablespoons	peanut oil or lard
3 tablespoons	all-purpose flour
Two	2½-pound chickens, each cut into 8 pieces (I use Northwind Farms chickens; substitute your own small local chickens or one 5-pound chicken)
	Salt and freshly ground black pepper
1	medium onion, diced
2	celery stalks, diced
2	medium green bell peppers, cored, seeded, and diced
1	medium red bell pepper, cored, seeded, and diced
3	garlic cloves, chopped
12 ounces	okra (fresh or frozen), sliced
6 cups	chicken stock or reduced-sodium broth
2	bay leaves
¼ teaspoon	cayenne pepper, or to taste
5 cups	chopped collard greens (about 1 large bunch)

Cook the sausage in a large Dutch oven (preferably cast-iron) over medium heat until it is browned but not crisp, about 5 minutes. Use a slotted spoon to transfer the sausage to a bowl, and discard the rendered fat.

Add 3 tablespoons of the oil and the flour to the Dutch oven, and stir with a wooden spoon. Then cook the roux over medium-low heat, stirring constantly, until it is a deep dark brown, about 15 minutes. Set aside.

In a large sauté pan or skillet, heat the remaining 1 tablespoon oil over medium-high heat. Season the chicken parts with salt and pepper and sear them, turning to brown them on all sides for 7 to 8 minutes; do this in batches to prevent crowding, transferring pieces to a plate as they brown. Set aside the browned chicken. Add the onion, celery, bell peppers, and garlic to the same skillet and cook, stirring occasionally, until the vegetables are tender, about 5 minutes. Add the okra and cook for another 5 minutes.

Meanwhile, heat the chicken stock in a saucepan until just simmering; keep it hot.

Put the Dutch oven back on the heat. Whisk 1 cup of the warmed stock into the roux. Add the bay leaves, cayenne, and ¼ teaspoon black pepper. Stir in the cooked vegetables, and add the browned sausage and chicken. Add just enough additional stock to cover, and stir again. Cook, uncovered, until the chicken is very tender and the sauce is thick, about 45 minutes. (Add a bit more stock occasionally if necessary to keep the mixture thick and fluid.) During the last 10 minutes of cooking, stir in the collard greens. Season with salt and pepper if necessary. Discard the bay leaves, and serve.

Serve over white or brown rice, or even couscous.

VARIATIONS

- Toss in some fresh corn kernels during the last few minutes of cooking.
- Add 8 ounces pork tasso (Cajun-cured smoked meat; we get ours from Mountain Products Smokehouse in LaGrangeville, New York), trimmed and cut into ¼-inch pieces.
- Substitute kale or chard for the collard greens.
- Substitute chicken sausage for the pork.

LEFTOVERS

So good the next day!

NUTRITION

Okay, the nutritionist is going out on a limb a bit with the fat (it's the roux!), but gumbo is also rich in protein and chock-full of veggies that are filled with vitamins, minerals, and phytochemcials.

ECONOMY $$

Overall a rather inexpensive meal for six (with leftovers). Less expensive than a seafood gumbo.

Hudson Valley Salad with Low-Fat Horseradish-Chive Dressing

MAKES 4 TO 6 SERVINGS

I put this salad on the Just Salad menu as a celebration of the harvest that takes place just north of our five New York City locations. It's a simple vegetarian salad that highlights the ingredients that grow so well in the Hudson Valley. Combined with the zesty horseradish-chive dressing, it makes for a tasty and healthy meal or first course. At Just Salad, we chop all of our salads with a triple-blade mezzaluna knife. If you'd like the same chopped effect at home, use two large chef's knives, one in each hand, with all the salad ingredients except the croutons and pumpkin seeds—toss them in, along with the dressing, after chopping

Low-fat horseradish-chive dressing

½ cup	low-fat sour cream (if not available, combine reduced-fat and fat-free)
1½ tablespoons	prepared horseradish cream sauce (available in most supermarkets; if not, combine 2 teaspoons freshly grated horseradish root with 1 teaspoon lemon juice and 1 tablespoon sour cream)
2 tablespoons	white wine vinegar
1 tablespoon	Dijon mustard
	Salt and freshly ground black pepper
1 teaspoon	confectioners' sugar (optional)
2 tablespoons	chopped fresh chives

Hudson Valley salad

4	medium beets (about 2 to 3 inches in diameter)
3 cups	diced peeled butternut squash
1 tablespoon	olive oil
	Salt
1½ cups	broccoli florets
12 ounces	baby spinach (about 12 cups)
1	medium apple, peeled, cored, and diced
1⅓ cups	whole-grain croutons (made from your favorite whole-grain bread or use your favorite brand)
½ cup	toasted pumpkin seeds

Preheat the oven to 375°F.

To prepare the horseradish-chive dressing, combine the sour cream, horseradish cream, vinegar, and Dijon mustard in a food processor and puree until smooth. Add 2 tablespoons water, or more, to thin to the desired consistency. Season with salt and pepper and sugar, if using, and stir in the chives. Store, covered and refrigerated, for up to 5 days.

Wrap the beets tightly in aluminum foil (red and gold separately) and roast them in the middle of the oven until fork-tender, 45 to 60 minutes, depending on their size. Let the beets rest in the foil for 15 minutes. Then carefully open the foil, letting any residual steam escape, and transfer the beets to a cutting board. With a small sharp knife, cut off the stems and peel the beets. Cut the beets into "rustic" bite-size pieces.

Place the butternut squash in a baking dish that is just large enough to hold it in a single layer. Drizzle with the olive oil, season with salt, and toss to combine. Roast until the squash can be easily pierced and is lightly browned, 20 to 25 minutes. Set aside to cool.

Bring 1 inch of water to a boil in a saucepan with a steamer (if you do not have a steamer put the florets directly in the water). Add the broccoli, reduce the heat to a low boil and cook until the broccoli is easily pierced with a fork or paring knife. Place in an ice bath to cool. Drain and set aside.

In a large bowl, combine the spinach, butternut squash, beets, broccoli, and apple. Add the dressing and toss to combine. Season with salt and pepper if necessary, stir in the croutons, and sprinkle with the toasted pumpkin seeds. Serve immediately.

VARIATIONS

- Add 4 ounces of your favorite crumbled or shredded cheese, such as feta, goat cheese, Manchego, or cheddar.
- Give it a protein boost with grilled shrimp, chicken, or even a few hard-boiled eggs.
- Substitute your favorite dressing; this salad works well with a simple vinaigrette or more assertive flavors like sherry-shallot (page 276) or even a blue cheese dressing.
- Enjoy the horseradish-chive dressing as a low-fat alternative to dress other salads.

NUTRITION

The vibrant colors tell all in this salad: lots of vitamins, minerals, and protective phytochemicals.

ECONOMY $

Portobello and Bell Pepper Sloppy Joes

MAKES 4 SERVINGS

Portobellos provide the meatiness, and harvest peppers offer contrast with a little sweet and spice. We get our fresh bells from Hearty Roots Farm. Enjoy this recipe with my sloppy joe sauce or take a shortcut, adding 1½ cups of your favorite BBQ sauce plus ½ cup water.

4 tablespoons	olive oil
2	medium onions, thinly sliced
2	garlic cloves, chopped
1	small green bell pepper, cored, seeded, and cut into long thin strips
1	small red bell pepper, cored, seeded, and cut into long thin strips
9	large portobello mushrooms (about 18 ounces), gills removed, cut into ¼-inch-thick slices
	Salt and freshly ground black pepper

Sauce

1 cup	tomato sauce, homemade (see page 290) or canned
2 tablespoons	tomato paste
1 teaspoon	dried oregano or 2 teaspoons fresh oregeno
1 tablespoon	Worcestershire sauce
1 teaspoon	Tabasco sauce, or to taste

4	whole-grain hamburger buns, toasted

Heat 2 tablespoons of the olive oil in a large skillet over medium heat. Add the onions, garlic, and bell peppers and cook, stirring or tossing often, until soft, about 10 minutes.

Increase the heat to medium-high and add the remaining 2 tablespoons olive oil and the mushrooms. Cook, tossing or stirring occasionally, until the mushrooms are soft and all the released water has evaporated, 8 to 10 minutes. Season with salt and pepper to taste.

Reduce the heat to medium and add all the sauce ingredients. Stir in ¾ cup water and cook, stirring often, until the mixture is thick, about 15 minutes.

Adjust the seasoning if necessary. Serve between your favorite toasted whole-grain hamburger buns or "open face."

- Add shredded cheddar when assembling the sandwich.
- Add eggplant strips when sautéing the vegetables.
- Omit the peppers and increase the mushrooms by 6 ounces.
- Substitute seasonal local mushrooms for the portobellos.

LEFTOVERS

Enjoy reheated on the stovetop or in the microwave.

NUTRITION

Peppers are rich in carotenoids and vitamins A and C. Mushrooms lend selenium as well as other minerals and phytochemicals.

ECONOMY $$

Pizzoccheri alla Valtellinese

Buckwheat Pasta with Cheese and Savoy Cabbage

MAKES 6 TO 8 SERVINGS

This is one of my favorite pasta dishes of all time. Although it is a traditional dish of Valtellina, an area in the Lombardia region of Italy that borders Switzerland, it is prepared throughout the north of Italy during the autumn and winter months, really anywhere that cabbage is grown. Often served in the little agriturismi and osterie in the Veneto region of Italy, where I once lived, this is the perfect hearty, rustic, and healthy dinner to fortify and warm you up after a day of skiing, hiking, or working outdoors. If you do not have time to prepare the buckwheat pasta, purchase long, wide ribbons (like pappardelle) of dry buckwheat pasta, cook them according to the package instructions, and toss with the savory sauce.

Buckwheat pasta

2½ cups	all-purpose flour
1½ cups	buckwheat flour
Pinch	salt
5	large eggs, lightly beaten
¼ cup	whole milk

Sauce

2	medium potatoes, peeled and diced
1 head	Savoy cabbage, cored and sliced into thin strips
6 tablespoons	unsalted butter (¾ stick), cut into cubes
10	fresh sage leaves
3	garlic cloves, minced

	Freshly ground black pepper
8 ounces	Bitto cheese, diced (This is the classic cheese of Valtellina. If you cannot find it, substitute Fontina.)
½ cup	freshly grated Grana Padano or Parmesan cheese (optional)

To prepare the pasta, combine the all-purpose and buckwheat flours on a flat work surface. Season with the salt. Make a well in the center and pour the eggs and the milk into the well. Using a fork, gradually incorporate the flour into the egg mixture. Using your hands, gather the dough together and knead it, adding a little more flour if it is sticky, until it forms a smooth ball. Wrap the dough in plastic wrap and let it rest in the refrigerator for at least 30 minutes or up to 1 day.

Using a pasta machine or a rolling pin on a lightly floured surface, roll the dough to about ⅛-inch thickness. Trim it to a neat rectangular shape, and then cut it into ½-inch-wide, 4-inch-long strips. Lightly dust the pasta with flour and transfer it in one layer to a sheet pan or store in an airtight container for up to 3 days until ready to cook.

Bring a large pot of water to a boil (if you have a pasta pot with an insert, this is ideal). Season the water with salt. Put the potatoes in the insert and plunge it into the boiling water. After 6 minutes, add the cabbage. Cook for another 2 to 3 minutes, until the vegetables are tender. Remove the insert and drain the vegetables. Keep the water at a boil for the pasta.

Cook the pasta in the boiling water until al dente, 2 to 4 minutes.

Meanwhile, heat the butter and the sage in a large skillet over medium-high heat, and cook until the butter browns slightly and smells nutty and the sage leaves become crisp. Add the garlic and cook for another minute. Add the reserved potatoes and cabbage and cook, tossing, to warm through.

Drain the pasta, reserving ½ cup of the cooking water. Add the pasta to the skillet, season with black pepper, and toss, blending all the ingredients. If the mixture is too thick, add a little of the reserved cooking water. Remove the skillet from the heat and add the Bitto cheese; toss again.

Portion the pizzoccheri onto serving plates, and serve with the grated cheese, if using.

SERVING SUGGESTION

Enjoy with a glass of northern Italian white wine, such as a Tocai or a Gavi.

VARIATIONS

- Add diced carrots when cooking the potatoes.
- Substitute your favorite semi-firm to firm cheese for the Bitto or Fontina. Consider Gruyère, Manchego, or cheddar.

LEFTOVERS

Best enjoyed immediately.

NUTRITION

Cabbage is a cancer-fighting cruciferous vegetable. Both potatoes and cabbage are rich in vitamin C.

ECONOMY $$

Gigi Tagliatelle Bolognese

MAKES 6 TO 8 SERVINGS

This hearty sauce from the Emilia-Romagna region of Italy can be tossed with just about any kind of pasta, but it is especially divine with fresh tagliatelle or other long pasta such as fettuccine. Our Bolognese sauce is made with Northwind Farms ground beef and pork in a sixty-forty ratio. Nothing beats a piping hot plate of this pasta on a chilly day. More often than not, it's my Sunday midday meal in between shifts at the restaurant. I guess many others feel the same, as it is ordered the most on Sunday and the refrigerated shelves of Gigi Bolognese sauce clear by the end of the day at Gigi Market. If you don't wish to make the homemade pasta, enjoy the Bolognese sauce with 2 pounds of store-bought fresh fettuccine.

Tagliatelle

1 pound	Italian extra-fine 00 flour or cake flour (3 cups)
4	large eggs
¼ cup	extra-virgin olive oil
1 teaspoon	salt
	Cornmeal, for dusting the pasta

Bolognese sauce

2 tablespoons	olive oil
1½ pounds	ground beef
1 pound	ground pork; or 8 ounces ground pork and 8 ounces pancetta, finely chopped
1	carrot, finely chopped
1	small onion, minced
½ stalk	celery, minced
2	garlic cloves, minced
½ cup	dry white wine
1 cup	beef, veal, or chicken stock, or reduced-sodium broth
1 tablespoon	tomato paste
One	28-ounce can whole peeled San Marzano tomatoes, with juice
1 tablespoon	chopped fresh thyme
2 teaspoons	chopped fresh rosemary
¼ cup	chopped fresh flat-leaf parsley
½ teaspoon	kosher salt
¼ teaspoon	freshly ground black pepper
1 cup	whole milk (optional)
1 tablespoon	all-purpose flour (optional)
⅓ cup	freshly grated Grana Padano or Parmesan cheese

To prepare the tagliatelle, place the flour in a mound on a pasta board or clean work surface. Using your fingers, make a center well. Place the eggs, oil, salt, and 1 tablespoon water in the well. Again using your fingers, mix the liquid ingredients together. Then begin pulling in flour from the inside rim of the well. Continue to pull the flour into the liquid until it is mostly mixed together. Using both hands, gather the mixture together in a ball and begin kneading it, picking up stray pieces of dough as you work it. Continue kneading until you have a smooth, elastic ball, about 5 minutes. Wrap the dough in plastic wrap and refrigerate it to rest for 30 minutes.

Meanwhile, to prepare the Bolognese sauce, heat the olive oil in a large skillet over high heat. Add the ground beef and cook, breaking up the chunks with a spatula, until it is evenly browned, about 7 minutes. Use a slotted spoon to transfer the meat to a plate; set aside.

Return the skillet to medium heat and add the pork (or pork and pancetta). Cook, stirring frequently, until just cooked through, about 2 minutes. Add the carrot, onion, celery, and garlic and cook until the vegetables are tender, about 4 minutes. Return the ground beef to the skillet. Add the wine, stock, tomato paste, tomatoes, thyme, rosemary, half of the parsley, and the salt and pepper. Bring to a boil. Then lower the temperature to a slow simmer, cover, and cook for 40 minutes.

For a creamier, thicker Bolognese sauce,

whisk just enough of the milk into the flour to make a creamy paste. Whisk in the remaining milk, and then pour the mixture into the simmering Bolognese sauce; cook, stirring often, for 5 minutes. (You can store the sauce, covered and refrigerated, for up to 4 days, or freeze it in a quart container for up to 2 months.) If cooking the pasta immediately, keep the sauce at a low simmer.

Line a sheet pan with parchment paper. Set the pasta machine roller on the widest setting. Cut the ball of dough into 2 pieces. Flatten one of the pieces of dough into a rectangle and feed it through the pasta machine rollers. Fold the ends into the center (as if you were closing a book), and feed the pasta through the rollers again with the seam vertical. Repeat two or three more times to widen the pasta sheet, and then send the sheet (without folding) through the pasta machine six or seven more times, gradually lowering the setting and lightly dusting with flour to prevent sticking, until you have a long, paper-thin sheet of pasta. Cut this sheet into 12-inch rectangles and place them on the parchment paper. Repeat the whole process with the second piece of dough. Fit the pasta machine with the tagliatelle attachment (fettuccine and tagliatelle are generally interchangeable). Roll each pasta sheet through the machine. Toss the long strands with some cornmeal to prevent sticking until ready to cook.

Bring a large pot of water to a boil and season it with salt.

Cook the tagliatelle in the boiling water

until al dente, 2 to 3 minutes. Drain, and quickly return the pasta to the pot; it should still have some cooking water on it. Add the hot Bolognese sauce, the Grana Padano, and the remaining parsley, and stir or toss to combine. Serve immediately, piping hot.

hot Bolognese sauce, the Grana Padano, and the remaining parsley, and stir or toss to combine. Serve immediately, piping hot.

SERVING SUGGESTIONS

Top the tagliatelle with a generous scoop of fresh ricotta (page 288) and enjoy with a medium-bodied Italian red such as a Sangiovese, Barbera d'Asti, or Dolcetto d'Alba.

NUTRITION

This high-carb, high-protein dish is certainly hearty. It sticks to the bones after a day of outdoor work or play.

ECONOMY $$

VARIATIONS

• Omit the pork or pancetta and add more beef.
• Enjoy the Bolognese between layers of lasagna or on top of Parmesan risotto.
• We offer the option of fresh traditional or whole-wheat tagliatelle; enjoy the Bolognese with either.

Creamy Mushroom Polenta "Lasagna"

MAKES 8 ENTRÉE OR 12 APPETIZER SERVINGS

This is a nice vegetarian option with a twist: lasagna noodles are replaced with polenta that has been cooked, chilled, and sliced. The mushroom filling is a rich counterpoint to the polenta. I use Wiltbank Farm mushrooms; you can substitute your favorite local seasonal mushrooms or even domestic white button or cremini. The dish stands up well to a full-bodied red wine.

Polenta

1 teaspoon	kosher salt
1½ cups	medium-grind stone-ground cornmeal (most brands found in the supermarket will work well)
1 tablespoon	olive oil
½ cup	freshly grated Grana Padano or Parmesan cheese

Mushroom filling

¼ cup	olive oil, plus extra for the baking dish
2 pounds	fresh shiitake and oyster mushrooms, tough stems removed, thinly sliced
5 or 6	fresh sage leaves, roughly chopped
2 tablespoons	chopped fresh flat-leaf parsley
1½ tablespoons	all-purpose flour
2 cups	half-and-half; or 1 cup 2% or whole milk and 1 cup heavy cream

	Salt and freshly ground black pepper
1½ cups	shredded Fontina cheese

Bring 4 cups water to a boil in a medium heavy-bottomed saucepan. Add the kosher salt, reduce the heat to a simmer, and gradually whisk in the cornmeal, a small amount at a time. Reduce the heat to low and cook the polenta, stirring often, until tender, about 20 minutes. Remove the pan from the heat and stir in the olive oil and Grana Padano. Pour the polenta into a shallow 9 x 17-inch baking dish and spread it out evenly with a spatula. Set aside until thoroughly cool.

Preheat the oven to 350°F.

Heat the olive oil in a large nonstick skillet over medium-high heat. Add the mushrooms, sage, and parsley, and cook, tossing or stirring occasionally, until the mushrooms have released all of their liquid and are beginning to turn golden, about 12 minutes. Add the flour, stirring until it is no longer visible. Add the half-and-half and cook until the sauce is thick, 4 to 5 minutes. Season with salt and pepper to taste, and set aside.

Cut the cooled polenta into quarters. Then trim the quarters slightly so they will fit in a 13 x 9 x 2-inch (3-quart) baking dish. Grease the bottom and sides of the baking dish with olive oil, and place 2 slices of polenta on the bottom. Spoon half of the mushroom mixture over the polenta, and top it with half of the shredded Fontina. Place the other two pieces of polenta over the cheese and top with the remaining mushrooms. Cover the baking dish with aluminum foil and bake until heated through, 20 to 25 minutes.

Increase the oven temperature to 400°F. Remove the foil and top the "lasagna" with the remaining Fontina. Cook until the cheese is bubbly and golden, 10 to 12 minutes. Serve piping hot.

SERVING SUGGESTIONS

Enjoy as an entrée or serve with roasted chicken, pork, or beef.

VARIATIONS

- Substitute 4 cups mixed roasted or grilled vegetables for the mushrooms. Mix with 1½ cups tomato sauce before layering.
- Use mozzarella (fresh or smoked) instead of the Fontina.
- Substitute thyme for the sage.
- Use the mushroom ragù to fill traditional pasta lasagna, toss with pasta, or top canapés.

LEFTOVERS

Reheats well in a microwave.

NUTRITION

Stone-ground cornmeal is usually a whole grain and provides ample amounts of B vitamins, minerals (iron, magnesium, and phosphorus), and fiber. Depending on where they are cultivated, mushrooms can offer significant selenium. For a lower-calorie, lower-fat dish, prepare Enlightened Béchamel (page 281) to replace the flour/half-and-half mixture.

ECONOMY $$

Three Local Cheese Risotto Gratin

MAKES 4 ENTREES OR 6 APPETIZER SERVINGS

As a nutritionist, I am often asked about my secret dietary indulgences. Hands down, it's cheese. I'm a nosher, and a great-quality cheese always satisfies. Cheese making has seen a resurgence in the Hudson Valley, as innovative craftspeople have taken over old dairies. Every style is available, from New York State cheddars to cheeses in the classic Italian, French, and Spanish traditions. Enjoy this simple gratin using cheeses that celebrate your local bounty.

⅓ cup	unseasoned dried bread crumbs
¼ cup	freshly grated Grana Padano or Parmesan cheese
6 cups	chicken stock or reduced-sodium broth
2 tablespoons	olive oil
1	small onion, diced
1½ cups	Italian rice (preferably Carnaroli, Superfino Arborio, or Semifino Vialone Nano)
½ cup	dry white wine
	Salt and freshly ground black pepper
2 tablespoons	unsalted butter
2 ounces	Old Chatham Sheepherding Company Ewe's Blue, Gorgonzola dolce, or other creamy blue-style cheese, crumbled or dice
2 ounces	Coach Farm Triple Cream Aged Goat Cheese or other triple-cream goat's or sheep's milk cheese, crumbled or diced
2 ounces	Sprout Creek Farm Batch 35 or other pungent, earthy cheese, such as Robiola, Morbier, or Taleggio, crumbled or diced

Grease a 2-quart casserole with butter or olive oil cooking spray, and set it aside. Mix the bread crumbs and Grana Padano together in a small bowl, and set it aside.

Pour the stock into a saucepan and bring it to a simmer. Keep it at a low simmer.

Heat the olive oil in a medium heavy-bottomed saucepan over medium heat. Add the onion and cook until softened, 3 to 4 minutes. Add the rice and cook, stirring constantly, until it looks chalky and you can see a white dot in the center of each grain, about 2 minutes. Add the wine and cook, stirring, until it is almost completely absorbed. Stir in 1 cup of the hot stock, season with salt and pepper to taste, and bring to a boil. Cook at a low boil, stirring frequently. When most of the liquid has been absorbed, add another cup of stock. Continue adding small ladles of stock as the rice absorbs the liquid. After 15 minutes, taste a grain of rice; it should be tender but firm, and the mixture should have movement but no excess liquid. If it requires more cooking, add a touch more stock and cook for another 1 to 2 minutes.

Remove from the heat and whip in the butter and cheeses. Season with more salt and pepper if necessary.

Place a rack 6 inches below the heat source and preheat the broiler.

Transfer the risotto to the prepared casserole and top with the bread crumb mixture. Place the dish under the broiler and broil for about 3 minutes, or until the top is golden. Serve immediately.

VARIATION

Omit the bread crumb topping and the broiling, and serve as a creamy classic risotto.

LEFTOVERS

Reheat in the microwave.

NUTRITION

This rather rich dish can be a moderately portioned side dish. A little goes a long way with this much flavor.

ECONOMY $$

Winter Pasta Salad with Chicken, Mushrooms, and Radicchio

MAKES 6 TO 8 SERVINGS

Winter needs a little color. Radicchio adds some pizzazz, crunch, and pleasantly bitter flavor to contrast with the earthy mushrooms in this pasta salad. Prepare it with or without the chicken.

8 ounces	dry orecchiette or farfalle pasta
3 tablespoons	olive oil
12 ounces	fresh shiitake mushrooms, stems discarded, caps sliced
	Salt and freshly ground black pepper
1	small head radicchio, shredded
12 ounces	boneless, skinless chicken breasts, cut into bite-size pieces
1	garlic clove, minced
¼ cup	dry white wine
1 teaspoon	Dijon mustard
¼ cup	chicken stock or reduced-sodium broth
¼ cup	freshly grated Grana Padano or Parmesan cheese

Bring a pot of salted water to a boil. Add the pasta and cook until al dente, following the package directions. Drain, and transfer to a large bowl. (The pasta can be cooked ahead of time: place it in a large bowl and drizzle with a little olive oil to keep it from sticking together.)

Heat 2 tablespoons of the oil in a large skillet over moderately high heat until it is hot but not smoking. Add the mushrooms, season with salt and pepper, and cook, tossing or stirring occasionally, until they are tender and golden brown, 5 to 7 minutes. Transfer the mushroom mixture to the pasta bowl. In the same skillet, sauté the shredded radicchio for a minute. (Don't let the radicchio cook too long; you want it to retain some crunchiness.) Add it to the pasta.

Season the chicken with salt and pepper.

Heat the remaining 1 tablespoon oil in the same skillet over medium-high heat. Add the garlic and sauté until slightly browned. Add the chicken and sauté until lightly browned and cooked through, 7 to 10 minutes. Add the white wine and let it reduce to a few teaspoons. Add the mustard and cook, stirring, for 1 minute. Add the stock and simmer for a minute. Then stir in the Grana Padano. Remove the skillet from the heat and add the chicken mixture to the pasta. Toss to blend. Serve warm, at room temperature, or cold.

VARIATIONS

• Add some cooked white beans and/or a cup of peas.
• Substitute shrimp for the chicken

ECONOMY $$

A fairly inexpensive, easy-to-prepare meal.

NUTRITION

Colorful radicchio is chock-full of antioxidants.

Fusilli with Mushrooms and Swiss Chard

MAKES 4 SERVINGS

This simple and healthy pasta dish will perfume your kitchen with the aromas of shallots and mushrooms. The "sauce" is made quickly while the pasta cooks. Use whatever cooking green suits you to replace the chard, and any seasonal mushrooms that look good; trim the gills on large ones.

1 large bunch	green Swiss chard (Do not use red chard, as it will discolor the pasta.)
12 ounces	dry fusilli pasta
¼ cup	olive oil
4	large shallots, sliced lengthwise
10 ounces	fresh shiitake or domestic mushrooms, stems removed, caps sliced
¼ teaspoon	salt
	Freshly ground black pepper
2 tablespoons	chopped fresh flat-leaf parsley
⅓ cup	freshly grated Grana Padano or Parmesan cheese

Bring a pot of salted water to a boil. Add the pasta and cook until al dente, following the package instructions.

Meanwhile, in a large skillet (preferably nonstick), heat the oil over medium heat. Add the shallots and cook, tossing or stirring, until softened, 2 to 3 minutes. Increase the heat to medium-high and add the mushrooms and the sliced chard stems. Season with the salt and pepper to taste, and sauté, tossing or stirring occasionally, until the liquid has completely evaporated from the mushrooms, and the shallots and mushrooms are golden and tender, 5 to 7 minutes. Stir in the reserved chard leaves and the parsley, and cook for about 2 minutes, or until the liquid has mostly evaporated and the leaves are wilted.

Drain the pasta, reserving ⅓ cup of the cooking water. Return the pasta and the reserved cooking water to the cooking pot. Add the chard-mushroom mixture and the Grana Padano, and mix until well combined. Serve piping hot.

Trim off the ends of the Swiss chard stems. Cut out the triangular inner stem of each leaf, and cut the inner stems into ¼-inch-thick slices. Coarsely chop the leaves and set aside, separately.

VARIATIONS

- For protein, add leftover chicken or slices of kielbasa or sausage when sautéing the shallots.
- Add roasted red peppers, zucchini, or diced butternut squash (microwave for 3 to 4 minutes before adding to the sauté pan) when sautéing the mushrooms.
- Substitute chopped kale or collard leaves for the chard.
- Use whatever short pasta shape you like instead of the fusilli.

NUTRITION

One serving provides more than 60 percent of your daily requirement for vitamins A and C.

ECONOMY $

Stewed North African–Spiced Chicken Thighs over Whole-Wheat Couscous

MAKES 4 TO 6 SERVINGS

What can I say: I'm a "bad" nutritionist—I rarely eat boneless, skinless chicken breasts. I'd rather have a little bit of the full-flavored thigh, with skin and bone, especially if the chicken comes from Northwind Farms. And don't I make up for it with the whole-wheat couscous? This balanced meal takes less than 15 minutes of active cooking time. Enjoy it for a weekday supper—or any day.

¼ cup	chopped walnuts or almonds
1 tablespoon	peanut oil
1½ pounds	bone-in, skin-on chicken thighs
	Salt and freshly ground black pepper
2	garlic cloves, minced
1	medium onion, diced
1	celery stalk, diced
1	medium red bell pepper, cored, seeded, and cut into thin strips (optional)
2	medium sweet potatoes, peeled and quartered
¼ cup	raisins
½ teaspoon	ground cumin
½ teaspoon	ground turmeric
½ teaspoon	garam masala (see Note, page137)
⅛ teaspoon	cayenne pepper
2 tablespoons	all-purpose flour
½ cup	dry white wine, or ½ cup water plus a squeeze of lemon juice
1 cup	chicken stock or reduced-sodium broth
1 cup	whole-wheat couscous (found in many supermarkets and natural foods stores)

Toast the walnuts or almonds in a small skillet over medium heat until fragrant, 2 to 3 minutes; set aside.

Heat the peanut oil in large nonstick skillet over medium-high heat. When the oil is hot, season the chicken with salt and pepper and add it to the skillet. Cook, shaking the pan and turning the chicken pieces occasionally, until they are golden brown and crisp, about 8 minutes. Transfer the chicken to a plate or a rimmed baking sheet.

Pour off all but about 2 tablespoons of the

fat in the skillet. Add the garlic, onion, celery, and bell pepper to the skillet and cook, stirring, until softened, about 5 minutes. Add the sweet potatoes, raisins, and spices, and cook for another minute or two. Then sprinkle the flour over the vegetables and stir until it is no longer visible. Add the wine, scraping the pan to dissolve the browned bits. Cook until the wine is almost completely reduced, about 1 minute. Stir in the stock. Return the chicken and any released juices to the skillet. Cook, simmering, until the chicken is cooked through and the sweet potatoes are tender, 20 to 25 minutes.

Meanwhile, to prepare the couscous, bring 1½ cups water to a boil in a medium saucepan. Add ½ teaspoon salt and gradually stir in the couscous. Remove the pan from the heat, cover, and let stand for 5 minutes. Then fluff the couscous with a fork.

Spoon the chicken and sauce over the couscous. Sprinkle with the walnuts or almonds, and serve.

SERVING SUGGESTION

Enjoy immediately, with a tossed salad and some crusty bread to mop up the sauce.

VARIATIONS

• Substitute mixed chicken parts (halved breasts, drumsticks, and thighs) for the thighs.
• Use dried cherries or currants instead of the raisins.
• Add diced apples or pears during the last 5 minutes of cooking.

LEFTOVERS

Reheats well on the stovetop or in the microwave.

NUTRITION

Whole-wheat couscous is made from unrefined semolina. It contains all the vitamins, minerals, and protective phytochemicals found in whole grains.

ECONOMY $$

Biscuit-Topped Chicken and Root Vegetable Stew

MAKES 4 TO 6 SERVINGS

I love the one-pot feature of this soul-stirring fall or winter stew, which goes from stovetop to oven straight to the table. Its presentation, with colorful vegetables peeping between the biscuits, might just be the trick to get picky eaters to try root vegetables. For die-hard potato lovers, a diced medium potato can replace the turnip. But this substitution was not necessary for my dear friend Donna Grover, writer and professor of literature at nearby Bard College, who was astonished by her son Malcolm's full acceptance of this dish as is!

Chicken stew

2 tablespoons	olive oil
2	celery stalks, thinly sliced
2	medium carrots, sliced on the diagonal
1	medium onion, chopped
1	garlic clove, minced
12 ounces	boneless, skinless chicken breasts, cut into bite-size pieces
	Salt and freshly ground black pepper
¼ cup	dry white wine
1	small sweet potato, peeled and cut into 1-inch cubes
1	medium turnip, peeled and cut into ½-inch cubes

4 cups	chicken stock or reduced-sodium broth
2	thyme sprigs
1	bay leaf
1½ teaspoons	cornstarch

Biscuits

1 cup	sifted all-purpose flour
1 teaspoon	baking powder
½ teaspoon	baking soda
½ teaspoon	salt
2 tablespoons	canola oil
1 cup	low-fat buttermilk
⅓ cup	grated cheddar cheese

Place a 9- or 10-inch Dutch oven over medium heat and add the olive oil. When the oil is hot, add the celery, carrots, onion, and garlic. Cook, stirring often, until the vegetables have softened, 8 to 10 minutes.

Season the chicken with salt and pepper. Increase the heat to medium-high, add the chicken, and cook until lightly browned, 5 to 7 minutes. Add the white wine and reduce it slightly, 30 seconds. Stir in all the remaining stew ingredients except the cornstarch. Simmer over low heat, partially covered, until the vegetables are tender, 35 to 40 minutes.

While the stew simmers, prepare the biscuits: In a large bowl, combine the flour, baking powder, baking soda, and salt, and stir with a fork to blend. Add the oil and buttermilk, and mix until the ingredients are just incorporated. Set aside.

Preheat the oven to 375°F.

Stir the cornstarch into ¼ cup water to form a slurry. Stir this into the simmering stew and cook for 2 to 3 minutes, until thickened.

Drop tablespoons of the biscuit dough over the top of the stew. Transfer the pot to the oven, and bake for 20 minutes. Sprinkle the cheddar over the biscuits, return the pot to the oven, and bake for another 5 minutes, until the cheese is melted and slightly browned. Serve immediately.

VARIATIONS

- Add chopped or sliced rutabaga or parsnips with the celery and carrots.
- Add peas or chopped cooking greens during the last few minutes of cooking.
- Substitute pork or beef for the chicken; the stewing time needed to tenderize may increase, so add about 1 cup extra stock or broth.
- Use turkey instead of chicken.
- Substitute ⅓ cup whole wheat flour for ⅓ cup of the all-purpose flour.
- Make individual pot pies in small casseroles.
- *Indian:* Some curry, turmeric, a pinch of garam masala, and a spoonful of spicy mango chutney will steer you in this direction.
- *Mexican:* Use bell and chile peppers, beans, corn, and chili powder.
- *Thai:* Use red or green curry paste, cilantro, and coconut milk.

LEFTOVERS

This dish reheats well—the microwave works best.

NUTRITION

This dish is high in protein, vitamins, minerals, and phytochemicals while moderate in fat.

ECONOMY $$

Orange-Cranberry-Crusted Leg of Lamb

MAKES 6 TO 8 SERVINGS

You can't beat the presentation of a bone-in leg of lamb, and this recipe is a showstopper.
I serve it during the holidays and throughout the autumn and winter. The dish is easy to prepare,
allowing you to enjoy time with friends and family. The tart elements of cranberry and orange
cut through the richness of the lamb, and the result is a delicious balance of flavors.

One	6- to 8-pound bone-in leg of lamb
14	thin slices garlic (from 3 to 4 cloves)
14	very small thyme sprigs
	Slivered zest of 1 orange
1 cup	whole-berry cranberry sauce, homemade or canned
	Grated zest of 1 orange
¼ cup	fresh orange juice
3 tablespoons	pure maple syrup
2 tablespoons	Dijon mustard
1	small shallot, quartered
¼ teaspoon	garam masala (see Note, page 137), or a pinch of cinnamon
1 cup	unseasoned dried bread crumbs
	Salt and freshly ground black pepper

Preheat the oven to 325°F.

Trim the lamb of all but a ¼-inch-thick layer of fat. Cut fourteen ½-inch-deep slits all over the lamb with a small sharp knife, and insert a slice of garlic, a thyme sprig, and a sliver of orange zest into each slit.

Combine the cranberry sauce, grated orange zest, orange juice, maple syrup, mustard, shallot, and garam masala in a food processor and pulse a few times, until the cranberries and shallots are chopped. Add the bread crumbs, season with salt and pepper to taste, and pulse until just combined.

Place the lamb, fat side up, on a rack in a shallow roasting pan. Spread the cranberry mixture over the top and sides of the lamb. Roast for 2½ to 3 hours, until an instant-read thermometer inserted 2 inches into the thickest part of the meat (and not touching bone) reaches 125°F. Remove the lamb from the oven and allow it to rest for 10 minutes. (It will finish cooking to 135° to 140°F for medium.)

SERVING SUGGESTION

Transfer the lamb to a warm serving platter and surround it with fresh herb sprigs (thyme, rosemary, and parsley) and orange slices.

VARIATIONS

- *Seasonal:* Consider using other fresh local fruits, such as blueberries or currants, in place of the cranberries. Pat the crust on top of a butterflied boneless leg of lamb and grill outdoors in the summer.
- *Asian:* Substitute lime for the orange juice and zest, ¾ cup hoisin sauce for the cranberry sauce and maple syrup, and Chinese five spice powder for the garam masala.
- *Indian:* Eliminate the thyme and maple syrup. Substitute lemon for the orange, and mango chutney for the cranberry sauce. Add 1 tablespoon curry powder.
- *Provençal:* Substitute ½ cup olive tapenade for the cranberry sauce, and lemon juice and zest for the orange. Eliminate the garam masala and maple syrup.

LEFTOVERS

The obvious use for lamb leftovers is in sandwiches, such as panini and wraps. Also consider shredding the meat and stirring it into a risotto, stew, soup, or chili. A hearty lamb chili is the perfect next-day way to feed hungry holiday guests.

NUTRITION

The average cut of lamb is "lean" by FDA standards. Compared to other meats, lamb contains very little marbling (fat throughout the meat), since most lamb fat is on the outside edges of the meat and is easily trimmed. Lamb is a delicious red meat alternative to beef, providing satisfying flavor and protein without adding too many calories (less than 175 per 3-ounce serving). Lamb also contributes many essential nutrients, such as protein, B vitamins, selenium, zinc, and iron. As part of a balanced diet, rich in a variety of vegetables, fruits, and whole grains, lamb fits. The orange and cranberry crust ups the flavor and the antioxidants.

ECONOMY $$$

A leg of lamb, at approximately $4 per pound, serves many and provides delicious leftovers. Don't forget to boil the bone to make stock for lamb soup, stew, and risotto.

Lavender Pork Rib End Roast

MAKES 4 TO 6 SERVINGS

This succulent roast is easy to prepare, gorgeous to look at, and best of all, wonderful to eat. Lavender grows in the herb garden right outside my kitchen door, and by late fall it needs to be gathered up. I love using fragrant lavender with red meat, game, and game birds in addition to pork. A little goes a long way and won't overwhelm the flavor of the dish.

One	4-pound loin pork rib end roast, Frenched
6	garlic cloves, sliced in half
24 to 36	lavender leaves (around ¼ cup, loosely packed)
	Salt and freshly ground black pepper
1 tablespoon	olive oil

Preheat the oven to 350°F.

Trim any excess fat off the pork roast. Cut twelve ¼-inch-wide slits into the roast, and stuff each one with a garlic half and 2 or 3 lavender leaves. Generously sprinkle the roast with salt and pepper. Place the meat in a small roasting pan, slightly larger than the roast itself. Drizzle with the olive oil.

Roast for about 1¼ to 1½ hours, or until the internal temperature reaches 150°F. Let the roast rest for 10 minutes before carving.

SERVING SUGGESTIONS

Delicious served with red cabbage and a root vegetable gratin (see page 170).

VARIATIONS

Rosemary, thyme, and sage work well.

LEFTOVERS

Slice the leftover pork for sandwiches or shred it for quesadillas.

NUTRITION

Pork is a good source of B vitamins, especially thiamin; adequate thiamin is essential for optimal metabolic and healthy neurologic function.

ECONOMY $$$

Hudson Valley Cassoulet

MAKES 10 TO 12 SERVINGS

I specifically identify my Hudson Valley vendors in this recipe to demonstrate how a favorite French cold-weather classic can take on a local feel. Try to purchase local meats and vegetables to create your own version, but remember that the idea is to try to purchase more locally, not to create work—use the best quality products you can find in your markets.

2	Moulard duck breasts (I get mine from Hudson Valley Foie Gras)
	Salt and freshly ground black pepper
3 tablespoons plus 1½ teaspoons	olive oil
1 pound	Mountain Products Smokehouse smoked bacon or other thick-cut bacon, cut into lardons (about ⅓ inch wide and 1 inch long)
2½ pounds	Mountain Products Smokehouse smoked pork garlic sausage (see Note)
1	large onion, peeled and diced
2	celery stalks, diced
8 ounces	Wiltbank Farm oyster or shiitake mushrooms (or a combination)
2	garlic cloves, minced
2 tablespoons	tomato paste
1 teaspoon	red pepper flakes
½ cup	dry white wine

1 pound	dried cannellini or cranberry beans
12 cups	stock, reduced-sodium broth or water
¼ teaspoon	ground cloves
½ cup	freshly grated Grana Padano or Parmesan cheese
1 cup	unseasoned dried bread crumbs

Note: Garlic sausage is available in many supermarkets and in gourmet markets. Coleman's is one all-natural brand to look for. If you cannot find garlic sausage, simply substitute any good-quality pork sausage.

Pat the duck breasts dry. Using a sharp knife, score the skin in a crosshatch pattern; be careful not to cut into the meat below. Season the breasts with salt and pepper.

In a large braising pan or rondeau (preferably with a lid), heat the 1½ teaspoons olive oil over medium heat until it is hot but not smoking. Add the duck breasts, skin side down, and sear them until fat is rendered and the skin is golden brown and crisp, 10 to 12 minutes. Transfer them to a plate and set aside.

Drain off all but about 2 tablespoons of the fat from the pan, and cook the bacon until crisp, about 8 minutes. Again drain off all but about 2 tablespoons fat, leaving the bacon in the pan. Return the pan to medium-high heat and add the onion, celery, mushrooms, and garlic. Cook, stirring often, until the vegetables are softened and lightly browned, 8 to 10 minutes.

Meanwhile, cut the duck breasts into bite-size pieces.

Add the duck, tomato paste, and red pepper flakes to the pan and cook, stirring, for 1 minute. Then add the white wine and deglaze the pan. Cook until the wine has reduced to a couple of tablespoons, about 1 minute. Then add the beans, stock, and cloves. Partially cover the pan and simmer until the beans are thoroughly cooked, the meat is tender, and the mixture is thick, about 2 hours.

When the cassoulet is almost done, preheat the oven to 400°F. Lightly grease a 4-quart casserole.

Season the cassoulet with salt and pepper to taste, and transfer it to the prepared casserole. In a small bowl, combine the Grana Padano, bread crumbs, and remaining 3 tablespoons olive oil, and stir to combine. Top the cassoulet with the bread crumb mixture and bake, uncovered, until it is bubbly and the top is browned, 12 to 15 minutes. Let cool slightly, and serve family-style in the center of the table.

VARIATIONS

- Prepare individual cassoulets in ramekins.
- Use confit duck legs (whole) instead of breasts.
- Use any type of white bean instead of the cannellini.
- Add cubed lamb leg, goose, and/or pork shoulder.
- Omit the mushrooms.
- For a shortcut, use canned beans (rinsed and drained), cut the stock in half, and reduce the cooking time slightly.

LEFTOVERS

The cassoulet reheats well and tastes great the next day.

NUTRITION

No doubt, this is a hearty winter dish. If you wish to cut back on the richness, use turkey sausage, substitute chicken thighs for the duck, and omit the bacon. The beans certainly add a health benefit.

ECONOMY $$

Pretty economical for 10 to 12 servings. Substitute chicken breasts for the duck to further reduce the cost.

L'Anitra Arrosta con Salsa di Pere Balsamico

Whole Roasted Duck with Pear Balsamic Sauce and Herb Spaetzle

MAKES 8 SERVINGS

You'll be in heaven when you encounter the aromas of roasting duck, pears, and ginger. The experience will only improve when you sit down to enjoy the crispy duck with the naturally sweetened balsamic pear sauce. This is definitely a great dish for entertaining, but it is certainly easy enough for a Sunday family meal.

Duck

2	Northwind Farms or Hudson Valley Foie Gras ducklings (4 to 5 pounds each), or 2 Peking ducklings
2	medium carrots, chopped
2	celery stalks, chopped
2	medium onions, chopped
2	medium pears, cored and chopped
One	3-ounce piece of fresh ginger, peeled and chopped
	Salt and freshly ground black pepper

Balsamic pear sauce

2 tablespoons	unsalted butter
3	shallots, minced
2	garlic cloves, minced
1	medium carrot, diced
1	celery stalk, diced
2	pears, peeled, and diced
⅓ cup	good-quality balsamic vinegar
½ cup	Valpolicella, Nebbiolo, or other red wine
4 cups	rich veal stock, from your butcher, or frozen from a gourmet store

Herb spaetzle

¾ cup	cold whole milk
3	large eggs
1 tablespoon	chopped fresh flat-leaf parsley
1 teaspoon	chopped fresh sage
Pinch	ground nutmeg
2 cups	all-purpose flour
	Olive oil, for tossing
4 tablespoons	unsalted butter (½ stick)

Preheat the oven to 275°F. Long low-temperature roasting will result in moist meat and crispy skin.

To prepare the ducks, first rinse and dry them well. Combine the carrots, celery, onions, pears, and ginger in a medium mixing bowl. Trim off any loose fat from the necks and tails of the ducks, cut off the wings at the elbow, and reserve the gizzards. Season the cavities of the ducks with salt and pepper, and then stuff the cavities with the vegetable/ginger mixture. Truss the ducks: With the midpoint of a long piece of kitchen twine at the neck, drape the twine over the legs, pull it under the feet, push the tail end in, and tie firmly. Season the duck skin with salt and pepper.

Pierce the skin all over with the tip of a sharp knife, being careful not to puncture the meat. Place the ducks, breast side down, on a rack in a roasting pan. Place the necks and gizzards in the roasting pan, and pour 2 cups of water into the pan (this will prevent the fat drippings from burning). Roast for 2½ to 3 hours; after the first hour, baste with the drippings every 25 minutes or so. When the ducks are done, the legs should move easily. Let rest for 10 minutes before carving.

While the ducks cook, prepare the balsamic pear sauce: Heat the butter in a medium saucepan over medium-high heat. When it is bubbly, add the shallots and garlic. Cook, stirring, until they begin to soften and brown, 3 to 4 minutes. Then add the carrot, celery, and pears. Cook, stirring often, until the vegetables

and pears are nicely golden, about 10 minutes. Add the balsamic vinegar and cook until it has almost completely reduced. Then add the wine and cook until it has reduced by half. Add the veal stock and bring to a boil. Reduce the heat and simmer, stirring occasionally, for 45 minutes, until the sauce has thickened enough to coat the back of a spoon and the pears and vegetables are very soft. Leave the sauce chunky, or strain it through a sieve into a bowl. Adjust the seasoning with salt and pepper. Keep the sauce warm until you're ready to serve the duck.

Shortly before you are ready to serve the duck, prepare the spaetzle: Bring a large pot of salted water to a boil. While the water is heating, combine the milk, eggs, parsley, sage, 1 teaspoon salt, and nutmeg in a food processor; blend until smooth, about 30 seconds. Add the flour and pulse until just well combined, about 30 seconds.

Working in batches and using a spaetzle maker, a colander with medium holes, or a slotted spoon, press the dough through the holes, letting it drop into the boiling water; stir gently to prevent sticking. Simmer until the spaetzle float to the surface, 3 to 4 minutes, and then cook for another 30 seconds. Using a slotted spoon or a skimmer, transfer the spaetzle to a large bowl. Toss them with a drop of olive oil while you cook the remaining batches.

Heat the butter in a large skillet over medium-high heat. When it is frothy, add the spaetzle and cook, gently tossing or stirring occasionally, until the dumplings are coated with butter and heated through, 2 to 3 minutes. Season with salt and pepper to taste. Set aside, loosely covered to keep warm.

Carve the ducks, dividing them first into quarters; then halve the breast and leg pieces. Place one breast half and one leg half on each serving plate. Drizzle with the balsamic pear sauce, and serve with a generous spoonful of spaetzle.

SERVING SUGGESTIONS

A glass of Valpolicella Classico or Nebbiolo would complement the duck nicely.

VARIATIONS

- Substitute apples for the pears.
- Add strips of orange or lemon zest to the vegetable stuffing and grated zest to the balsamic pear sauce.
- Prepare a stock or gravy for another use from the pan drippings and cavity filling.
- Puree the sauce for a more refined pear-flavored sauce.
- Instead of the spaetzle, serve the duck with mashed or roasted potatoes or sweet potatoes, polenta, or risotto.

LEFTOVERS

Enjoy the duck and sauce reheated. Spaetzle can be pan-fried until crispy in butter or olive oil the next day.

NUTRITION

Once the fat renders from the young duckling to the bottom of the pan, it is reasonably lean. Duck is high in protein and particularly rich in the B vitamin niacin.

ECONOMY $$$

Classic Meat Loaf with Tomato Maple Glaze

MAKES 6 TO 8 SERVINGS

I've never trusted people who don't like meat loaf (although of course I bend the rule
for vegetarians). What's not to like? Enjoy this classic meat loaf all year long, but especially
when you need a good hearty comfort meal in the dead of winter. This one is made extra-yummy
by using Northwind Farms ground beef and pork. Try to find a source of local ground
beef and pork, or get the best quality available in your supermarket.

Glaze

½ cup	tomato sauce, either homemade (page 290) or canned
1 tablespoon	pure maple syrup
1 tablespoon	tomato paste

Meat loaf

¾ cup	unseasoned dried bread crumbs, or 1 cup instant oatmeal
1	small onion, finely diced
1	celery stalk, finely diced
1	medium carrot, finely diced
¼ cup	milk
2 tablespoons	ketchup
2 tablespoons	tomato paste
2 tablespoons	chopped fresh flat-leaf parsley
1 tablespoon	Dijon or yellow mustard
1 tablespoon	Worcestershire sauce

3	large eggs
¼ teaspoon	smoked paprika, or more for a smokier flavor
1¼ pounds	ground beef
1¼ pounds	ground pork
	Salt and freshly ground black pepper

Preheat the oven to 325°F.

First, prepare the glaze: Mix the tomato sauce, maple syrup, and tomato paste together in a small bowl. Set aside.

Combine all the meat loaf ingredients except the ground beef, ground pork, and salt and pepper in a large mixing bowl; stir well to combine. Add the meat, season with salt and pepper, and using a wooden spoon or your hands, work the ingredients into the meat until just blended; don't overmix. Transfer the meat mixture to a 9 x 5 x 3-inch loaf pan and press to form it into a loaf shape.

Roast for 40 minutes. Then spread the glaze over the top of the meat loaf and roast for another 15 minutes, until the loaf is bubbly and cooked through (the internal temperature should reach 155°F). Let it stand for 10 minutes in the pan before unmolding, slicing, and serving.

SERVING SUGGESTIONS

Mashed potatoes are an obvious choice. Try it with polenta as well.

VARIATIONS

- *Add vegetables:* Diced zucchini or mushrooms will add nutrients and release their water as they cook, helping to keep the meat loaf moist.
- *Go Italiano:* Try seasoning the meat loaf as you would meatballs. Skip the mustard, Worcestershire sauce, and paprika and add ⅓ cup grated Parmesan and some fresh chopped or dried oregano and marjoram.
- *Southwestern:* Add corn kernels, chili seasoning, and some hot sauce; omit the Worcestershire. A chipotle BBQ sauce would be a good glaze here.

LEFTOVERS

Meat loaf never stays around long. It's funny how you can eat only so many burgers, but meat loaf keeps you coming back for more. If you do have leftovers, prepare a sandwich on your favorite bread with whatever filler fixings you have available.

NUTRITION

Both pork and beef are rich in protein, iron, zinc, and B vitamins. Enjoy this meal with a whole grain and a colorful vegetable side dish.

ECONOMY $$

Good-quality beef and pork do cost more, but the ground cuts are less than the "prime."

Dinner in a Flash: Baby Chicken with Endive and Radicchio

MAKES 4 SERVINGS

This easy one-pan dish takes only minutes of prep time and makes the perfect Sunday (or any day) family meal. With one small chicken this can be a romantic dinner for two. By adding another baby chicken or using a more common roaster, you can have dinner for four easily. Placing the lemon and herbs under the chicken skin keeps the meat flavorful and moist. Add some cut-up new potatoes to the roasting pan for a complete meal. Serve with a glass of wine.

1 lemon, well rinsed

8 fresh sage leaves

2 baby Northwind Farm poussins or young chickens or one 3- to 4-pound roasting chicken, butterflied and backbones removed

1 medium or 2 small onions, cut into 6 or 8 wedges with the root end intact

1 small radicchio, rinsed and cut into 6 wedges with the core end intact

1 Belgian endive, rinsed and cut into 4 wedges with the core end intact

¼ cup olive oil

Salt and and freshly ground black pepper

Preheat the oven to 375°F.

Using a sharp paring knife, remove the zest from the lemon in long strips and stuff the strips and the sage leaves under the chicken skin. Place the chicken in a large shallow roasting pan, skin side up. Arrange the wedges of onion, radicchio, and endive around the chicken. Make sure the pan holds everything in one layer. (This ensures that the chicken skin will brown nicely while the vegetables caramelize.) Drizzle the chicken and vegetables with the olive oil, and sprinkle with salt and pepper.

Roast for about 45 minutes for the baby chickens and up to 1½ hours for the larger roasting chicken. Midway through the cooking, give the pan a shake and turn the vegetables over. The chicken is cooked through when the thigh meat juices run clear when pierced with a fork. Cut the chickens into eighths and serve on a platter surrounded by the roasted vegetables.

SERVING SUGGESTION

Mashed or roasted potatoes or sweet potatoes would be fine alongside.

VARIATIONS

The vegetables can vary with the seasons. Other fall/winter vegetables include turnips, rutabaga, sweet potatoes, or butternut squash (all cut into medium dice). In the spring, asparagus and mushrooms can be added during the last 20 minutes of roasting. Summer choices include bell peppers and zucchini.

LEFTOVERS

The chicken can be sliced and piled into sandwiches for a next-day treat.

ECONOMY $$

Lentils Stewed in Red Wine and
Last Season's Tomatoes

For centuries lentils and all kinds of legumes have sustained people, providing great flavor and much-needed protein for hardworking bodies. Perhaps that accounts for the Italian tradition of eating lentils on New Year's Day for good luck, good health, and good fortune. This dish is great alone as a delicious vegetarian stew, or served alongside any number of meat, poultry, or seafood preparations. Some of my favorites include cotechino, fresh pork sausage, a traditional fixing from Modena, Italy; grilled or roasted Italian sausage; roasted or braised chicken, duck, or venison; or grilled or seared salmon or monkfish.

Cooking the meaty lentils in a balanced red wine, such as a Valpolicella Classico from the Veneto, and last season's jarred tomatoes lends just the balance of fruit and acidity. I highly recommend the French or Italian lentils that are sold with their seed coat on; these keep their form and texture during cooking.

1 cup	French or Italian dried lentils
2 tablespoons	olive oil
1	small onion, diced
1	bay leaf
½ cup	fruity but dry red wine
1½ cups	home-canned tomatoes, or one 14-ounce can stewed tomatoes
1	thyme sprig
1	oregano sprig
	Salt and freshly ground black pepper

Rinse the lentils in cold water, and drain.

Heat the olive oil in a 2-quart saucepan over medium heat. Add the onion and sauté, stirring often, until soft, about 10 minutes. Add the lentils and bay leaf and cook, stirring, for 1 to 2 minutes. Pour in the red wine and cook until reduced by about half, about 1 minute. Add the tomatoes, 1½ cups water, and the herb sprigs. Cover the pan and simmer, stirring gently occasionally, for 30 minutes. Then uncover and cook for another 5 to 10 minutes, or until the lentils are tender and the liquid has evaporated. Season with salt and pepper to taste. Discard the bay leaf and the thyme and oregano sprigs, and serve warm or at room temperature.

- Add some smoked paprika with the onions, and puree the stewed lentils with some olive oil in a food processor to make a vegetarian "mousse."
- Omit the tomatoes and prepare with a total of 3 cups water or broth.
- Add diced celery, carrot, and/or bell peppers when sautéing the onion.

LEFTOVERS

These lentils are great added to soups or stews, tossed with salads, or mixed with cooked grains.

NUTRITION

With their meaty, peppery flavor, lentils can easily make you forget that meat is in fact lacking—a great ingredient to consider if you're trying to shift to a more plant-based diet. Lentils are one of the best sources of folate.

ECONOMY $

Next-Day Roasted Vegetable Frittata

MAKES 6 SERVINGS

A frittata, an Italian flat omelet, can be made with limitless choices of vegetables and herbs and is a quick and healthy dish for any meal. Just about any leftover cooked vegetables can be added as long as they do not contain a lot of water (try Gigi Seasonal Roasted Vegetables, page 262, or Winter Vegetable Hash, page 260).

3 tablespoons	olive oil
1	medium potato, peeled and cut into small chunks
½ to ¾ cup	sliced fresh shiitake and oyster mushrooms
2 tablespoons	chopped fresh flat-leaf parsley
2 tablespoons	chopped scallions, white and light green parts
2 cups	leftover roasted vegetables (such as onions, carrots, celery, and butternut squash)
10	large eggs
3 or 4	wedges leftover roasted acorn or butternut squash
1 cup	crumbled goat cheese, or other cheese on hand
	Salt and freshly ground black pepper

Preheat the oven to 350°F.

Heat the olive oil in a 14-inch ovenproof nonstick skillet over medium-high heat. Add the potato and mushrooms and cook, tossing or stirring often, until they are lightly browned, about 7 minutes. Add the parsley, scallions, and leftover vegetables and cook to heat them up, about 5 minutes.

While the vegetables are heating, lightly beat the eggs in a medium bowl.

Arrange the vegetables so that they're evenly distributed in the skillet, and pour the eggs over them. Cook over medium-high heat, using a spatula or wooden spoon to gently pull the edges of the eggs toward the center and rotating the skillet to allow the uncooked egg to move to the edges. In a minute or so the eggs will start to look about midway set. Reduce the heat to low. Arrange the wedges of roasted acorn squash in a decorative pattern on top of the frittata. Sprinkle the goat cheese over the surface, and season with salt and pepper to taste.

Bake the frittata in the oven until puffed up and beautifully browned, 15 to 20 minutes. Serve hot from the oven or at room temperature. Cut wedges directly from the skillet or slide the frittata onto a serving platter and then slice.

SERVING SUGGESTION

The frittata needs nothing more than a salad to complete a satisfying meal.

VARIATIONS

- *Vegetables:* Frittatas are great platforms for all kinds of leftover vegetables, or of course you can cook the vegetables from scratch. The main issue is to make sure the vegetables are not too watery. If you use fresh zucchini, for example, sauté it well to reduce the amount of water that the vegetable will give off when it's cooking with the eggs.
- *Fall/winter:* Use butternut squash, radicchio, endive, escarole, and dark hearty greens (spinach, kale, collards).
- *Spring:* Try artichokes, asparagus, chives, fava beans, peas, mushrooms, radishes, spinach, spring onions, and watercress.
- *Summer:* Use basil, eggplant, peppers, summer squash, all types of tomatoes.

LEFTOVERS

Now we're talking about leftovers of leftovers! Frittatas really are best eaten the day they're made, but they do reheat beautifully if you're tempted to save a piece for lunch the next day.

NUTRITION

Eggs are a delicious and high-quality protein source. If your budget permits, select omega-3-rich eggs; omega 3s are great for your skin and overall health.

ECONOMY $

Winter Vegetable Hash

Hash comes from the French verb hacher, *to chop.*
This exactly describes this mélange of seasonal vegetables.

1	medium celery root, peeled and cut into ¼- to ½-inch dice
2	large carrots, cut into ¼-inch dice
6 tablespoons	olive oil
1	medium butternut squash, peeled and cut into ½-inch dice
1½ pounds	Corola or Yukon Gold potatoes, cut into 1-inch dice
2	medium onions, chopped
2	garlic cloves, minced
6	fresh sage leaves
2 tablespoons	chopped fresh flat-leaf parsley
	Salt and freshly ground black pepper

Preheat the oven to 400°F.

Spread the celery root and carrots on a rimmed baking sheet (the vegetables should fit in one layer), and drizzle with 2 tablespoons of the olive oil. Toss to coat. Repeat with the butternut squash, potatoes, and another 2 tablespoons olive oil on a second baking sheet. Place both sheets in the oven and roast, stirring once midway through, for 15 to 20 minutes, until all the vegetables are tender and lightly browned.

When the vegetables are done roasting, heat the remaining 2 tablespoons olive oil in a large skillet or sauté pan over medium-high heat. Add the onions, garlic, and sage and cook, tossing or stirring, until the onions are soft and lightly browned, about 7 minutes. Turn up the heat and add the roasted vegetables to the pan. Cook, tossing or gently stirring occasionally, until the vegetables are hot, golden, and crispy on the edges. Add the parsley and season with salt and pepper. Serve hot or at room temperature.

For a full meal, top with an over-easy egg.

- *Spring:* Omit the celery root and the squash; substitute leeks for the onions; add asparagus and peas at the end of the cooking time.
- *Summer:* Substitute zucchini, yellow squash, and corn for the squash and celery root; add the diced vegetables at the end of cooking. Substitute basil for the sage. When just off the heat, stir in halved cherry tomatoes.
- *Winter/fall:* Substitute fresh thyme or rosemary leaves for the sage.
- *Any season:* Add diced pancetta or bacon while sautéing the onions.

A great vegetable addition to an omelet or a frittata (see page 258), or to fill a burrito or quesadilla.

Rich in vitamins A and C, as well as B vitamins, potassium, magnesium, and fiber.

Gigi Seasonal Roasted Vegetables

MAKES 6 TO 8 SERVINGS

At Gigi Trattoria and Gigi Market, roasted vegetables are a year-round contorno, *or side dish. Winter calls for root vegetables, such as turnips, parsnips, potatoes, and carrots, but this recipe can adapt to the harvest of each season. This simple combination pairs well with the rich, layered flavors in the Orange-Cranberry-Crusted Leg of Lamb (page 244).*

Further simplify the dish, if desired, by limiting the vegetable combinations: use just carrots, parsnips, and onions, or just turnips and potatoes, for example. And don't waste time with perfect vegetable cuts; this is a rustic side dish.

6   baby turnips, peeled and halved, or 2 medium turnips, peeled and cut into quarters or sixths

3   medium parsnips, peeled and cut diagonally into 1- or 1½-inch-thick slices

3   medium carrots, cut diagonally into 1- or 1½-inch-thick slices

2   medium sweet potatoes, peeled and cut roughly into 2-inch chunks

2   medium potatoes, peeled and cut roughly into 2-inch chunks

2   medium onions, cut into 6 wedges with the root end intact

3   rosemary sprigs

2   garlic cloves, crushed

3 tablespoons   olive oil
Salt and freshly ground black pepper

Preheat the oven to 450°F.

Place all the vegetables, the rosemary sprigs, and the garlic in a large mixing bowl. Drizzle with the olive oil, and toss. Spread the vegetables in an even layer on a large rimmed nonstick baking sheet (if not using nonstick, line it with parchment paper and spray with cooking spray). Roast for 15 minutes, or until the edges of the vegetables are golden brown. Then turn the vegetables, using a spatula that is safe for nonstick cookware.

Lower the heat to 375°F and continue roasting until the vegetables are crispy on the outside and tender when pierced with a knife, 15 to 20 minutes. Remove the rosemary sprigs, and season with salt and pepper as soon as you pull the sheet from the oven. Serve hot, warm, or at room temperature.

VARIATIONS

As you change vegetables through the seasons, cut the vegetables to size based on their cooking time (the shorter the vegetable's cooking time, the larger the cut-up size). Do the same with water-filled vegetables such as zucchini.

- *Spring:* Try asparagus, baby carrots, potatoes, and leeks.
- *Summer:* Try eggplant, summer squash, and tomatoes.
- *Fall/winter:* Try Brussels sprouts, carrots, root vegetables, and onions.

LEFTOVERS

Roasted vegetables reheat well in the oven or microwave. Enjoy leftovers added to an omelet or frittata (see page 258).

NUTRITION

Absolutely loaded with protective vitamins, minerals, and phytochemicals.

ECONOMY $

Basic Sautéed Cooking Greens

MAKES 4 SERVINGS

Cooking greens grow well in the Hudson Valley and are best in the spring and fall, when sweetened by a touch of frost. Collards, kale, chard, turnip greens, and spinach can generally be cooked the same way—the only difference is the cooking time (greens with thicker, tougher stems like kale will require a few more minutes of cooking).

3 tablespoons	olive oil
1	small onion, diced
4	garlic cloves, thinly sliced lengthwise
Pinch	red pepper flakes
10 cups	chopped collards, kale, chard, turnip, or spinach leaves
	Salt and freshly ground black pepper
⅓ cup	vegetable or chicken stock, reduced-sodium broth, or water

Heat the olive oil in a large nonstick skillet over medium heat. Add the onion, garlic, and red pepper flakes and cook, stirring, until the onion has softened and the garlic is just beginning to brown, about 5 minutes. Increase the heat to medium-high, add the cooking greens, and season with salt and pepper to taste. Use kitchen tongs to move greens from the bottom to the top of the skillet, coating most of the greens with the oil. Add the stock, cover the skillet, and simmer for 5 minutes. Remove the cover and continue cooking until all the liquid has evaporated. Season with more salt if necessary. Serve immediately.

SERVING SUGGESTION

A perfect side dish. Consider adding a drizzle of good olive oil and a bit of grated or shaved Parmesan over each serving.

VARIATIONS

• Add bacon when sautéing the onion.
• Color and sweeten it up with chopped roasted red peppers.

LEFTOVERS

Great in omelets, burritos, soups, or rice.

NUTRITION

A powerhouse source for vitamins A and C.

Fruited and Spiced Three-Grain Pilaf

Winter definitely needs a little spice in the Hudson Valley. Here's some: dried cherries and apricots and North African spices complement the toastiness of this mixed whole-grain blend. Enjoy this pilaf with just about all fall and winter entrées. Since most whole grains have similar cooking times, you can mix and match your favorites along with your favorite spice or herb blends. There are a variety of blended whole grains on the supermarket shelves that have the "100 percent whole-grain" seal, making them an "excellent source."

2 tablespoons   olive oil

½   small onion, minced

1   bay leaf

¼ cup   dried cherries

¼ cup   minced dried apricots

1   dried ancho or chipotle chile (optional)

1 teaspoon   crushed caraway seeds

½ teaspoon   ground cumin

½ teaspoon   ground coriander

1 cup   whole-grain rice blend (for example, ⅓ cup rye berries, ⅓ cup pearl barley, ⅓ cup brown rice)

½ teaspoon   salt

Heat the olive oil in a medium saucepan over medium heat. Add the onion and bay leaf and cook until the onion softens, about 3 minutes. Add the dried fruit, chile (if using), and spices, and cook for another 2 to 3 minutes or until the fruit has softened. Add the rice blend and cook, stirring, for 1 minute. Then add 2½ cups water and the salt, and bring to a boil. Reduce the heat, cover the pan, and simmer for 45 minutes or until the grains are tender. Fluff the pilaf with a fork, and serve immediately.

For a quick meal, mound this salad over baby greens and crumble feta or goat cheese on top.

- Prepare with one grain or seven grains—most whole grains tend to cook in 45 to 50 minutes.
- Other dried fruit to consider includes golden raisins and currants.
- Swap Indian spices (curry, turmeric) or Italian herbs (oregano, marjoram, thyme) for the North African spices. Omit the dried fruit with the Italian herb mixture.
- To make risotto or a filling, add ½ cup more water. After 45 minutes, when the mixture is still slightly soupy, stir in some grated Parmesan (or grated or shredded cheese of your choice). Enjoy immediately as "risotto" or cool slightly and use to stuff cabbage or peppers before baking.
- Add some cooked or canned and drained beans.

Fluff and reheat in the microwave, or add a bit of liquid and reheat on the stovetop.

Three whole-grain servings are recommended daily because they contain innumerable nutrients and phytochemicals that refined grains do not. They are also satiating, which helps with weight loss or weight maintenance.

Pear-Cranberry Upside-down Cake

MAKES 8 TO 10 SERVINGS

*Oh, to take a walk through Mead Orchards during late summer or early fall!
As if the variety of pears wasn't dazzling enough, this perfectly kept orchard,
with its amazing eastern views to the Berkshires and western views to the
Catskill Mountains, will cause you to happily delay your picking.*

Topping

1	firm pear (Bartlett and D'Anjou are fine), peeled, cored, and sliced
⅓ cup	dried cranberries
¾ cup	packed light brown sugar
4 tablespoons	unsalted butter (½ stick), plus extra for greasing the pan

Cake

1⅔ cups	all-purpose flour
3 tablespoons	medium-grind yellow cornmeal (polenta)
1½ teaspoons	baking powder
½ teaspoon	salt
1 teaspoon	ground cinnamon
½ teaspoon	ground nutmeg
8 tablespoons	unsalted butter (1 stick), at room temperature
¾ cup plus 1½ teaspoons	granulated sugar
4	large eggs, separated
1½ teaspoons	pure vanilla extract
⅓ cup	whole milk
⅓ cup	whole plain yogurt

Preheat the oven to 350°F.

To make the topping, grease a 9 x 9 x 3-inch baking dish well with butter. Lay the pear slices across the bottom and sprinkle the dried cranberries evenly over them. In a small saucepan over medium heat, melt the brown sugar and butter together until the mixture is foaming and the sugar has dissolved. Pour the sugar-butter mixture over the pears and cranberries. Set aside to cool slightly.

To make the cake, whisk together the flour, cornmeal, baking powder, salt, cinnamon, and nutmeg in a large bowl. In a standing mixer, cream the butter and ¾ cup granulated sugar together until light and fluffy. Add the egg yolks, one at a time, mixing after each addition, and then stir in the vanilla extract. In a small bowl, combine the milk and yogurt. Alternate adding the dry ingredients and the milk-yogurt mixture to the sugar-butter mixture, mixing briefly with each addition.

In a separate medium bowl, whip the egg whites and the remaining 1½ teaspoons granulated sugar until they form soft peaks. Fold one quarter of the whites into the cake batter. Continue gently folding in the remaining whites until combined. Pour the batter over the pears and place the baking dish on the center rack in the oven. Bake the cake for 60 to 65 minutes, until a toothpick inserted in the middle comes out clean.

Transfer the baking dish to a cooling rack and let it sit for 5 minutes. Then invert a flat platter over the baking dish, and holding them together, invert quickly and carefully. Lift off the baking dish. The caramel sauce from the topping should be still quite liquid and will slowly drip down the sides of the cake. Some of the fruit may slide; just gently nudge it back into place.

SERVING SUGGESTIONS

Enjoy warm with ice cream, whipped cream, or gelato or at room temperature as a snack or a sweet pick-me-up.

VARIATIONS

- *Summer:* Use sliced fresh peaches instead of pears and cranberries. Add ¼ teaspoon ground ginger to the cake batter.
- *Winter:* Use firm bananas, sliced lengthwise, in place of the pears. Pineapple is a classic, too. Use a small pineapple, cored and sliced, and omit the cinnamon and nutmeg from the cake batter.

LEFTOVERS

Yummy for 2 to 3 days.

NUTRITION

Pears are a good source of vitamin C and are among the highest-fiber fruits.

ECONOMY $

Chocolate Banana Panettone Bread Pudding

MAKES 12 SERVINGS

'Tis the season for panettone! The colorful boxes decorate Gigi Trattoria and Gigi Market
throughout the holidays. As we get close to Christmas Day, the Gigi managers and
I start giving them away to good customers as they leave the restaurant.
Whatever's left (and still fresh) will go into our panettone bread puddings in January.

3	large eggs
3	large egg yolks
½ cup	sugar
1½ cups	whole or 2-percent milk
1½ cups	heavy cream
2	ripe bananas, mashed
1 teaspoon	pure vanilla extract
2	small panettones (4 to 6 ounces each), cut into 1- to 2-inch pieces (see Note)
1 cup	semisweet chocolate chips

In a large bowl, beat the eggs, yolks, and sugar together until well blended. Add the milk, cream, bananas, and vanilla, and mix thoroughly. Add the panettone pieces and mix. Stir in the chocolate chips. Set the mixture aside for 10 to 15 minutes so that the bread absorbs the liquid.

Preheat the oven to 350°F. Lightly grease twelve 4-ounce ramekins with butter.

Spoon the pudding mixture into the prepared ramekins, filling them up to three-fourths full. Place the ramekins in a large roasting pan and add enough hot water to the pan to reach halfway up the sides of the ramekins. Cover the pan with aluminum foil and bake for 40 to 45 minutes, or until the puddings are puffed and golden.

Note: Panettones differ from baker to baker. Some are very sweet and cakelike, while others are just an enriched bread, usually containing dried and/or candied fruit. Taste and decide whether you need to add all the sugar to the recipe, or slightly less.

SERVING SUGGESTIONS

Serve warm or at room temperature with ice cream, frozen yogurt, or gelato.

VARIATIONS

- Substitute half a loaf of challah or brioche (10 to 12 ounces) for the panettone. Check to make sure the bread you are using isn't overly sweet. If it is, cut back on the sugar slightly.
- Omit the chocolate and bananas and prepare with pears (or apples) and dried cranberries.
- To serve family-style, make one large bread pudding in a greased 13 x 9 x 2-inch baking dish.

LEFTOVERS

Refrigerate the leftovers for up to 2 days, and reheat in the oven or microwave.

NUTRITION

Not only rich in potassium, bananas also contain an array of B vitamins including thiamin, riboflavin, niacin, B_6, and folic acid. They're also a good source of vitamin A and fiber.

ECONOMY $

Gigi Biscotti

MAKES 4 DOZEN

Gigi biscotti are a presence on our cookie plate at Gigi Trattoria and sell by the bagful
at Gigi Market. A good biscotto is a rare find—not a tooth breaker, but
still firm to the bite. Enjoy our salute to this popular Italian treat.

1½ cups	almonds, pistachios, or hazelnuts
1 cup	unsalted butter (2 sticks), at room temperature
2 cups	sugar
¼ teaspoon	pure vanilla extract
4	large eggs
Pinch	salt
1½ teaspoons	baking powder
5¼ cups	bread flour
2 teaspoons	medium-grind yellow cornmeal (polenta)
6 ounces	dried fruit, such as cherries, cranberries, or chopped apricots

Preheat the oven to 200°F. Lightly grease two 18 x 13-inch sheet pans with butter or cooking spray. Set aside.

Toast the nuts in a medium skillet over medium heat. Shake the pan for even browning and cook until fragrant, 2 to 4 minutes.

In a standing mixer, cream the butter and sugar together on low speed. Add the vanilla and then the eggs, one at a time, mixing after each addition. Add the salt, baking powder, flour, and cornmeal, mixing slowly until incorporated. Add the fruit and nuts and mix until combined. The dough will be thick.

Remove the dough from the mixer and divide it into quarters. On a well-floured surface, roll each quarter into a long log that extends the length of a sheet pan and is about 1 inch thick.

Place 2 logs on each prepared sheet pan, making sure they are at least 2 inches apart. Bake for 2 hours, until the dough cracks slightly but is still pale in color. You may see a little brown on the edges, but not too much. Remove the sheet pans from the oven and let the biscotti logs cool.

Increase the oven temperature to 300°F. With a sharp knife (preferably serrated), cutting on the diagonal, slice each log into ¼-inch-thick slices. Place them on their sides on the baking sheets. (You should get 12 slices out of each log.) Place the baking sheets in the oven and bake for 5 to 10 minutes, or until the biscotti feel completely dried out. Let cool completely on wire racks, and then store in an airtight container.

SERVING SUGGESTIONS

Enjoy with ice cream or gelato, Gigi Cioccolata Calda (opposite) or Gigi Affogato (page 188), a cup of espresso, or simply on their own.

VARIATION

For chocolate biscotti, replace ½ cup of the bread flour with ½ cup good-quality unsweetened cocoa powder. Add 1½ cups semisweet chocolate chips to the dough in place of the dried fruit or the nuts.

ECONOMY $

Gigi Cioccolata Calda

MAKES ENOUGH MIX FOR 9 SERVINGS

Gigi's thick and rich cioccolata calda reminds me of the fact that I could never wait until pudding had cooled and thickened to dig in. When I indulge in a mug, I envision myself in a ski lodge in Cortina d'Ampezzo, or somewhere else wonderful. Then I regroup, ready to shovel my walk.

3 cups	good-quality unsweetened cocoa powder (we use Valrhona)
¼ cup	cornstarch
½ cup	confectioners' sugar
1½ cups	granulated sugar
Pinch	ground cinnamon
Pinch	salt
1 cup	milk (per serving)

Sift all the dry ingredients together into a bowl. Store in a sealed glass jar for up to 2 months.

For each serving, scald 1 cup milk in a small saucepan over medium heat. Whisk in ⅓ cup of the cioccolata mix, and cook, whisking constantly, until creamy and thickened, about 2 minutes.

VARIATIONS

- Enjoy with a dollop of whipped cream or marshmallows—we make homemade ones at Gigi Market.
- Spike it with chocolate liqueur or your favorite spirit.

ECONOMY $

Gigi Basics

Gigi Sherry-Shallot Vinaigrette

This signature dressing complements our two most popular salads, the Stagione, which is simply Chris Regan's incredible Sky Farm mesclun mix, and the Barbina (page 146), those same greens and herbs tossed with roasted beets, butternut squash, toasted walnuts, and crumbled Coach Farm goat cheese. The dressing recipe has evolved over the years into this divine blend. Make sure the olive oil you select is on the lighter, more delicate side, so that it does not overwhelm the sherry and shallot flavors.

½ cup good-quality sherry vinegar

2 shallots, finely minced

1 tablespoon Dijon mustard

1 cup olive/canola oil blend (combine ½ cup of each if you cannot find the blend)

⅓ cup Gigi Minimal Mayonnaise (page 280) or your favorite brand

Salt and freshly ground black pepper

Combine the vinegar, shallots, and Dijon mustard in a food processor, and pulse a few times to combine. With the motor running, slowly drizzle the oil through the feed tube. Continue mixing until all the oil is incorporated and the dressing is slightly emulsified. Pulse in the mayonnaise. Taste, and add salt and pepper as needed. Store, covered and refrigerated, for up to 1 week.

Gigi Lemon Vinaigrette

*I love this vinaigrette on arugula leaves, with shavings of Parmigiano-Reggiano
or Grana Padano cheese. I originally prepared this recipe for
Just Salad, but it is now a Gigi favorite too.*

⅓ cup	fresh lemon juice (from about 2 lemons)
1 tablespoon	minced shallots
1½ teaspoons	Dijon mustard
1 teaspoon	confectioners' sugar
1 teaspoon	grated lemon zest
¼ teaspoon	salt
1 cup	olive/canola oil blend (combine ½ cup of each if you cannot find the blend)

Combine all the ingredients except the oil in a food processor, and pulse a few times to combine. With the motor running, slowly drizzle the oil through the feed tube. Continue processing until all the oil is incorporated and the dressing is emulsified. Taste, and adjust the seasoning as needed. Store, covered and refrigerated, for up to 1 week.

Pesto for All Seasons

MAKES ABOUT 2 CUPS

I think it's time to liberate pesto from being just a summertime dish. This recipe is for a classic basil pesto, but that's only a jumping-off point. Feel free to substitute arugula or watercress in the spring, summer, or fall, or try dandelion greens or mustard greens for a spicier winter pesto. For an utterly new but delicious approach, try swapping cooked beets for the basil.

1½ cups	fresh basil leaves
1 teaspoon	chopped garlic
½ cup	extra-virgin olive oil
¼ cup	grated Grana Padano or Parmesan cheese
1 teaspoon	chopped oil-packed anchovies (optional)
1 teaspoon	grated lemon zest
⅓ cup	pine nuts, toasted
	Salt and freshly ground black pepper, to taste

Place the basil, garlic, and ¼ cup of the olive oil in a food processor, and pulse a few times. Add the Grana Padano, anchovies (if using), lemon zest, pine nuts, and salt and pepper, and pulse to combine. While the processor is running, pour the remaining ¼ cup olive oil through the feed tube. You should have a nice smooth puree. Add a bit of cold water, if desired, to thin.

The pesto can be used immediately, or you can refrigerate it for several days. Pesto is best consumed right away, but I have been known to freeze it in ice cube trays for a reminder of summer flavor during the long days of winter.

Roasted Red Pepper Pesto

MAKES ABOUT 2 CUPS

Another riff on pesto to enjoy as a base for a Skizza (page 28), as a spread to
enjoy with cold vegetables, tucked into a frittata, or tossed with pasta.

2 cups	chopped roasted red peppers (see below)
2 teaspoons	chopped garlic
¼ cup	grated Grana Padano or Parmesan cheese
1 teaspoon	salt
2 teaspoons	salt-packed capers, rinsed of any excess salt
1 teaspoon	smoked paprika
2 tablespoons	minced fresh flat-leaf parsley
1 teaspoon	Dijon mustard
	Salt and freshly ground black pepper, to taste
½ cup	extra-virgin olive oil

Place all the ingredients except the olive oil in a food processor, and pulse a few times to combine. While the processor is running, slowly pour the olive oil in through the feed tube. You should have a nice smooth puree. Taste, and correct the seasoning.

Use the pesto immediately or refrigerate, covered, for several days.

Roasted Red Peppers

Preheat the oven to 475°F. Halve and core 5 large red bell peppers.

In a large bowl, combine the pepper halves and 2 tablespoons olive oil, tossing them to evenly coat. Spread them on a baking sheet, season with salt and pepper, and roast for 20 minutes. Transfer the hot peppers to a bowl and cover with plastic wrap. Set aside to cool for at least 30 minutes. When the peppers are cool, remove and discard the skins.

Gigi Minimal Mayonnaise

*Sometimes simple is best. This mayonnaise requires few ingredients and is a snap
to prepare. It is delicious all by itself but is also a part of both Gigi Market's
and Gigi Trattoria's standard repertoire of dressings and sauces.*

2	large egg yolks, at room temperature
¼ teaspoon	salt
¼ teaspoon	Dijon mustard
1 teaspoon	fresh lemon juice
¾ cup	sunflower, vegetable, or canola oil
¼ cup	extra-virgin olive oil

Put the egg yolks in a bowl, add the salt, mustard, and lemon juice, and whisk lightly to blend. In a separate bowl, whisk the sunflower oil and olive oil together. With the whisk in one hand and the bowl of oil in the other, slowly drip the oil onto the egg yolk mixture, drop by drop, whisking all the time. Within a minute you'll notice the mixture beginning to thicken. When that happens, you can add the oil a little faster—in a thin drizzle.

Continue adding the oil until it has all combined with the yolks. You should have a beautiful, thick yellow mayonnaise. Taste to correct the seasonings, adding a touch more salt or lemon juice if desired. Cover and refrigerate until ready to use or store for up to 3 days.

Béchamel, Two Ways

MAKES ABOUT 1½ QUARTS

Béchamel, also known as white sauce, is one of the "mother sauces" of French cuisine.
Classically béchamel is made with a base of equal amounts of butter and flour. My two hats,
nutritionist and chef, led me to provide both classic and "enlightened" versions of
béchamel. For cheese béchamel, stir in 2 cups shredded cheddar or 1 cup
grated Parmesan during the last minute of cooking.

Classic Béchamel

6 cups	whole or 2-percent milk
8 tablespoons	unsalted butter (1 stick)
½ cup	all-purpose flour
Pinch	ground nutmeg
	Salt and freshly ground black pepper

Enlightened Béchamel

6 cups	2-percent milk
½ cup	all-purpose flour
Pinch	ground nutmeg
Pinch	cayenne pepper
	Salt and freshly ground black pepper

Heat the milk in a saucepan over medium heat until it is steaming hot (do not let it boil). Keep it at this temperature.

Melt the butter in a heavy-bottomed saucepan over medium-low heat. Stir in the flour and cook, stirring constantly, until the paste bubbles, 2 to 3 minutes; don't let it brown. Whisk in the hot milk and nutmeg and bring to a boil. Cook, whisking constantly, until the sauce thickens, 5 minutes. Season with salt and pepper to taste. Lower the heat and cook, stirring, for 2 to 3 minutes more.

Heat the milk in a saucepan over medium heat until it is steaming hot (do not let it boil).

Place the flour in a medium saucepan and whisk in ½ to ¾ cup of the hot milk, just enough to form a smooth, creamy paste; there should be no lumps of flour. Slowly add the remaining milk, whisking constantly, until fully blended. Add the nutmeg and cayenne, and season with salt and pepper to taste. Over medium heat, gradually bring the mixture to a boil, whisking often. Cook until thickened, about 5 minutes.

Gigi Tomato Salsa

MAKES 3½ CUPS

We use Mr. Mink's tomato harvest to prepare this salsa, which we like to serve with grilled or roasted fish and shellfish (such as shrimp, snapper, or tuna) as well as grilled Northwind Farms baby chickens. This salsa also tops crostini or bruschetta (drain it before topping) and is the base for Mr. Mink's Panzanella (page 78).

4 cups	diced seeded fresh tomatoes (3 large tomatoes)
½ cup	finely diced red onion or thinly sliced scallions (white and light green parts)
⅓ cup	fresh lemon juice
½ cup	extra-virgin olive oil
2 small	jalapeño peppers, halved, seeded, and finely chopped
1 teaspoon	salt
⅓ cup	chopped fresh flat-leaf parsley

Combine tomatoes, red onion, lemon juice, olive oil, jalapeño peppers, and salt in a large bowl. Mix well, cover, and let sit at room temperature for 1 hour. The salsa will keep for 1 day, refrigerated. Add the parsley just before serving.

Salsa Through the Seasons

Summer
- *Black or white bean:* corn and tomato, avocado (optional), lime juice, fresh cilantro or parsley
- *Peach:* red onion, jalapeño, lime juice, fresh cilantro or parsley
- *Plum:* red onion, jalapeño, ground coriander, serrano chile, lime juice, honey
- *Cucumber:* scallions, lemon juice, fresh cilantro, fresh mint or parsley, tomato (optional)
- *Cantaloupe:* cucumber, scallions, fresh cilantro, lime juice and zest, splash of orange juice, jalapeño

Fall
- *Apple/pear:* red onion, lemon or lime juice, cumin, fresh ginger, fresh cilantro or parsley, honey or sugar

Spring
- *Baby vegetables:* carrots, radishes, scallions, fresh tarragon, parsley, rice vinegar, lemon juice, sugar or honey

Winter
- *Tropical:* pineapple and/or mango, red onion, lime juice and zest, jalapeño or serrano chile, fresh parsley or cilantro

Gigi Salsa Verde

MAKES 1¼ CUPS

Each basket of crispy Gigi Tuscan Fries served at Gigi Trattoria and Gigi Market comes with Gigi Salsa Verde. By popular demand, we began retailing the salsa at Gigi Market in 2007. It also makes a great sandwich spread.

1 cup	Gigi Minimal Mayonnaise (page 280) or your favorite brand
2 tablespoons	chopped fresh flat-leaf parsley
2 tablespoons	chopped fresh basil
3 tablespoons	chopped well-rinsed salt-packed capers
3 tablespoons	chopped cornichons
	Salt and freshly ground black pepper, to taste

In a medium bowl, stir together the mayonnaise, chopped herbs, capers, and cornichons. Taste, and add a bit of salt and/or pepper if desired. (Alternatively, you can pulse the ingredients in a food processor—just keep it a little chunky and interesting, not too fine a chop.)

Keep refrigerated and use within 3 days.

Gigi Tuscan Fries

MAKES 4 SERVINGS

*Gigi Tuscan Fries keep our customers coming in the doors of Gigi Trattoria and Gigi Market;
they certainly have fans, young and old. We use top-quality potatoes and fry them in peanut
oil with a few sprigs of fresh rosemary and sage. The presentation is colorful, flavorful,
and abundant—one order can easily be enjoyed by a table of 4 during the meal or while sipping
cocktails. In addition to our classic version, we offer them with a Parmesan dusting.*

3 quarts	peanut oil
1 pound	skin-on potatoes, cut into ⅜-inch fries (or your favorite fry style)
3 sprigs	fresh rosemary
3 sprigs	fresh sage
	Salt
½ cup	freshly grated Grana Padano or Parmesan cheese (optional)

Heat the peanut oil to 375°F in a large Dutch oven or home fryer. Place the potatoes in a fry basket and cook until golden and crispy, about 8 minutes. During the last 30 seconds of cooking, add the herbs. Drain thoroughly, then transfer the fries and herbs to a large bowl. While tossing the fries and herbs in the bowl, season with salt and Grana Padano or Parmesan, if using. Serve immediately with Salsa Verde (opposite), if desired.

NUTRITION

Peanut oil is pricier than other oils, but it results in a crispier and healthier fry. Purified safe for most allergies. We clearly indicate its use on our menus.

Gigi Caesar Dressing

MAKES 2½ CUPS

The Gigi Caesar is classic and simple. We lightly coat top-quality romaine lettuce with our tasty Caesar dressing and finish the salad with a topping of Grana Padano shavings. Knowing that many people like to up the protein in their salads, we offer the following add-ons to all our salads: seared organic salmon, imported white anchovies, sliced organic free-range chicken breast, or pan-seared shrimp.

¼ cup	mashed roasted garlic (recipe follows)
1 tablespoon	chopped oil-packed anchovies
¼ cup	Dijon mustard
¼ cup	fresh lemon juice
1 teaspoon	dried oregano
2 tablespoons	white wine vinegar
¼ cup	extra-virgin olive oil
1 cup	Gigi Minimal Mayonnaise (page 280) or your favorite brand
	Salt and freshly ground black pepper, to taste

Place the roasted garlic and anchovies in a food processor and pulse to combine. Add the mustard, lemon juice, oregano, and vinegar and mix well. With the machine running, slowly drizzle in the olive oil; you'll see the mixture thicken. Add the mayonnaise and pulse to combine. Taste to see if you need to add any salt or pepper. Keep refrigerated and use within 3 days.

Roasted Garlic

Preheat the oven to 350°F.

Cut the very tops off 4 or 5 heads of garlic to expose the cloves. Place the garlic in a small baking dish. Add ¼ cup olive oil and season with salt and pepper to taste; toss to coat. Cover the dish tightly with aluminum foil. Bake until the garlic skins are golden brown and the cloves are tender, about 50 minutes. Let the garlic cool. Squeeze the garlic cloves from papery skins. Store the whole head, wrapped in foil, for up to 3 days. Use roasted garlic in salad dressings, dips, and spreads.

Gigi Fig Jam

MAKES 1 QUART

*We use this delicious jam on our cheese plate and as the base
for the ever-popular Skizza Bianca (page 29).*

2 tablespoons	olive oil
2	medium shallots, roughly chopped
2 teaspoons	chopped fresh rosemary
12 ounces	dried Calmyra figs, chopped (about 2½ cups)
2 tablespoons	dry red wine
1 tablespoon	dry white wine
	Salt and freshly ground black pepper

Heat the olive oil in a medium saucepan over medium-high heat. Add the shallots and cook until softened, about 3 minutes. Add the rosemary and figs, and cook for another 3 minutes, until the figs soften slightly. Add the wines and 4 cups of water, and bring to a boil. Then reduce the heat and simmer until the figs are very soft, about 30 minutes. Remove the pan from the heat and let cool.

Puree the mixture in a food processor until smooth. Season with salt and pepper to taste. Store, covered and refrigerated, for up to 1 week.

Gigi Homemade Fresh Ricotta

MAKES 1 CUP

Ricotta is so delicious when fresh, and it's super-easy to prepare. Get whatever great-quality milk you can find locally to get started (we use Hudson Valley Fresh). We include our fresh ricotta on appetizer plates and use it to top some of our pastas and Skizzas.

8 cups	whole milk
1 cup	fresh lemon juice
1 tablespoon	unsalted butter, at room temperature
½ teaspoon	salt
1 teaspoon	finely chopped fresh herbs, such as parsley, thyme, basil, sage, etc. (optional)

Heat the milk in a large saucepan over medium heat at 170°F, until scalding. Remove the saucepan from the heat and add the lemon juice. Set the milk-lemon mixture aside for about 5 minutes, until the milk begins to curdle.

Line a colander with a double layer of cheesecloth, and pour the milk mixture into it. Allow the water to drain out thoroughly and the curds to remain. Gather the cheesecloth into a ball and gently squeeze out some of the remaining water. Place the ricotta in a bowl, and whisk in the butter and salt. If you like, whisk in the herbs.

Serve immediately, or place in a tightly sealed container and refrigerate for up to 3 days.

Stone Fruit BBQ Sauce

Use peaches, plums, or nectarines to create this sweet and spicy sauce for grilled poultry,
fish (salmon or shrimp), or pork chops. At Gigi, we use BBQ sauces made
from seasonal fruits to sauce our famous Skizzas.

2 cups	diced ripe peaches, plums, or nectarines (about 3 medium to large)
2 cups	ketchup
½ cup	packed light brown sugar
1	shallot, minced
2 teaspoons	grated fresh ginger
¼ teaspoon	ground cloves
¼ teaspoon	cayenne pepper, or to taste
¼ cup	white wine vinegar
2 tablespoons	Worcestershire sauce
4 tablespoons	unsalted cold butter (½ stick), cut into cubes
	Salt and freshly ground black pepper

In a medium saucepan, combine all the ingredients except the butter, salt, and pepper. Bring to a boil over medium-high heat, stirring to blend the ingredients. Then reduce the heat and simmer, partially covered, for 20 minutes. Add a few tablespoons of water if necessary to thin the sauce slightly. Remove the pan from the heat, whisk in the butter, and season with salt and pepper to taste.

Basic Tomato Sauce

MAKES ABOUT 4 CUPS

During the winter, canned tomatoes taste best. But by summer, canned tomatoes from last year's harvest can taste almost bitter. To solve that problem, we sauté the onion in this sauce for a long time, until it is almost caramelized and sweet. This cooked tomato sauce is quite different from the quick-cooking sauce we prepare during the blissful six weeks that we enjoy fresh local tomatoes. This classic tomato sauce works its way onto some of our Skizzas and is the base for our Arrabbiata Sauce (opposite).

¼ cup olive oil

1 large onion, finely chopped

2 rosemary sprigs, leaves removed and chopped fine, stems discarded

Two 28-ounce cans whole San Marzano tomatoes, chopped, with juices

¼ cup chopped fresh basil

Salt and freshly ground black pepper

In a wide-bottomed pot, heat the olive oil over medium heat. Add the onion and cook slowly until it is very soft, with a light brown color, 6 to 8 minutes. Add the rosemary and stir, cooking the rosemary in the oil to impart its flavor, about 2 minutes. Add the tomatoes, turn the heat to low, and simmer, uncovered, until the sauce is richly colored with a shiny, almost glossy appearance; this can take from 45 minutes to an hour. Add the chopped basil toward the end of cooking, along with salt and pepper to taste.

The sauce can be used immediately in any number of dishes, including a simple plate of spaghetti. Covered and refrigerated, the sauce will keep for up to 6 days; it can also be frozen for up to 6 months.

Arrabbiata Sauce

This sauce is easily and quickly made from a basic pomodoro, *or tomato, sauce. Try the Gigi homemade version, or spike up your favorite brand with the ingredients below. In the summer, make this with a fresh tomato sauce. Penne Arrabbiata is one of the most popular pastas at Gigi. Its simplicity should not fool you—it's all about using the right amount of deliciously spicy sauce to just coat the pasta, and it should be served piping hot. A sprinkle of good-quality grated Parmigiano-Reggiano or Grana Padano is the only thing you might want to consider adding.*

2 tablespoons	extra-virgin olive oil
1 tablespoon	chopped garlic
1	shallot, finely chopped
¼ cup	dry red wine
4 cups	Basic Tomato Sauce (opposite)
2 tablespoons	chopped fresh basil
1 teaspoon	red pepper flakes
¼ teaspoon	salt

Heat the olive oil in a large skillet over high heat. Add the garlic and shallot and sauté until soft and just beginning to brown, about 3 minutes. Add the wine and cook until reduced to a tablespoon or two, about 1 minute. Add the basic tomato sauce and the remaining ingredients and bring to a simmer; cook for 2 to 3 minutes.

For penne arrabbiata, toss the hot sauce into cooked penne immediately after draining. Add a generous handful (about ⅓ cup) of freshly grated Grana Padano or Parmesan. Toss again and serve immediately.

Buttera Sauce

MAKES 4 TO 5 CUPS

*I always joke with Gigi chef Wilson Costa about the revolt we would have on our hands
if I ever removed our Rigatoni with Buttera Sauce from the menu. Like the
Tagliatelle Bolognese (page 229), it is trustworthy and stalwart—the
dish you crave for comfort and guaranteed satisfaction.*

2 tablespoons	fennel seeds, toasted
2 tablespoons	olive oil
1	carrot, finely chopped
1	medium onion, finely diced
2	celery stalks, finely diced
2	garlic cloves, minced
½ cup	chopped fresh flat-leaf parsley
¼ cup	chopped fresh sage
2	rosemary sprigs, leaves removed and chopped fine, stems discarded
1½ pounds	Northwinds Farms sausage, crumbled
½ cup	dry white wine
One	15-ounce can whole San Marzano tomatoes, chopped, with juices
½ cup	heavy cream
½ cup	fresh or frozen peas

Toast the fennel seeds in a small skillet over medium heat until fragrant and lightly brown, 2 to 3 minutes, set aside.

Heat the olive oil in a large skillet over medium heat. Add the carrot, onion, celery, and garlic and cook until softened, 5 to 7 minutes. Add the herbs and allow them to cook slightly and release their aromas, 1 minute.

Increase the heat to high and add the pork. Cook, stirring occasionally, until browned, 5 to 7 minutes. Add the wine and deglaze the pan, scraping up any brown bits. Cook until the wine has reduced slightly. Add the tomatoes and the fennel seeds. Lower the heat to a slow simmer, cover the skillet, and cook, stirring occasionally, for 40 minutes. During the last 3 minutes of cooking time, when the mixture is slightly thick, stir in the cream and the peas. Serve immediately.

Gabbi's Gruel

MAKES 4½ QUARTS

*I'm a registered dietitian, not a vet, and therefore do not claim that this is a
100-percent-balanced diet for dogs. What I do know is that my eight-year-old black Labrador
enjoys this "supplement" to her traditional feed—what dog ever turns down liver? She looks great
and it makes me feel nurturing to put a big pot of this "gruel" on the stovetop. I make
large batches (it freezes well) and spoon a few tablespoons into each meal.
Northwind Farms provides some poultry parts from their cleaned fowl.*

3 pounds	chicken livers, rinsed and chopped
3 pounds	ground turkey or chicken
1 pound	chicken or turkey giblets
2	medium sweet potatoes, peeled and roughly chopped
10 ounces	frozen spinach, or 2 large bunches fresh spinach
½ cup	pearl barley

Combine all the ingredients in a large saucepan or a soup pot, and add just enough water to cover (about 6 cups). Stir to combine, and bring the mixture to a boil. Then reduce the heat and cook, stirring often in the beginning to prevent the proteins from sticking to the bottom of the pot, until thick and gruel-like, about 1½ hours.

Store, covered, in the refrigerator, for up to 5 days, or freeze in 2-cup or 1-quart containers for up to 2 months.

Food and Entertaining

In the late 1990s I lived for a year in northern Italy, helping to run a restaurant and perfect (or at least improve!) my Italian. I lived in a charming small town called Bassano del Grappa, just over an hour outside of Venice. Up until then I had spent my whole working life in New York City, so with this move, life changed dramatically. The two places could not have been more different. But what quickly became apparent to me then, and in all the regions I've traveled to since, is how naturally convivial life is in Italy. If three people get together, man, it is officially a party—no reason needed. I love that. I love that sense of expansiveness and spontaneity. In Italy, no matter how busy you are, there is always time to have a little fun. Maybe that's why over the past decade almost all my vacation time has been spent there. It has great people, wonderful food and wine, and beautiful urban and rural treasures.

Life in the Hudson Valley lends itself to a similarly genial spirit. Unlike the many years of socializing in New York City, where my friends and I met primarily in restaurants, the character of the Valley encourages more sharing of your personal space. Yes, entertaining occurs in restaurants, but more often we share great stories, laughs, food, and festivities in our homes, often in a very impromptu fashion. I always keep sparkling wine and good cheese on hand, as I never know when Claire, Edris, Toni, or Tabetha might stop by. In fact, after years of restaurant life, I've found that many of my friends have similarly odd schedules and days off. To us, Sunday is Friday.

Nowadays, whether I'm hosting a sit-down dinner or a New Year's Eve cocktail party, entertaining at home is a way for me to stay in touch with my friends, many of whom have busy, jam-packed lives like my own. One of the benefits of owning a restaurant, market, and catering business is that you see what makes for a successful party or a dull evening. It's about energy, and for that, there is no magic recipe. Rather, it's all in the mix. Like a bartender, you combine people, good food, and plenty of drinks and then toss in some ambience. What you pour out is an experience. The question is, how much of each do you need to create a wonderful time?

In my opinion, people are, hands down, the most important part of any evening. Everything else—food, flowers, good lighting, and so on—just helps people connect. And it is that person-to-person connection that makes events memorable. Now, I do think that food and drink are great social helpers. It doesn't have to be anything fancy. It just has to be of great quality.

Living in the country, even in a fairly sophisticated place like the Hudson Valley, means that entertaining is less formal. My company, Gigi Catering, does events all year long throughout the Valley and what we find works best is a more natural, clean, and informal style of presentation and approach. A rustic elegance, as we like to say here. We provide this service in private homes, stately historic sites, at Gigi Market, and, most recently, as the exclusive caterer for Vassar College's Alumnae House.

My staff and I look at every event we cater as if it is our own. What would I like to see? What would I like to eat? What's in keeping with the surroundings and the season? The food should be impeccably fresh and full-flavored, but doesn't need to be overly manipulated or fussy. It should look inviting, but taste even better.

Ultimately, we share food in order to share ourselves. It's our way of providing nourishment and comfort to those we care about. Planning a party, even a simple get-together, does require a little forethought and organization, but you shouldn't feel so overwhelmed that you decide to nix the idea altogether. Plus, there are very few rules anymore. You can do what you like and what works. With help from my dear friend and colleague, catering and events director John Storm, here are some of the things I've learned over the years. Of course, make it fit your own particulars. Nothing is set in stone.

- Have a general game plan in mind, including how many people will come and how much you want to spend. Take your budget seriously. You don't want that cranky feeling afterward when you realize you've spent too much. It will take away the pleasure of the event.
- Consider your space. I personally don't favor entertaining that requires extensive redecorating, refurbishment, or new furniture. (Again, consider that possible cranky feeling!) But sometimes you can move things around to accommodate your event. Need to set up a bar somewhere? Look at a corner of your entryway as a possible space, or a spot underneath the staircase. Get creative and have fun.
- As much as we all want to be the perfect host, we can't do it all!

Consider hiring someone to help. It could be a bartender to mix drinks, someone to help serve dinner, or a late-night helper to clean up after the last guest heads out the door. You want to enjoy the festivities as much as your guests do.

- It's perfectly acceptable to limit the alcoholic beverages you wish to offer. Beer, white and red wine, and a specialty cocktail is a perfect drinks menu.

- Open seating for a casual dinner/holiday party is fine, and it adds to the energy of the table. If it's a formal setting (and these don't happen all that often), just remember that boy/girl, boy/girl is still very nice.

- General rules for beverages:

  - There are approximately 60 glasses of wine per case.
  - There are approximately 70 glasses of Champagne per case.
  - There are approximately 20 drinks in a 750ml bottle of liquor.
  - How much ice? Plan on 2.5 to 4 pounds per person. That may seem like a lot, but remember, ice melts and you'll need it for mixing cocktails, for water glasses, and for chilling white wine or Champagne. If you don't have an ice tub to chill your wine

or beer in, don't fret. Use the bathtub in a bathroom the guests won't see!

  - Depending on your crowd and the length of your event, assume 1 to 2 cocktails or 2 to 3 glasses of wine per guest.

- Food looks its very best, I believe, on a plain, solid background. I prefer simple white china when I entertain. For dinner buffets, various sizes of white serving bowls, platters, and tureens are preferable. They can be any shape—oval, rectangular, and/or square—but do keep in mind how heavy they are. It may look beautiful, but if it takes two arms and a squat to lift that platter off the shelf, imagine how heavy it will be when laden with delicious food!

- Find a good match between amount of food and size of tray. You want your platters to look full and abundant. I generally prefer 18 x 9 inches for rectangular platters, 16 x 11 inches for ovals, and 12- to 16-inch-diameter round bowls. They are all "human-friendly" sizes. I sometimes lay out my bowls and platters on the table beforehand to get a visual image of how everything will fit. Leave a little space. You don't want it to look like too tight a squeeze.

- I'm constantly asked how much food will serve how many people. Generally, about 6 to 8 ounces of protein (beef, chicken, or fish) per person works well along with about 4 ounces of vegetables and starchy dishes. To calculate how much you'll need, take the guest count and multiply it by the suggested ounces. Then divide by sixteen in order to get the number of pounds of food to buy. For example, if twelve people are coming for dinner and you decide to serve green beans, multiply 12 x 4 ounces for a total of 48 ounces. Then divide by 16 to get to 3 pounds. Always round up; better to have a little extra than not enough!
- Let the season be your guide when it comes to crafting a menu. For dinner buffets you can have one or two main protein dishes (depending on your guest count), one or two simple and flavorful vegetable selections, a light starch, perhaps a grain or bean salad, and a green salad.
- For a more formal dinner party where people are seated and served, play it safe and go with menu items that are universal and recognizable. Your culinary tastes may be far ranging, but have a little mercy on the guest who really just likes a nice piece of grilled steak or chicken! I think it's a great idea to serve several vegetable dishes since you may have one or more guests who prefer to eat a vegetarian meal. They will greatly appreciate your consideration.
- Remember that no matter what, the majority of all dinner parties or get-togethers end up in the kitchen anyway!

MIGLIORELLI FARM

Migliorelli Farm brings together my whole premise of "Hudson Valley Mediterranean." When I asked Ken Migliorelli the best way to keep small local farms and farming communities healthy, his response reminded me of my long-departed Italian grandmother: "Eat fresh food. That will keep you and everyone around you healthy."

As one of the most experienced and diverse farmers in the area, Ken Migliorelli represents the third generation in his Italian-American family to grow food for a living. His grandfather, Angelo, immigrated to the United States from the town of Lazio and farmed in the Bronx beginning in the 1930s. Angelo's son, Rocco, and his uncle ran a dairy there for a few years, and when Ken was ten his father bought 135 acres in Tivoli, where Ken still lives.

By local standards, Migliorelli Farm is a large operation, with eight hundred acres cultivated for fruits and vegetables, and Ken is one of the "old heads" here—a local spokesperson for making the business of farming a permanent feature of life in the Hudson Valley, even during financially

difficult times. He voices the concerns of other farmers that the near-perfect growing conditions of the Valley are a treasured resource and should never be developed into strip malls or housing tracts. Working with a local conservancy group, Scenic Hudson, Ken placed the farm's development rights under a conservation easement in 1998, keeping his patch of heaven as farmland forever, producing wholesome food for locals and for greenmarket customers in New York City.

I love visiting Migliorelli Farm. It reflects Ken's exuberant approach to life. He cultivates more than a hundred and thirty varieties of fruits and vegetables, including the original strain of broccoli rabe brought by his grandfather to America more than seventy years ago. He is a specialist in hard-to-find ethnic vegetables and greens, and he treasures the unique, unusual, or simply weird. It makes farming more interesting, and his customers, especially chefs, like it too. For years Ken grew only vegetables, but now he leases land with orchards on it. "It feels good to stretch up," he says. "Growing veggies for so many years, I bent down all the time. With fruit you get a chance to be aboveground!"

The farmers' market phenomenon, beginning in the early 1980s, made farming a sustainable livelihood for Ken, and the "eat local" movement of the past few years has really raised customer awareness and patronage of the markets where he sells his produce. He has been a member of the famous Union Square Greenmarket since 1983 and today sells at more than thirty farmers' markets around New York City during the summer and fall. He also maintains two local farm stands, one in Red Hook and one in Rhinebeck, to provide fresh food to the community. The farm supports Ken, fifteen full-time workers, and thirty-five seasonal workers during the summer. There is plenty of work for everyone.

Ken and I walk up the hill to his house, which sits at the high point on his property with a sweeping view of the farm. He built the house himself, and its terra-cotta floors, central woodstove, and colored oak and pine ceiling beams remind me of the rustic farmhouses of northern Italy: snug and warm and welcoming. We talk about his future plans, and whether his kids will someday take over the family business. He hopes so, but he is letting their interests and growth direct the path. He is enthusiastic about exploring new techniques in controlled-atmosphere storage and greenhouse growing, so that he can extend his selling season to almost year-round. He is optimistic that he can continue doing what he loves. "You don't get rich," Ken confides, "but overall, farming is a great life."

Farming in the Hudson Valley attracts so many different kinds of people; there is no "one size fits all." That's part of the charm of living here. We are happy to support all kinds of farms: CSAs, wholesalers, direct-to-market sellers, and value-added artisans producing highly indiosyncratic products. Thanks to the continued hard work and careful land conservation efforts of local farmers like Ken Migliorelli, we lucky locals can purchase an unusually wide variety of fruits and vegetables grown almost literally in our backyards. That is something to treasure.

Migliorelli Farm, 46 Freeborn Lane,
Tivoli, New York 12583
845-757-3276
www.migliorelli.com

Celebrating Through the Seasons

I've collected recipes from each season that make entertaining flavorful and festive. Enjoy my suggestions or adapt them by following some of the "variations" offered on each recipe. *Cin-cin!*

SPRING

In like a lion . . .

Out like a lamb . . .

SUMMER'S BOUNTY BUFFET

FALL HARVEST DINNER

WINTER FIRESIDE DINNER

SOUL-WARMING WINTER LUNCH

Sources

The fabulous farms and small businesses listed highlight some of my favorites in the Hudson Valley. The list is not exhaustive in terms of the wide variety of quality product here in the Valley, just a sampling of the relationships we at Gigi hold near and dear. To find fresh local foods near you, check out the resources listed below.

Amazing Real Live Food Co.
124 Chase Road, Pine Plains, NY 12567
Phone: 518.398.0368
Farmer/Producer/Contact: Rory Chase and
Peter Destler
Email: rory@amazingreallive.com
Web: http://amazingreallive.com
     Committed to producing restorative food and drink in the Hudson Valley. Products containing essential probiotics, dense nutritional values, and key digestive enzymes, which the human body naturally thrives on. Farmer's Cheeses (perfectly plain, fresh dill, roasted garlic, jalapeño, basil garlic, sun-dried tomato, horseradish. Other cheeses include: probiotic camembert and queso blanco. Kombucha elixirs (pure kombucha, ginger root extract, goji berry juice, seasonal fruit infusions. Lacto-ferments (old fashioned sparkling sauerkraut, kim chi, pickled cucumber, green bean, and asparagus). Probiotic ice cream coming soon.

Awesome Farm
223 Pitcher Lane, Tivoli, NY 12571
Phone: 845.332.1929
Farmer/Producer/Contact: Owen O'Connor and KayCee Wimbish
E-mail: info@awesomefarmny.com
Web: www.awesomefarmny.com
     Pastured poultry, grass-fed lamb, eggs, vegetables, pelts, and yarn

Beth's Farm Kitchen
P.O. Box 113, Stuyvesant Falls, NY 12174
Phone: 800.331.5267
Farmer/Producer/Contact: Beth Linsley
E-mail: info@bethsfarmkitchen.com
Web: www.bethsfarmkitchen.com
     Chutneys, jams, marmalades, pickles and relish, zany and specialty jellies

Cedar Heights Orchard
7 Crosby Lane, Rhinebeck, NY 12572
Phone: 845.876.3231
Farmer/Producer/Contact: Arvia and Bill Morris
E-mail: info@rhinebeckapples.com
Web: www.rhinebeckapples.com
     Apples, apples, apples

Chutney Unlimited
52 Pioneer Street, Cooperstown, NY 13326
Phone: 607.547.7272
Farmer/Producer/Contact: Tanna Roten
E-mail: info@chutneyunlimited.com
Web: www.chutneyunlimited.com
     Chutneys, spreads, garam masala, Tuscan salt

Coach Farm
105 Mill Hill Road, Pine Plains, NY 12567
Phone: 518.398.5325
E-mail: info@coachfarm.com
Web: www.coachfarm.com
     Fresh curd, soft and aged goat cheese, goat cheese grating sticks, spreads (regular, flavored, and reduced-fat), Yo-Goat (goat's milk yogurt)

The Currant Company
59 Walnut Lane, Staatsburg, NY 12580
Phone: 800.CurrantC, 800.287.7268
Farmer/Producer/Contact: Greg Quinn

E-mail: info@currants.com
Web: www.currants.com
    Fresh (seasonal) and frozen black currants, Currant-C juice, black and red currant plants

Feather Ridge Farm
47 Bogdanffy Road, Elizaville, NY 12523
Phone: 845.756.2381
Farmer/Producer/Contact: the Bogdanffy Family
E-mail: katie@featherridgeeggs.com
Web: www. featherridgeeggs.com
    Eggs and egg products

Fitting Creek Farm
1191 Route 22, Ghent, NY 12075
Phone: 518.828.7007
Farmer/Producer/Contact: Walter Blank
E-mail: fittingcreek@usadatanet.net
    Maple syrups, pure maple sugar, maple pepper seasoning, maple nuts, maple BBQ sauce, vinegar and mustards, honey

Fix Bros Fruit Farm
215 White Birch Road, Hudson, NY 12534
Phone: 518.828.4401 or 518.828.7560
Farmer/Producer/Contact: Linda and Robert Fix
E-mail: fixfarm@aol.com
Web: www.fixbrosfruitfarm.com
    Four generations of Hudson Valley farmers offer sweet and sour (red and black) cherries, peaches, nectarines, apples, pumpkins, gourds—wholesale and pick-your-own

Gadaleto's Seafood Market
246 Main Street # 1, New Paltz, NY 12561
Phone: 845.255.1717
Farmer/Producer/Contact: Nat Gadaleto
E-mail: info@gadaletos.com
Web: www.galdaletos.com
    Super fresh wild and sustainable seafood species. Great restaurant on site!

Grazin' Angus Acres
125 Bartel Road, Ghent, NY 12075
Phone: 518.392.3620
Farmer/Producer/Contact: Dan and Susan Gibson
E-mail: dan.gibson@grazinangusacres.com
Web: www.grazinangusacres.com
    Grass-fed and finished Black Angus—no antibiotics, no hormones, no grains

Greig Farm
223 Pitcher Lane, Red Hook, NY 12571
Phone: 845.758.1234
Farmer/Producer/Contact: Norman Greig
Web: www.greigfarm.com

    Pick-your-own fruits and vegetables (apples, blueberries, pumpkins, raspberries)

Grey Mouse Farm
22 Grey Mouse Road, Saugerties, NY 12477
Phone: 845.246.3405
Farmer/Producer/Contact: Sallie and Kathy Kreda
Web: www.greymousefarm.com
    Preserves, BBQ sauces, fruit butters, spreads, garlic, pickles

Harney and Sons Fine Teas
P.O. Box 665, Salisbury, CT 06068
Phone: 800.TeaTime
E-mail: ht@harney.com
Web: www.harney.com
    More than 250 single-estate and blended teas, as well as five flavors of fresh-brewed bottled iced tea. Visit their café/tea house in Millerton, NY.

Harpersfield Cheese
Brovetto Dairy, P.O. Box 216, Harpersfield, NY 13786
Phone: 845.373.7022 or 607.278.6622
Farmer/Producer/Contact: Glenn Golovin
Email: ronrinfar@aol.com
Web: www.harpersfieldcheese.com
    Naturally aged, crafted Tilsit-style cheeses. The base cheese is sold raw or aged (4 to 6 months). Seasonal flavors include: hops, caraway, jalapeño, Ommegang beer, dill, lavender. Harney & Sons tea flavors include: herbal rosemary, green rea, lapsang souchong.

Hawthorne Valley Farm
327 Route 21C, Ghent (Harlemville), NY 12075
Phone: 518.672.7500
Farmer/Producer/Contact: Rachel Schneider and Lelia Cafaro
Web: www.hawthornevalleyfarm.org
    Certified organic bakery, dairy (farmstead yogurt, quark, and cheeses), 250-member CSA (over forty vegetables), biodynamic farm, lacto-fermented vegetables (sauerkraut), grass-fed beef, and farm-raised pork

Hearty Roots Community Farm
P.O. Box 277, Tivoli, NY 12583
Phone: 845.943.8699
Farmer/Producer/Contact: Miriam Latzer and Benjamin Shute
E-mail: heartyroots@heartyroots.com
Web: www.heartyroots.com
    More than forty types of fruits and vegetables grown without chemical pesticides or synthetic fertilizers. Check out their Farm Share program on their website.

Hudson Valley Fresh
Hudson Valley Fresh is a not-for-profit dairy cooperative dedicated to preserving the agricultural heritage of the Hudson

River Valley and promoting it as one of the premier food regions of the United States. More than seven dairy farms in the Hudson Valley provide cow's milk that meets the strict standards of Hudson Valley Fresh.
47 South Hamilton Street, Poughkeepsie, NY 12601
Phone: 845.264.2372
Farmer/Producer/Contact: Samuel Simon
E-mail: info@hvfresh.com
Web: www.hudsonvalleyfresh.com
    Premium-quality dairy products. whole, skim, low-fat, and chocolate milk, half-and-half, heavy cream, sour cream

Hudson Valley Homestead
102 Sheldon Lane, Craryville, NY 12521
Phone: 518.851.7336
E-mail: sales@hudsonvalleyhomestead.com
Web: http://www.hudsonvalleyhomestead.com
    Vinegars, mustards, rubs, salad dressings, savory sauces, dips, and spreads

J. B. Peel Coffee and Tea
7582 North Broadway, Red Hook, NY 12571
Phone: 800.231.7372
Farmer/Producer/Contact: Gil Klein
E-mail: jbpeel@citlink.com
Web: www.jbpeelcoffee.com
    Numerous types of coffee roasted with care onsite and a wide selection of teas

Katchkie Farm/Great Performances
34 Fischer Road Ext., Kinderhook, NY 12106
Phone: 518.758.2166
Farmer/Producer/Contact: Bob Walker
E-mail: info@katchkiefarm.com
Web: www.katchkiefarm.com
    More than thirty different varieties of vegetables, as well as a selection of culinary herbs are available at farmers' markets in the Hudson Valley and NY metro areas. The Sylvia Center at Katchkie Farm is a nonprofit organization designed to improve the lives of at-risk children by giving them the opportunity to connect with nature and learn about nutritious and healthy eating through joyful hands-on experiences.

Lively Run Goat Farm
8978 County Road 142, Interlaken, NY 14847
Phone: 607.532.4647
Farmer/Producer/Contact: Steven and Susanne Messmer
E-mail: contact@livelyrun.com
Web: www.livelyrun.com
    Chevre (plain, lemon thyme and rose peppercorn, lemon thyme, dill, fine herb, garlic and pepper, rose peppercorn, herbes de provence), Cayuga blue, feta produced from Alpine, Nubian, Saanen, and South African Boer breeds, as well as crossbreeds

Markristo Farm
Route 23, Hillsdale, NY 12529
Phone: 518.325.4261
Farmer/Producer/Contact: Martin and Christa Stosiek
E-mail: growing@markristofarm.com
Web: www.markristofarm.com
    Certified organic family-owned market garden and farmers' market, offering a diverse crop of vegetables, cut flowers, and bedding plants to restaurants, farm stands, resorts, conference centers. CSA shares now available.

Mead Orchards
15 Scism Road, Tivoli NY 12583
Phone: 845.756.5641
Farmer/Producer/Contact: Chuck Mead
E-mail: meadorchards@yahoo.com
Web: www.meadorchards.com
    Apples, pears, peaches, plums, apricots, and nectarines, and more than forty types of vegetables available at their farm stand, pick-your-own, and in farmers' markets throughout the Hudson Valley and NY metro area

Migliorelli Farm
46 Freeborn Lane, Tivoli, New York 12583
Phone: 845.757.3276
Farmer/Producer/Contact: Ken Migliorelli
E-mail: farm@migliorelli.com
Web: www.migliorelli.com
    Services local restaurants and more than thirty farmers' markets in the Hudson Valley, capital, and NY metro areas, offering more than 130 fruits and vegetables. Operates two farm stands in Dutchess County.

Mink Farm
1067 County Route 6, Germantown, NY 12526
Phone: 518.537.4232
Farmer/Producer/Contact: Irving Mink
    Wide variety of gorgeous heirloom tomatoes

Montgomery Place Orchards
P.O. Box 24, Annandale-on-Hudson, NY 12504
Phone: 845.758.6338
Farmer/Producer/Contact: Thalia and Doug Finke
    More than sixty varieties of apples over the growing season; U-pick, farm market

Mountain Products Smokehouse
47 Burdick Road, LaGrangeville, NY 12540
Phone: 845.223.7900
Farmer/Producer/Contact: Thomas and Katherine Gary
E-mail: sales@mountainproductssmokehouse.com
Web: www.mountainproductssmokehouse.com
    Only natural apple and hickory wood chips in state-of-the-art stainless-steel smokehouses produce perfectly smoked cheeses, bacon, poultry, fish, and ham.

Northwind Farms
185 West Kerley Corners Road, Tivoli, NY 12583
Phone: 845.757.5591
Farmer/Producer/Contact: Richard and Jane Biezynski
Web: www.northwindfarmsallnatural.com
    Naturally raised Bronze Heritage and Holland White turkeys, ducks, chicken (Cornish hens, poussin, broilers, fryers, roasters), guinea hens, rabbits, goats, British White and Angus cattle, pork and pork products including preservative-free kielbasa and bacon

Old Chatham Sheepherding Company
155 Shaker Museum Road, Old Chatham, NY 12136
Farmer/Producer/Contact: Tom and Nancy Clark
Email: cheese@blacksheepcheese.com
Web: www.blacksheepcheese.com
    Sheep's milk Camembert, Ewe's Blue, sheep's milk yogurt, and ricotta

Palatine Valley Dairy
68 East Main Street, Nelliston, NY 13410
Phone: 518.993.3194
Farmer/Producer/Contact: Earl and Carol Spencer
E-mail: cheesymomma@palatinecheese.com
Web: www.palatinecheese.com
    Cheddar cheeses (more than twenty varieties) and cheese curds

Provich Provisions
P.O. Box 152, Pine Plains, NY 12567
Phone: 845.337.5930
Farmer/Producer/Contact: Joe Popovich
    Fresh mozzarella rated "best in the Hudson Valley"

Ray Tousey Honey and More
1783 Route 9, Germantown, NY 12526
Phone: 518.537.5353
Farmer/Producer/Contact: Ray Tousey
    Wide variety of honeys, candles, beeswax for soap and candle crafters. Ray also offers a variety of fruits: currants, gooseberries, raspberries, and heirloom tomatoes, as well as fresh fruit juices, preserves, and his own unique brand of cassis sweetened with honey rather than sugar.

Ronnybrook Farm Dairy
310 Prospect Hill Road, Ancramdale, NY 12503
Phone: 518.398.8000
Farmer/Producer/Contact: Ronnie, Rick, and Sid Osofsky
E-mail: info@ronnybrook.com
Web: www.ronnybrook.com
    Wide variety of milks, yogurts, ice creams, crème fraîche, butter, and eggnog

RSK Farm
13255 Route 23A, Prattsville, NY 12468
Phone: 518.229.3195

Farmer/Producer/Contact: Bob and Sandy Kiley
    Extensive varieties of potatoes including Corola, Adirondack Blue, and fingerlings

Sky Farm
122 Boston Corners Road #A, Millerton, NY 12546
Phone: 845.698.0953
Farmer/Producer/Contact: Chris Regan
    Baby arugula and gourmet salad mix, including over thirty varieties of greens, herbs, edible flowers, and "wild" plants

Sprout Creek Farm
34 Lauer Road, Poughkeepsie, NY 12603
Phone: 845.485.8438
E-mail: info@sproutcreekfarm.org
Web: www.sproutcreekfarm.org
    European-style cheeses made with cow's milk from grass-fed Jersey, Guernsey, Milking Shorthorn, and Brown Swiss cows; educational and camp programs available

TWELVE
1552 Post Road, Fairfield, CT 06824
Farmer/Producer/Contact: Joe Faso
E-mail: info@twelvebeverage.com
Web: www.twelvebeverage.com
    Sparkling nonalcoholic beverage

Uncle Neilie's Maple Syrup
38 Mill Road, Rhinebeck, NY 12572
Phone: 845.876.3894
Farmer/Producer/Contact: Neil Kane
Email: neilbev81@hotmail.com
    Pure maple syrup and syrup products

Upstate Farms of Highland Inc.
P.O. Box 376, Red Hook, NY 12571
Phone: 845.756.3803
Farmer/Producer/Contact: Michael Kokas and Jan Greer
    Specialty Hudson Valley produce

Wild Hive Farm
2411 Salt Point Turnpike, Clinton Corners, NY 12514
Phone: 845.266.5863
Farmer/Producer/Contact: Don Lewis
Web: http://www.wildhivefarm.com
    Micro mill and bakery/café; small batch artisan bakery products using their own freshly milled stone-ground whole germ flour from local organic grains, such as hard red spring wheat, soft white winter wheat, spelt, rye, triticale, oats, and corn

Wiltbank Farm
102 Charles Smith Road, Saugerties, NY 12477
Phone: 845.246.4169
Farmer/Producer/Contact: Gary Wiltbank
    Oyster and shiitake mushrooms

BREWERIES, WINERIES, AND DISTILLERIES

Adair Vineyards
52 Allhusen Road, New Paltz, NY 12561
Phone: 845.255.1377
E-mail: adairwine@aol.com
    Seyval Blanc, Vignoles, Foch and Millot

Alison Wines and Vineyard
231 Pitcher Lane, Red Hook, NY 12571
Phone: 845.758.6335
Farmer/Producer/Contact: Richard Lewit
E-mail: info@alisonwines.com
Web: www.alisonwines.com
    Seyval Blanc, Rose, Red Barn Red, Merlot, Fraise, Cassis

Brotherhood Winery
100 Brotherhood Plaza, Washingtonville, NY 10992
Phone: 845.496.3661
E-mail: wine@frontiernet.net
Web: www.brotherhoodwinery.net
    Merlot, Cabernet Sauvignon, Pinot Noir, and Ricolingo; limited releases of Mariage, Eiswien, Vintage Port, Blanc de Blanc, Grand Monarque, and Carpe Diem, a truly delightful Spumante

Chatham Brewing
30 Main Street, Suite 2, Chatham NY 12037
Phone: 518.697.0202
Farmer/Producer/Contact: Jake Cunningham, Tom Crowell, and Chris Ferrone
E-mail: beer@chathambrewing.com
Web: www.chathambrewing.com
    Amber ale, IPA, porter

Clinton Vineyards
450 Schultzville Road, Clinton Corners, NY 12514
Phone: 845.266.5372
Farmer/Producer/Contact: Phyllis and Ben Feder
Web: www.clintonvineyards.com
    Seyval Blanc, Seyval Naturel, Jubilee, Peach Gala, and Royale, all made with champeniose, and numerous dessert wines. Tours and tastings available.

Core Vodka by Harvest Spirits, LLC
3074 Route 9, Valatie, NY 12184
Phone: 518.261.1625
Farmer/Producer/Contact: Derek Grout and Tom Crowell
E-mail: harvestspirits@gmail.com
Web: www.harvestspirits.com
    Distilled spirits from local products

Keegan Ales
20 Saint James Street, Kingston, NY 12401

Phone: 845.853.7354
Farmer/Producer/Contact: Tommy Keegan
E-mail: beer@keeganales.com
Web: www.keeganales.com
    Old Capital, Mother's Milk, Hurricane Kitty

Millbrook Vineyards & Winery
26 Wing Road, Millbrook, NY 12545
Phone: 845.677.8383
Farmer/Producer/Contact: David Bova
Web: www.millbrookwine.com
    Cabernet Franc, Chardonnay, Pinot Noir, Tocai, Zinfandel, Hunt Country Red, and Villo Pillo extra-virgin olive oil from their Tuscan estate. Tours and tastings available at the lovely Millbrook, NY, vineyards.

Rivendell Winery
Farmer/Producer/Contact: Robert Ransom and Susan Wine
E-mail: rivendellwinery@vintagenewyork.com
Web: www.rivendellwine.com
    Chardonnay, dry Riesling, Northern Lights, Southern Lights, Interlude Blush, City Cab, Merlot, Merlot Reserve, Cabernet Sauvignon, and numerous seasonal wines

Tuthilltown Spirits Distillery
14 Gristmill Lane, Gardiner, NY 12525
Phone: 845.633.8284
Farmer/Producer/Contact: Ralph Erenzo
E-mail: Ralph@tuthilltown.com
    Spirit of the Hudson Vodka (made with 100 percent Hudson Valley apples), Corn Whiskey, Four-Grain Whiskey, River Rum, Baby Bourbon, Manhattan Rye Whiskey, Single Malt

Warwick Valley Winery & Distillery
114 Little York Road, Warwick, NY 10990
Phone: 845.258.6020
E-mail: wvwinery@warwick.net
Web: www.wvwinery.com
    Hard draft ciders, Cabernet Sauvignon, Merlot, Pinot Noir, Cabernet Franc, Riesling, Chardonnay, Harvest Moon (Cayuga/Vidal blend), Eau de Vie, Bartlett Pear Liqueur, Black Currant Cordial, and port. Apple and pear picking onsite; tasting and tours available.

NEW YORK STATE CONSERVATION GROUPS AND PROGRAMS

Pride of New York
www.prideofny.com
    The Pride of New York program was developed to promote and support the sale of agricultural and food products grown and processed within New York State. The program's growing membership now includes farmers and processors,

retailers, distributors, restaurants, and related culinary and support associations, all working together to bring you wholesome, quality New York State products.

Riverkeeper
www.riverkeeper.org
Their mission is to safeguard the ecological integrity of the Hudson River, its tributaries, and the watershed of New York City (protecting the city's drinking water supply) by tracking down and stopping polluters. Since 1983 Riverkeeper has investigated and brought to justice more than 300 environmental lawbreakers.

Scenic Hudson
www.scenichudson.org
E-mail: info@scenichudson.org
Scenic Hudson is dedicated to protecting and restoring the Hudson River, its riverfront, and the majestic vistas and working landscapes beyond as an irreplaceable natural treasure for America and a vital resource for residents and visitors. To date they have protected more than 25,000 acres in the Hudson Valley, much of it vital farmland.

NATIONAL SUSTAINABLE AGRICULTURE/ EAT LOCAL NETWORKS

The following resources can help you select seasonal, local fare where you live. Encourage food and beverage producers, as well as restaurants that highlight local products, to join these organizations to help interested parties find them.

Local Harvest
www.localharvest.org
The best organic food is what's grown closest to you. Use this website to find farmers' markets, family farms, and other sources of sustainably grown food in your area, where you can buy produce, grass-fed meats, and many other goodies. Find farms, CSAs, restaurant, grocery/co-ops, online stores, and farmers' markets in your local area.

National Resources Defense Council
www.nrdc.org/health/foodmiles/default.asp
Select your state and season to find out what products are being harvested in your locale as well as in neighboring states.

Oldways
www.oldwayspt.org/index.html
Oldways is the widely respected nonprofit "food issues think tank" credited with successfully translating the complex

details of nutrition science into the familiar language of food. It is best known for developing consumer-friendly health-promotion tools, including the well-known Mediterranean Diet Pyramid.

PickYourOwn.ORG
www.pickyourown.org/index.htm
This fabulous website helps you find pick-your-own farms near you; just plug in your zip code. It also alerts you to festivals and provides tips for pickling and canning.

Slow Food
www.slowfood.com
The Slow Food movement was founded by Carlo Petrini in Italy to combat fast food. It aims to preserve the cultural cuisine and the associated food, plants, seeds, domestic animals, and farming within an ecoregion. The movement has expanded globally to over 83,000 members in 122 countries. Check for a chapter (or conviva) in your area. We're lucky to have Hudson Valley Slow Food.

Sustainable Table
www.sustainabletable.org/home.php
Sustainable Table celebrates local sustainable food, educates consumers on food-related issues, and works to build community through food.

USDA Agricultural Marketing
www.ams.usda.gov
Great source for farmers' market facts and finding farmers' markets near you.

HUDSON VALLEY TOURISM BOARDS

For more information on the Valley, visit the websites of local tourism boards. My two favorites are:

Columbia County Tourism
www.bestcountryroads.com
Columbia County Bounty: www.columbiacountybounty .com

Dutchess County Tourism
3 Neptune Road, Suite Q-17
Poughkeepsie, NY 12601-5545
Phone: 845-463-4000
dctpa@DutchessTourism.com
Dutchess County Bounty website coming soon!

Acknowledgments

Without my friends, colleagues, and customers, this book would never have been possible. A huge debt is owed to the wonderful people at William Morrow, especially my editor, Cassie Jones, who saw the potential of this project from the outset and believed I could connect the dots among the many beliefs and concepts that are near and dear to me. I knew when I met her that my book had found its home, and that *Hudson Valley Mediterranean* would move from a hope to reality. My dear friend and literary agent, Miriam Altshuler, brought me to the wonderful HarperCollins team. Our shared love of food and the Hudson Valley was the initial spark that nourished the proposal.

One of the great lessons I've learned as the owner of Gigi Hudson Valley is that everything depends on teamwork. The same is true for writing a book. I am so grateful to have had the help of the Gigi Kitchen team, led by executive chef Wilson Costa; Gigi Market chef Steve Foley, pastry chef Ashley Kearns, Gigi Trattoria chef de cuisine Kevin Hermann, sous chef Mark Luciano, and all-around everything guy Nico Vasques when I've faced a mountain of recipes to test and a laundry list of questions. Their energy, enthusiasm, suggestions, and hands-on help made a daunting task fun, delicious, and efficient.

While I was locked up in the house cooking and writing, the restaurant and market continued to hum along due to the inestimable efforts of Derek Lauck, John Storm, Peggy Curik, and the incredibly talented teams they manage. Thank you all for your passion for food, wine, and service. It has made Gigi's reputation for warmth and conviviality shine throughout the Hudson Valley. I am so lucky to work with each one of you.

The beautiful photos in this book were taken either at the restaurant, at my home, or outside behind the red barn at Gigi Market. I am indebted to the creative efforts of Leonardo Frusteri, who focused tirelessly on getting that "just right" shot. Helping us out were my friends at Hammertown and High Falls Mercantile, whose beautiful plates and cloths are pictured.

There are many long days in this business, and it can be months before I get a chance to catch up with friends. I'd like to send a special thanks to my "soul sisters," who have encouraged me for years. Janet Crawshaw, publisher of *The Valley Table*, has been a supporter of Gigi from the beginning and has believed in my vision that delicious food and a healthy life go hand in hand. Also, I'd like to acknowledge the mentoring and friendship of Beth Shepard at ElectricPressRelease .com, whose advice and representation has been a treasure. Great big hugs to my crazy girlfriends, who know I adore cooking for them; Toni, Edris, Claire, Donna, and Tabetha—*grazie, grazie*. They're joined by a roving band of brothers—Sam, Michael, Andrew, Ted, Ed, Todd, and Marcus—who visit me often at Gigi Trattoria and allow me to pop into their dinner parties when my odd schedule allows. A longtime friend who lives far too far from the Hudson Valley is my French Culinary Institute classmate Susan Crescimanno-Ruffins. We two Sicilian girls have talked food and shared laughs and ideas for almost twenty years. This book would not have been possible without our ongoing dialogue.

I want to thank my colleagues at Just Salad, Nick Kenner and Rob Crespi, who understood my approach to food and health from the very start and gave me a space to do it in a fast-food venue. Also, a special thank-you to the management of Vaughan Foods. May we bring the Gigi "Skizza" to all of America very soon!

I also want to acknowledge the work of my fellow board members of the Wilderstein Historic Site, who seek to preserve the historic rural beauty of the Hudson Valley. Ned Sullivan and his wife, Tara, are not only devoted customers; his group at Scenic Hudson has protected more than 25,000 acres of precious land in nine counties, and created or enhanced many parks and preserves for public enjoyment. Mary Kay Verba and her team at Dutchess County Tourism help all the businesses, large and small, promote and market what they do within this majestic area and to outside groups. They're pros.

I raise a glass and toast all the customers who walk through the door with their ready appetites and good spirits. Their support and appreciation of what we do is an enormous gift. Finally, a special thank-you to the hardworking farmers of the Hudson Valley— and one beyond, Matt Little, who greatly informed me on the balance and harmony that can coexist between small- and large-scale farms. Their efforts make it a pleasure for me to eat, drink, and live here. Their passion makes my life a pleasure.

Index

D

Daikon, notes about, 7

Desserts. *See also* Cakes; Cookies and bars

Blackberry, Raspberry, and Apple Rustic Fruit Tart, 112–13

Chocolate Banana Panettone Bread Pudding, 269–70

Gigi Affogato, 188

Gigi Cider Doughnuts, 186–87

Gigi Summer Fruit Salad with Zabaglione, 115

Grilled Strawberries with Vanilla Gelato and Aged Balsamic, 60

Mead Orchard Chilled Peach Soup, 114

Dingle Pies (Irish-Style Lamb Pies), 24–25

Dips and spreads

Fresh Fava Bean Spread, 18

Gigi Fig Jam, 287

Gigi Minimal Mayonnaise, 280

Gigi Salsa Verde, 284

Pesto for All Seasons, 278

Roasted Red Pepper Pesto, 279

Sweet 'n' Sour Chicken Liver Mousse, 212–13

Sweet Pea Guacamole, 16–17

White Bean Spread, 22–23

Doughnuts, Gigi Cider, 186–87

Duck

Hudson Valley Cassoulet, 247–48

Whole Roasted, with Pear Balsamic Sauce and Herb Spaetzle (L'Anitra Arrosta con Salsa di Pere Balsamico), 249–51

E

Eggnog, Fresh Hudson Valley, 208–9

Eggplant

Fries, 109

notes about, 72–73

Parmesan, Enlightened, 90–91

Eggs

Asparagus Soufflé, 19–20

Next-Day Roasted Vegetable Frittata, 258–59

Entertaining, ideas and strategies for, 295–98

F

Fava Bean(s)

Barley, and Kale Soup, 216–17

Fresh, Spread, 18

notes about, 6

Spring (and Every Other Season) Lasagna, 39–41

Spring Vegetable Stew, 26–27

Fennel Watermelon Salad, 81

Fig Jam, Gigi, 287

Fincke, Talea and Doug, 120–22

Fish

Hudson River shad population, 4–5

Just Salad Immunity Bowl, 143–45

Roasted Marinated Salmon, 144

Salmon Burgers with Peach Salsa, 97–98

Sautéed Red Snapper with Herb Roasted Fingerling Potatoes and Sweet Pea Guacamole, 46–47

Seared Salmon over Spring Trifolati, 48–49

Sweet and Sour Cod "Saor," Venetian Style, 88–89

Tacchino Tonnato (Turkey with Tuna Caper Sauce), 99–100

Fregola Salad, Summer Garden, 84–85

Frittata, Next-Day Roasted Vegetable, 258–59

Fruit(s). *See also* Berries; Citrus; *specific fruits*

dried, notes about, 201–3

Fruited and Spiced Three-Grain Pilaf, 265–66

Gigi Biscotti, 271–72

Summer, Salad with Zabaglione, Gigi, 115

G

Gabbi's Gruel, 293

Garlic, Roasted, 286

Gnocchi, Gigi Potato, with Chicken and Pea Ragù, 36–38

Grain(s). *See also* Rice

Fava, Barley, and Kale Soup, 216–17

Mixed-Grain Risotto with Bok Choy, Radicchio, and Mushrooms, 150–51

Stewed North African–Spiced Chicken Thighs over Whole Wheat Couscous, 240–41

Summer Garden Fregola Salad, 84–85

Three-, Pilaf, Fruited and Spiced, 265–66

Wheat Berries, 145

Yellow Split Pea and Wild Rice Soup, 141–42

Green Beans

notes about, 119, 123

in Warm Dijon Vinaigrette, 180–81

Greens. See also Arugula; Cabbage; Chard; Kale; Radicchio; Spinach

Cooking, Basic Sautéed, 264

Gigi Barbina Salad, 146–47

Gigi BLT Salad with Roasted-Tomato Vinaigrette, 82–83

Jayne Keyes–Approved Hudson Valley Cajun Gumbo, 220–22

Just Salad Immunity Bowl, 143–45

salad, notes about, 11–13

from Sky Farm, 14–15

Spring and Fall Baby Beet Salad, 21

Watermelon Fennel Salad, 81

winter, notes about, 199–201

Guacamole, Sweet Pea, 16–17

Gumbo, Jayne Keyes–Approved Hudson Valley Cajun, 220–22

H

Ham. See Prosciutto

Hash, Winter Vegetable, 260–61

Hearty Roots Community Farm, 206–7

Horseradish-Chive Dressing, Low-Fat, 223–24

J